W9-CPQ-164

Ex-Library: Friends of
Lake County Public Library

REVOLUTIONARY
CUBA

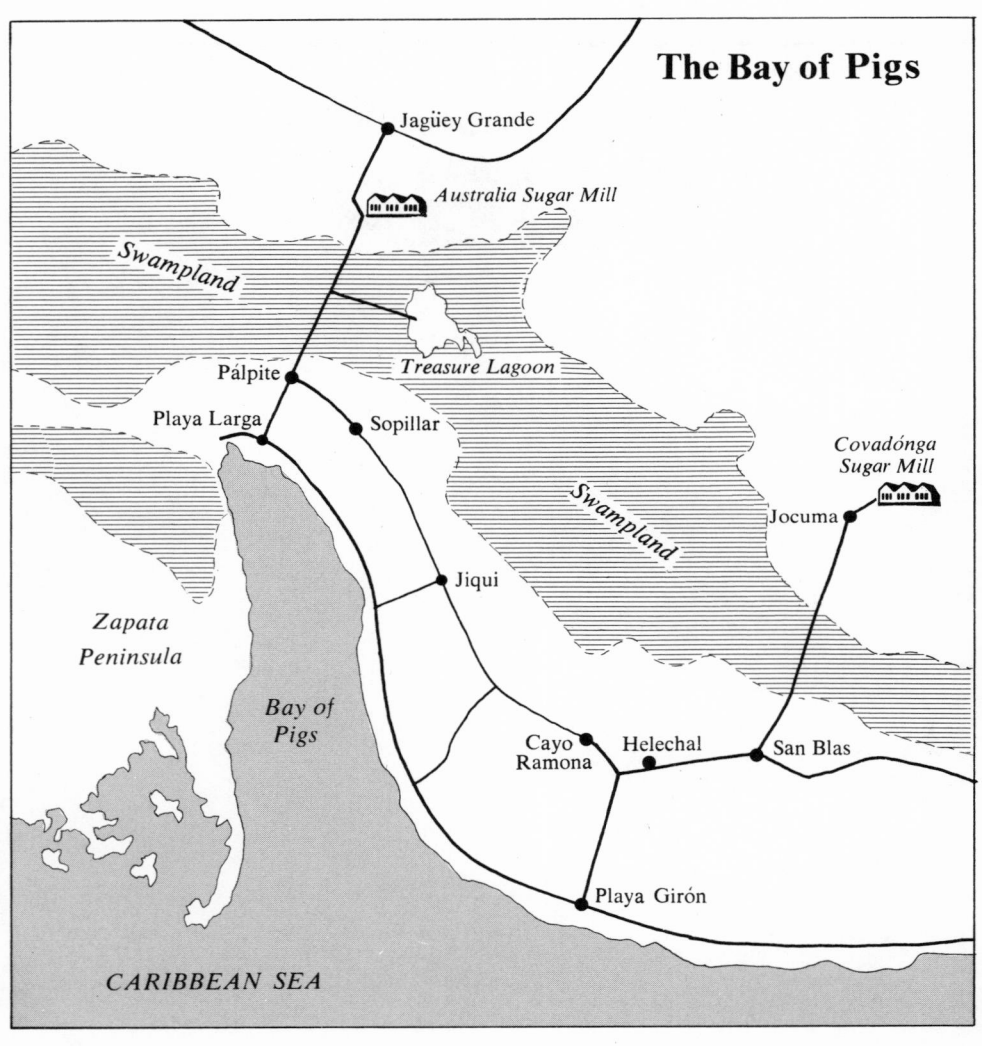

REVOLUTIONARY
CUBA

Terence Cannon

THOMAS Y. CROWELL   NEW YORK

LAKE COUNTY PUBLIC LIBRARY

11541950

Maps by Dyno Lowenstein

Copyright © 1981 by Terence Cannon
All rights reserved. Printed in the United States of America.
No part of this book may be used or reproduced in any manner
whatsoever without written permission except in the case of
brief quotations embodied in critical articles and reviews.
For information address Thomas Y. Crowell, 10 East 53rd Street,
New York, N. Y. 10022. Published simultaneously in Canada
by Fitzhenry & Whiteside Limited, Toronto.
Designed by Harriett Barton

Library of Congress Cataloging in Publication Data
Cannon, Terence.   Revolutionary Cuba.
Bibliograpy: p.
SUMMARY: A history of the Cuban Revolution based
on the writings and perspectives of its leaders and
on the author's travel and research in Cuba.
1. Cuba—History—Revolution, 1959. 2. Cuba—History—1959.
[1. Cuba—History—Revolution, 1959] I. Title.
F1788.C2564   972.91′064   77–26587
ISBN 0–690–01307–8

1   2   3   4   5   6   7   8   9   10
FIRST EDITION

FOR MY
MOTHER AND FATHER

ACKNOWLEDGMENTS

There are many individuals and organizations that aided and coun-
seled me in the research and writing of this book. I would especially
like to thank Professor Johnnetta Cole, Fernando Garcia, Florence
Johnson, Professor Cecelia and Harry Pollack, Sandy Pollack, Mag-
aly Quiala Martinez, Gail Reed, Ambassador Julian Rizo, Freddy
Torres, and the staffs of the Center for Cuban Studies and the Biblio-
teca Nacional de Cuba.

Grateful acknowledgment is also made to the following for permission to reprint copyrighted material: The Bobbs-Merrill Company,
Inc., for material on pages 52 and 68 (top) from *Fidel Castro* by Jules
Dubois, copyright © 1959 by The Bobbs-Merrill Company, Inc.;
Joan Daves and the Macmillan Publishing Company, Inc., for material on pages 69–70, 170, and 191 from *Venceremos! The Speeches and
Writings of Ernesto Che Guevara,* edited by John Gerassi, copyright
© 1968 by John Gerassi; Farrar, Straus and Giroux, Inc., for material
on pages 13, 32, and 34 from *The America of José Martí,* translated
by Juan De Onís, copyright © 1954 by the Noonday Press, Inc.;
International Creative Management for material on pages 159 and
164 from "Conversation with Fidel Castro" by Frank Mankiewicz,
which originally appeared in *Oui* Magazine, January 1975, copyright
© 1974 by Frank Mankiewicz; International Publishers Company,
Inc., for material on pages 8, 9, 10–11, 12, 14, 18, 19, 20–21, 21–22,
25, 26, 29, and 31 (paragraph 2) from *A History of Cuba and Its*

Relations with the United States, vols. I and II by Philip S. Foner, copyright © 1962, 1963; The MIT Press, Cambridge, Mass., for material on pages 169 and 175 from *Che: Selected Works of Ernesto Guevara,* edited by Rolando E. Bonachea and Nelson P. Váldes, copyright © 1969 by the Massachusetts Institute of Technology, and for material on pages 53, 58, 64 (first quotation), 66, 67, and 92–93 from *The Selected Works of Fidel Castro,* vol. I, edited by Rolando E. Bonachea and Nelson P. Váldes, translation and Introduction copyright © 1972 by the Massachusetts Institute of Technology; The Massachusetts Review, Inc., for excerpts from the poem "Tengo" on page 115 by Nicolás Guillén, translated by Robert Marquez, which originally appeared in *The Massachusetts Review,* vol. xi, no. 3, copyright © 1970 by The Massachusetts Review, Inc.; and the Monthly Review Press for material on pages 109 (bottom), 110, 128, and 162 from *The Economic Transformation of Cuba* by Edward Boorstein, copyright © 1968 by Edward Boorstein.

The quote on page ix by Nicolás Guillén is from *The Revolution and Cultural Problems in Cuba,* published by the Ministry of Foreign Relations, Havana, 1962; the quote on page 59 is from *La Sierra y el Llano,* edited by Edmundo Desnoes, Casa de las Américas, Havana, 1961; the quotes on pages 5, 6–7, and 65 are from Fidel Castro's *History Will Absolve Me,* Editora Política, Havana, 1964; the Battle of Alegría de Pio account on pages 74–75 is based on Che Guevara's *Episodes of the Revolutionary War* and Carlos Franqui's *El libro de los doce;* the quote on page 88 by Fidel Castro is reprinted from *The Selected Works of Fidel Castro,* vol. I, edited by Rolando E. Bonachea and Nelson P. Váldes, and appeared originally in "Cuban Rebels," by Andrew St. George, *Look* magazine, February 4, 1958; the material on pages 102–3 is from "En Ciudad Semejante" by Lisandro Otero in Rolando Cartaya's *Alma Mater,* January 1975; the section "How I Became a Communist" on pages 132–34 is from *Cuba–Chile,* published in Havana, 1972; the quote by I. F. Stone on page 154 is reprinted from *The Cuban Missile Crisis,* edited by Robert A. Divine, and appeared originally in "The Brink," *New York Review of Books,* April 14, 1966. The figures on page 149 are from the official Cuban report "History of an Agression," Ediciones Venceremos, Havana, 1964.

Contents

Preface

I wrote this book for people who are curious about Cuba and want something besides the common U.S. view of Cuban history; I have tried to communicate, as well as someone from the United States can, the view from there.

Most U.S. bookstores offer primarily the opinions of Cuban exiles, State Department analysts, and scholars with an anti-Cuban point of view. I chose, wherever possible, not to use their material, but to use Cuban books, magazines, archives, material from interviews with Cubans, and personal experience to reconstruct the *Cuban* opinion about their Revolution and the world they have helped to change.

In this task I was helped immeasurably by the fact that the Cuban Revolution has been one of the most open and frank in the world. Cubans are remarkably straightforward about their successes and failures, their heroics and their flops. The secret of understanding the Cuban Revolution, in my opinion, is to respect it, rather than to assume—as many in this country have—that Fidel Castro is crazy and the Cuban people cowed and oppressed.

The oral history of revolutionary Cuba is produced continuously by Fidel Castro and the other leaders of the Revolution. Their speeches, chats, press conferences, asides, and essays constitute a rich body of recorded history. The reader will find them quoted throughout.

The eight occasions I have been in Cuba, most recently in 1978, included travel, work, interviews with people on the street, in the communities, in factories, and elsewhere. I found that though it is surely not true that the Cuban people think monolithically, the vision held by their leaders is essentially that of a vast number of the people.

Much has necessarily been left out of this history. I have concentrated on the problems that the Cuban people have faced during the four centuries they have moved from primitive tribalism through slavery, feudalism, and capitalism to a socialist society, and what they have done to solve their problems.

The history of Cuba, like all histories, is the story of real people, with burning needs, in situations that they partially understand and do not wholly control. With all their limitations and great capacity for learning and sacrifice, it is people who make history. I wish I could have included even more of the human reality of the Revolution—the sounds of voices, the burning sun, the feel of work, the sense of exhilaration and fear. I have tried to communicate the sheer physical effort of history, what it takes to raise a society another step, the doggedness needed to accomplish necessary political ends.

An economist friend of mine who spent many years in Cuba once commented, "One of the things you learn when you live in Cuba a long time is that you must try to think the thing through in terms of the Cuban Revolution, not from your personal view, because it can look a lot different. The way to get an understanding of the situation in Cuba is to immerse yourself in what's there, see how the people look at it there."

In 1961 Cuba's poet laureate, Nicolás Guillén, urged Cuban writers and poets to take the history of Cuba as a fitting subject for literature, in these words:

This is the story of a small nation, apparently helpless, certified as dead, or at least dying, by many illustrious doctors; the story of a people enslaved by a brutal and insatiable enemy, who pounce upon that enemy and defeat him, and then turn on the accomplices of that enemy, who have betrayed their country, their family, their blood, and their bones, and defeat them too—a people who not only accomplish this, which, indeed, is quite a lot, but then begin to build their own house in the land of their ancestors, to live there in peace and freedom.

Doesn't this story deserve to be told? What nation in our America has been offered so much greatness by destiny? Doesn't that task—the task of relating historical events that seem more like marvelous tales—doesn't that task deserve to figure in the center of our lives?

PART I

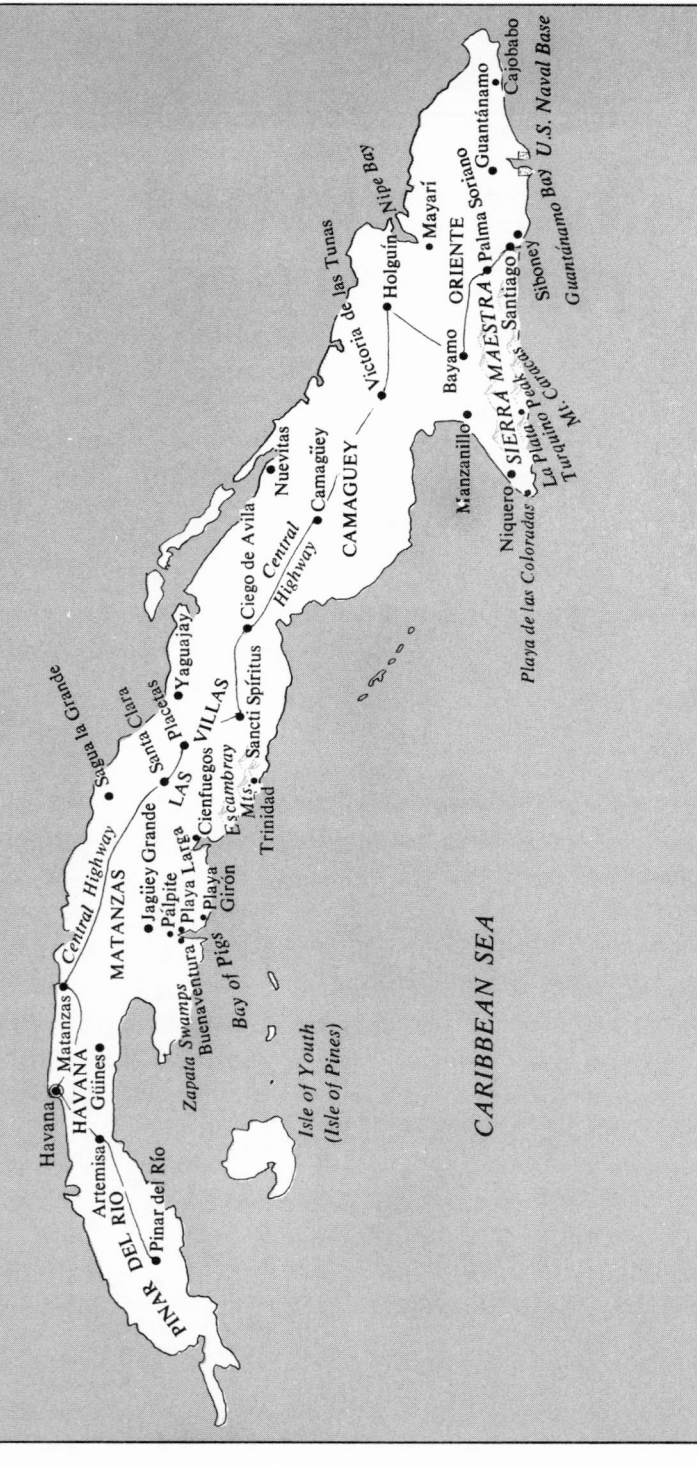

CUBA

PINAR DEL RÍO

Pinar del Río

Artemisa

HAVANA

Havana

Güines

Matanzas

Matanzas

MATANZAS

Central Highway

Sagua la Grande

Santa Clara

Placetas

Jagüey Grande

Palpite

Playa Larga

Buenaventura

Playa Girón

Zapata Swamps

Bay of Pigs

Cienfuegos

LAS VILLAS

Yaguajay

Escambray Mts.

Trinidad

Sancti Spíritus

Ciego de Avila

Central Highway

Camagüey

CAMAGÜEY

Nuevitas

Victoria de las Tunas

Holguín

Nipe Bay

Mayarí

Palma Soriano

Guantánamo

Cajobabo

ORIENTE

Bayamo

SIERRA MAESTRA

Santiago

Siboney

Guantánamo Bay

U.S. Naval Base

Manzanillo

Niquero

La Plata Peak

Turquino Mt.

Caracas

Playa de las Coloradas

Isle of Youth (Isle of Pines)

CARIBBEAN SEA

THE ATTACK

July 26, 1953

In the next hours, we shall win, or we shall be defeated, but in either case, listen well, comrades! In either case this movement will triumph. If we win this morning, it will hasten that to which Martí aspired. If the opposite occurs, the gesture will serve as an example to the people of Cuba, to seize the flag and move forward.

—FIDEL CASTRO TO HIS FOLLOWERS AN HOUR BEFORE THE ATTACK ON THE MONCADA GARRISON, July 26, 1953

The day before: To another passenger on the train, or to a policeman, he was a young man on the way to the Carnival, the sugar-harvest festival that brings all Cuba into the streets to dance and drink beer and watch the floats and fireworks. But when the train to Santiago paused in the foothills of the Sierra Mountains, he covered his face with a handkerchief and pretended to sleep.

There were too many people there who might recognize student militant Raúl Castro, kid brother of the impetuous Fidel, lawyer of street demonstrators and the poor. Fidel, who had tried to bring the dictator Batista to court for overthrowing the government, Fidel who dared to say openly, "To die for one's country is to live forever."

The train was weaving through the hills of Oriente, Cuba's easternmost province. It pleased him greatly, Raúl recalled later, to see the familiar places of his childhood. He felt proud that what he was about to do would take place in the province where he had grown up. During the trip he watched the landscape "greedily, as if for the last time." Tomorrow morning—July 26, 1953—he and Fidel and 123 other men and women would launch an armed attack on the second largest military garrison in the country, the Moncada garrison in Santiago, eastern headquarters of the military dictatorship.

At the Santiago station he was met by Abel Santamaría, second-in-command under Fidel, who took him to the Pearl of Cuba Hotel where he tried to eat. There were other revolutionaries in the dining room, each pretending to be alone. José Luís Tasende kept putting coins in the jukebox to liven things up; after all, they were supposedly there for the Carnival. There is a photo of Tasende taken by the Cuban army the next day: he is barefoot and drenched in blood, and stares directly at his executioners with the look of a man about to step into history.

RAÚL CASTRO: Each little room held only a bed, on which I lay down fully dressed and with both hands behind my head, eyes fixed on the high ceiling of the old hotel, my mind full of thoughts, and waited for the longest minutes of my life to pass.

As the walls that separated the rooms only went halfway to the ceiling one could hear clearly all the noises and music from the streets, and the sounds of the restaurant full of people eating and drinking, the jukeboxes giving out uninterrupted songs.

For an instant I thought that it was not right that while some danced and drank, or made love, completely diverted, we were there waiting to be called from one minute to the next to an imminent action. How many of the comrades were at that moment sitting in the restaurant having the last meal of their lives? Of the eighteen who made up this group, headed by comrade Tasende, I think that only three survived.

MELBA HERNÁNDEZ: Haydée [Santamaría] and I asked Fidel for instructions. He told us to stay in the house and wait until we got news of the results of the action. Haydée and I looked at each other, disappointedly. Until then, we were sure we'd be going with them, and now we felt like outcasts. I protested, saying that we were just as revolutionary as anybody else there and that it was unfair of them to leave us out because we were women. Fidel hesitated, and I knew that we had hit a sensitive spot. He finally answered that he was leaving it up to Abel.

As soon as Abel arrived, we ran to him and asked for his opinion. By then we had a good "defense attorney," Dr. Mario Muñoz, who said that he needed us to act as nurses. Abel and Fidel gave their permission, and Haydée and I began our preparations for going along.

FIDEL CASTRO: The final mobilization of men who came to this province from the most remote towns of the island was accomplished with admirable precision and in absolute secrecy. The attack began simultaneously at 5:15 A.M. in both Bayamo and Santiago . . . and, one by one, with an exactitude of minutes and seconds prepared in advance, the buildings surrounding the barracks fell to our forces.

Nevertheless, in the interest of accuracy and even though it may detract from our reputation, I am also going to reveal a fact that was fatal: due to a most unfortunate error, half of our forces, and the better armed half, at that, went astray at the entrance to the city and were not on hand to help us at the decisive moment.

Abel Santamaría, with twenty-one men, had occupied the City Hospital; with him went a doctor [Mario Muñoz] and two of our women comrades [Haydée Santamaría and Melba Hernández] to attend to the wounded. Raúl Castro, with ten men, occupied the Palace of Justice, and it was my responsibility to attack the barracks with the rest, ninety-five men.

The reserve group, who had almost all the heavy weapons, turned up the wrong street and lost their way in the city, with which they were not familiar. I must clarify that I do not for a moment doubt the valor of these men. They experienced great anguish and desperation when they realized they were lost. . . . Many of them, captured later, met death with true heroism.

MELBA HERNÁNDEZ: It was about 8 A.M. Abel remained as cool as could be. He called Haydée and me aside and said, "We're lost. You and I know what's going to happen to me. Find a place to hide in the hospital. You must stay alive no matter what. Somebody must live to tell what's happened here."

We ran along the hospital corridor and wound up in the children's ward.

FIDEL CASTRO: When I became convinced that all attempts to take the garrison had become quite futile, I began to withdraw our men in groups of eight and ten. Our losses in the battle had been insignificant; 95 percent of our casualties came from the army's inhumanity after the struggle.

Our plans were to continue the struggle in the mountains in case the attack on the regiment failed. . . . I was able to gather a third of our forces; but many of these men were now discouraged. About twenty of them decided to surrender; we shall see what became of them. The rest, eighteen men, with what arms and ammunition were left, followed me into the mountains.

MELBA HERNÁNDEZ: At 10 A.M. the soldiers found us in the children's ward. We were taken to the Moncada in a car and locked up in a big room that probably belonged to the officers' club, because I remember there were several pool tables there. And, lying under the tables, the boys who had already been through the horrors of torture cried in pain as their blood oozed out onto the floor. The soldiers would grab them in groups of four, take them away, and bring them back semiconscious. . . .

They took us to the barbershop, which, to all appearances, had been turned into a torture chamber. There was blood everywhere— on the floor, the walls, and even the ceiling. They pulled us outside, onto a small, narrow balcony. It looked as if the floor drain was clogged, and there was a pool of blood about half an inch deep around it. The breeze made little ripples in that pool of blood.

FIDEL CASTRO: Other methods were used. Frustrated by the valor of the men, they tried to break the spirit of the women. With a bleeding human eye in his hands, a sergeant went to the cell where our comrades Melba Hernández and Haydée Santamaría were held.

Addressing the latter and showing her the eye, he said, "This eye belonged to your brother. If you will not testify what he refused to testify, we will tear out the other." She, who loved her valiant brother above all things, replied full of dignity, "If you tore out an eye and he did not testify falsely, much less will I."

FIDEL CASTRO: From a shack in the mountains, I listened to the radio broadcast by the dictator on Monday, July 27, while there were still eighteen men in arms against the government. Those who never experience similar moments will never be acquainted with bitterness and indignation in life.

While the long-cherished hopes of freeing our people lay in ruins about us, we heard those crushed hopes gloated over by a tyrant more vicious, more arrogant than ever. . . .

In a cellar full of prisoners someone told Melba Hernández that it was July twenty-eighth. "Seventy-two hours of my life had gone by. It was July twenty-eighth and the long black night of July twenty-sixth had come to an end." Within a week, Fidel and several companions, who had fled to the mountains to continue the battle, were captured.

Asked at his trial in October 1953 if outside agitators had sponsored his attack, Fidel replied, "Yes. José Martí." Martí, "the father of Cuba," had led Cuba's war of independence against Spain fifty-eight years earlier.

Five years, five months, and five days after the attack on the Moncada garrison, General Fulgencio Batista fled by plane to Santo Domingo, exile, and death. Those who had led the attack governed the nation. A war of independence whose first battles had been defeated by the soldiers of Diego Columbus in 1510 was finally victorious.

THE FIRST CUBANS

As friends they had received them, the white men with the beards; they had regaled them with their honey and their corn, and even King Behechio gave a handsome Spaniard his daughter Higuemota as a wife, she who was like a wild pigeon and a royal palm. They showed them their mountains of gold and their rivers of golden waters, and their adornments all of fine gold and they had put on these adornments on their armor. And these cruel men hung them with chains; they took away their women and their sons; they put them in the depths of the mines to drag the weight of stone with their forehead, and divided them and marked them with a brand.

—*JOSÉ MARTÍ, The Age of Gold*

Of the race of human beings who first lived in Cuba's luxuriant semitropical woodlands, breathed its fragrant air, and marveled at the many bright birds and the red burst of sunrise over its eastern mountains, none remain. They were the Taínos and the Ciboneys, Caribbean Indians who themselves had come as refugees, driven by hunger or fiercer Indians, traveling in long canoes from the coasts of Florida, Puerto Rico, and South America.

The Taínos were of a stone-age culture; they used large seashells to make tools, implements, and musical instruments. They were peaceful; they hunted and fished and grew yucca, maize, beans, peanuts, squashes, peppers, fruits, and tobacco.

According to Cuban historian Fernando Portuondo, their villages were built around a central area that was both marketplace and dancing ground: "The diversion of the song and dance served as commemoration of great happenings and was used to transmit to the young people the traditions worthy to be preserved, the deeds of the ancestors, and the mystic vicissitudes of the race."

The Taínos held slaves—the prize of battles with the less advanced Ciboneys—but within their tribe there was much equality. There were no rich or poor Taínos, no tribesman who labored for others, no institution of private property. Included in the ruling group of chieftains, priests, and doctors were a number of women.

When the Spaniards first arrived, many of the Indians treated them with friendship and respect; it was a great mistake.

Christopher Columbus landed in Cuba on October 24, 1492. It was the "fairest island human eyes have yet beheld," he said; but as he reported to the king of Spain, "It is certain that where there is such marvellous scenery, there must be much from which profit can be made."

Europe needed wealth, for it produced no jewels, spices, or gold. Great changes were occurring there; a rising merchant class that would overthrow feudalism in the eighteenth and nineteenth centuries was beginning to emerge, and was in the process of amassing wealth by exploiting the resources of the New World.

In 1510, on the rumor that gold was to be found in Cuba, King Ferdinand of Spain ordered that the island be conquered. He instructed Diego Columbus, son of the famous explorer, to carry out the task. Columbus in turn delegated the job to Diego Velázquez, the richest planter in Hispaniola (the island that is now Haiti and the Dominican Republic). Velázquez embarked with three hundred men, expecting no difficulty.

The Indians of Hispaniola had resisted fiercely when the Spaniards first arrived on their island, but they were no match for Spanish firearms and armor and were soon crushed. The remnants of one people, the Guahabas, led by their chief Hatuey, chose to leave Hispaniola rather than face extermination. They embarked —four hundred men, women, and children—in canoes, landing in Cuba just ahead of Diego Velázquez's invasion force.

At first the Taínos of Cuba were suspicious, mistaking Hatuey's people for the warlike Caribs, from whom the Taínos themselves had fled. But Hatuey sent emissaries to convince them of their peaceful intentions. He explained what had happened in Hispaniola and the need to join together against their common enemy.

Hatuey told the chiefs (as later recorded by the Spanish priest Bartolomé de las Casas):

"You know the report is spread abroad that the Spaniards are ready to invade this island, and you are not ignorant now of the ill-usage our friends and countrymen have met with at their hands and the cruelties they have committed at Hispaniola. They are now coming hither to inflict the same outrages and persecutions upon us."

He held out before the chiefs a basket of gold and jewels. "Here is the god which the Spaniards worship," he cried. "For these they fight and kill; for these they persecute us and that is why we have to throw them into the sea. . . .

"They tell us, these tyrants, that they adore a God of peace and equality, and yet they usurp our land and make us their slaves. They speak to us of immortal soul and of their eternal rewards and punishments, and yet they rob our belongings, seduce our women, violate our daughters. Incapable of matching us in valor, these cowards cover themselves with iron . . . that our weapons cannot break. Doubtful even of their advantage, they use the ray which wounds us from a point our arrows cannot reach. . . . But they are few and we are many. They are fighting in this foreign land, and we on our own soil. They invoke a seditious God of blood and

Gold, and we have, on our side, a just and wise God. . . ."

His speech did not suffice. Suspicion of the foreign leader prevented the Indians of central and western Cuba from joining Hatuey. Rallying a few of the eastern tribes, Hatuey set up a vigil on the coast. When Velázquez and his soldiers landed on the deserted beach and entered the forest, the Indians attacked. It was the first battle for Cuba.

The iron and the mysterious "ray" of the conquistadores triumphed. Fighting valiantly, the Indians were slowly driven into the mountains. Hatuey organized them in guerrilla fashion, attacking and retreating, keeping the Spaniards on the defensive. For three months the invaders were bottled up in their fort at Baracoa. "For the first time since they had arrived in the New World," writes historian Philip Foner, "the Spaniards knew the meaning of fear. Dissension broke out in their ranks, and it was only because he was a forceful commander and a man of indomitable will that Velázquez was able to prevent open mutiny."

Velázquez changed his tactics. Making use of an Indian traitor, he was able to surround the mountain headquarters of Hatuey and capture him.

On February 2, 1512, Hatuey was tied to a stake at the Spanish camp. A priest approached him with a crucifix and inquired if Hatuey would accept Christianity before he died.

"Why?" asked Hatuey.

"So that you may go to Heaven, son."

"Do Christians go to Heaven?" asked Hatuey.

"Yes, if they die in the grace of God," the priest replied.

"If the Christians go to Heaven," said Hatuey, "I do not want to go to Heaven. I do not wish ever again to meet such cruel and wicked people as Christians, who kill and make slaves of the Indians."

The conclusion of the story is told by Bartolomé de las Casas. A village of twenty-five hundred Indians who welcomed the conquistadores, fed them, and gave them drink. When the Spaniards finished their meal, they set upon the Indians, slashing, disemboweling, and slaughtering them until their blood ran like a river.

Las Casas saw seven thousand children die of starvation after their parents had been shipped off to work in the gold mines. Of those sent to the mines, he said, the Spaniards "required of them tasks utterly beyond their strength, bending them to the earth with crushing burdens, harnessing them to loads which they could not drag, and with fiendish sport and mockery, hacking off their hands and feet, and mutilating their bodies in ways which will not bear description."

Those Indians who escaped murder, starvation, and disease were worked to death in the mines. By 1535—only twenty-five years later—when the small Cuban gold deposits were exhausted, it was estimated that there were no more than two thousand Indians in the entire island.

When the next census was taken a few centuries later, there were none at all. An entire people, who may have numbered a million before the Spaniards came, had been exterminated. Cuba had been integrated into the European colonial system.

THE CUBAN NATION

Let the world be grafted on our republics; but the trunk must be our own. . . . There are no lands in which a man can take greater pride than in our long-suffering American republics.

—*JOSÉ MARTÍ, Our America*

When the gold ran out, the conquerors lost interest. The king in Madrid decreed the death penalty for anyone leaving Cuba without permission, but the conquistadores, the settlers, the miners, and merchants streamed away to Mexico and Peru like pollen in a gold-seeking wind. By 1602 the island was virtually deserted.

Cuba remained a Spanish military bastion, the stepping-off point for the conquest of Latin America and the southern regions of North America. Still, there was coffee to plant and sugar to harvest, ships to unload. Someone had to do the work. The Indians had not survived the conquest, and the conquistadores had come from Europe to get rich, not to do backbreaking labor.

It was then that large shipments of black African slaves—first bought to work the almost depleted Jagua gold mines in 1524—began to arrive in Cuba in chains.

The British were the masters of the trade in slaves. They bought or captured Africans—almost all men—in Senegal, Guinea, the Congo delta and Angola, and as far away as Mozambique on the eastern shore of Africa, shipping them to the shores of America to replace the massacred Indians.

According to historian W. E. B. Du Bois, for every slave imported to the New World, five were killed in Africa or died on the high seas, resulting in the loss to Africa of some sixty million people. "It was the rape of a continent seldom if ever paralleled in ancient or modern history," Du Bois wrote.

The first Cuban slave revolt was recorded in 1533. Four slaves defended themselves to the death against a large force of soldiers sent by the terrified governor general. Afterward a law was passed forbidding blacks from carrying long knives or traveling in groups. These revolts continued until the 1880's, when slavery was abolished.

The history of black Cubans is in great part the history of Cuba itself. The census of 1774 showed that blacks and mulattoes, slave and free, totaled some 44 percent of the population. The fate of black Cubans determined the future of the country as a whole; of this, their masters were painfully aware.

By the time of the 1774 census, black Cubans were not alone in their revolt against tyranny, for Cuban society had changed greatly since the days of Columbus. Cuba had begun to prosper in the 1700's. Spain, bankrupt a century before, no longer was turning to its colonies for gold alone, but for wealth of all kinds —and in agricultural wealth, Cuba surpassed the gold mines of Peru and Mexico and all the jewels of captured Indian civilizations. Spain clamped a rigid monopoly over Cuba's agricultural trade. On pain of death, Cuban growers and merchants could trade only with Spain—only with certain cities in Spain in fact. Tobacco was heavily taxed; a state monopoly controlled by the Spanish king handled all tobacco sales.

At first the tobacco growers got around this by smuggling—selling secretly to British ships that landed on the coast at night. But in 1717, five hundred growers rose up in revolt. Such rebellions were put down harshly by Spanish authorities; in 1723 the governor general hung the bodies of rebellious growers from trees along the road to Havana as a warning to others.

At the top of this now complex society were the *Peninsulares,* the Spanish-born: they were the government officials, bureaucrats, and monopoly merchants. They were the aristocrats, who scorned the native-born Cubans and feared the slaves. They believed in the natural superiority of Spaniards over Cubans.

Below them was a new group, the *Criollos* (Creoles), born in Cuba, descendants of the Spanish and to some extent products of intermarriage between the Spanish conquerors and Indian or black women.

The Creoles were the cattle raisers, the tobacco and sugar planters, and, with the rise of cities, the lawyers, journalists, doctors, and teachers. Some were wealthy, owning great plantations and many slaves. Others were peasants, growers of handfuls of sugar.

By the late eighteenth century many black Cubans were free, having run away from their owners or having purchased their freedom. Though a few rose to be landowners, merchants, or professionals, racism forced the vast majority into day labor. Their hatred of the slave system was no less than the slaves', and many slave revolts were organized and led by free blacks, who had more opportunity to move openly about the island.

In the late eighteenth century two revolutions took place that profoundly influenced Cuban life. Documents from the first revolution were circulated secretly among the Creoles, who passed from hand to hand Spanish translations of Thomas Jefferson's *Declaration of Independence* and Thomas Paine's *The Rights of Man.* The ideas they contained were radical, but not offensive to the Creoles, who noted that the American revolutionaries had not gone so far as to free their slaves.

The second revolution was a different matter. In 1791 the slaves in the French-ruled portion of the nearby island of Hispaniola revolted. Led by Toussaint L'Ouverture, the black population drove out the French and two years after L'Ouverture's death in 1803 established the Negro Republic of Haiti, the first in the world. Secretly the blacks of Cuba, slave and free, rejoiced.

In June 1795, the Spanish governor of the Bayamo region in Oriente province was told by an informer that one Nicolás Morales, a free Negro, "tall in body, very robust, of dark color, marked with smallpox, straight hair, very cunning and about fifty-six years old," was urging black slaves and white farm workers to unite, arm themselves, and demand that the king declare the equality of the races, the abolition of excise taxes, and the distribution of the land to the poor, "since all the land is owned by the very rich."

Their demands would wait 164 years to be met. Most frightening to the slave owners was the fact that the Morales uprising, when crushed, was discovered to have involved whites, blacks, and mulattoes together.

A few years later, the fierce wind of independence swept over Latin America. The joint armies of the Venezuelan Creole Simón Bolívar and the Argentinian José San Martín drove Spain from their lands. Colombia in 1819; Central America and Venezuela in 1821; Mexico in 1822; Peru in 1824—all became independent. After the battle of Ayacucho, in Peru, on December 9, 1824, the defeated armies of Spain left the continent forever.

From this massive revolution, a decaying Spain preserved only two colonies on two Caribbean islands: Cuba and Puerto Rico.

The Spanish praised Cuba as "the ever-faithful isle" and rewarded its loyal Creole class with a lucrative and liberalized trade policy.

A good prophet in 1820 could have predicted that Cuba and Puerto Rico would create sharp problems for the United States 150 years later. Why? We must look northward to the United States of America and the question of slavery.

THE NEIGHBOR
TO THE NORTH

*These islands [Cuba and Puerto Rico] are natural appendages of
the North American continent. . . .*

—*SECRETARY OF STATE JOHN QUINCY ADAMS, 1823*

In September 1822, a secret representative of the rich Cuban
Creoles, a "Mr. Sanchez" (his real name is not known), traveled
to Washington, D.C., where he met with President James Monroe
and his Cabinet.

Mr. Sanchez and his fellow slaveholding Creole planters were
confronted with a problem. Sentiment in favor of Cuban independence from Spain was rising in the island, as were antislavery
agitation and revolts by black Cubans, slave and free. If Spain
withdrew from Cuba, as it was doing elsewhere in Latin America,
and if England or France then acquired Cuba, the slaves would
be freed. On the other hand, if Cuba became independent, the
slaves would free themselves.

Annexation to the United States was the Cuban planters' only
alternative. The United States was still half slave, and the Cuban
planters could count on the powerful Southern slaveowners to

help maintain the institution ninety miles from their shores. Mr. Sanchez suggested this to the Cabinet. The Cabinet was undecided. Secretary of State John Quincy Adams wrote in his diary:

> Mr. Calhoun* has a most ardent desire that the island of Cuba should become part of the United States, and says that Mr. Jefferson has the same. There are two dangers to be averted by the event: one, that the island should fall into the hands of Great Britain; the other, that it should be revolutionized by the Negroes.

Most future United States policy toward Cuba was foreshadowed in those words. From the day of that secret Cabinet meeting, United States policy stabilized around three propositions: (1) Cuba belongs to the United States; (2) all foreign influence must be kept out; (3) the revolutionary influence of the Cuban people must be contained.

The next year Secretary of State Adams made the policy of the United States perfectly clear:

> These islands [Cuba and Puerto Rico] are natural appendages of the North American continent, and one of them [Cuba] almost within sight of our shores, from a multitude of considerations has become an object of transcendent importance to the commercial and political interests of our Union. . . .
> There are laws of political as well as physical gravitation. And if an apple, severed by the tempest from its native tree, cannot choose but to fall to the ground, Cuba, forcibly disjoined from its own unnatural connection with Spain, and incapable of self support, can gravitate only toward the North American Union, which by the same law of nature cannot cast her off from her bosom. . . .

---

*John C. Calhoun (1782–1850), Southern proslavery leader, secretary of war under Monroe, later vice president.

In December 1823, President Monroe announced the famous doctrine that bears his name. The Monroe Doctrine declared that any attempt by European governments "to extend their system to any portion of this hemisphere" would be viewed by the United States "as dangerous to our peace and safety." At the same time, it noted that "with the existing colonies or dependencies of any European power we have not interfered and shall not interfere."

The Monroe Doctrine thus preserved Cuba as a Spanish colony, warning off all European rivals. Sooner or later Cuba would fall like a "ripe fruit" into the lap of the United States.

In vain did Cuba's revolutionaries appeal to the United States for support against the Spanish colonial government. The Monroe Doctrine, once set in motion, required John Quincy Adams, a liberal president for his time, to praise the despotic Spanish governor as ". . .precisely the man to tranquilize and conciliate the submission of the people of the island to their old government." (Later it would lead to United States intervention in Cuba's war of independence, President Eisenhower's military aid to the Batista tyranny, and President Kennedy's invasion at the Bay of Pigs.)

Disappointed, those Cubans who favored independence from Spain turned to their fellow Latin Americans for support. They appealed to Simón Bolívar, who had led the armies that drove Spain from South America. Bolívar agreed to send a united Mexican-Colombian military expedition to liberate both Puerto Rico and Cuba.

Washington reacted to the prospect of the "ripe apple" falling the other way—toward an independent Latin America—by obtaining the backing of England for a series of threatening notes to Mexico and Colombia, declaring that the United States would not "remain indifferent" to the freeing of Cuba.

The threats worked. Bolívar sadly told a delegation of Cuban revolutionaries, "We cannot set at defiance the American Government, in conjunction with that of England, determined on maintaining the authority of Spain over the Islands of Cuba and Puerto Rico. . . ."

The United States diplomat who delivered the threats wrote a revealing letter to his boss, Secretary of State Henry Clay, during the negotiations. "What I most dread," he wrote, "is that the blacks may be armed and used as auxiliaries. . . ."

"This country prefers that Cuba and Porto Rico should remain dependent on Spain," wrote Clay. "This Government desires no political change of that condition."

During the twenty-year period before the American Civil War, however, Cuba came within several hair-breadths of becoming a state of the United States.

In the 1840's the Creole planters renewed their agitation for annexation to the United States, driven by fears of a slave revolt, heightened by the discovery in 1844 that free blacks, slaves, and a few white Cubans had been meeting for three years in the province of Matanzas. They were planning a revolt to establish a republic in which slavery would be abolished and in which blacks and whites would have full equality.

Exposed by informers, the conspiracy was crushed. The Spanish authorities arrested more than four thousand people. Black suspects were lashed to ladders and whipped to obtain confessions, giving the conspiracy the name it is known by, *La Escalera* (The Ladder).

The fervor for annexation finally foundered on its own contradictions. The government of Spain warned the wealthy planters that any attempt to wage an annexationist revolt against Spain would be met with the ultimate weapon—emancipation. Spain would free the slaves. That was sufficient. Cuban annexationist leader Gaspar Cisneros argued in vain that "an army of fifty thousand Americans would immediately land in Cuba to the assistance of the white population." By 1850 annexationism was waning among the Creoles.

But it picked up in the United States.

It was the era of expansion, of Manifest Destiny, of acquisition of the Southwest, California, and Texas. The federal government, slaveowner-dominated and eager for new territories, had its eyes set on Cuba. "We must have Cuba," said Secretary of State (later President) James Buchanan. "We can't do without Cuba, & above all we must not suffer its transfer to Great Britain. . . . Cuba is already ours, I feel it in my finger ends."

There were three ways of getting Cuba: buying it, invading it, or waging war with Spain. First the United States tried to buy it. In 1848, President Polk offered Spain $100,000,000 but was refused.

Then began a series of intrigues on the part of several administrations, culminating in the infamous Ostend Manifesto of 1854 in which the United States ambassadors to England, France, and Spain argued that the immediate annexation of Cuba was essential to the "security" and "repose" of the United States. Once exposed, the scheme failed.

The Southern slaveowners, however, had an even grander vision: a slave empire to be won by ousting Spain from Cuba, restoring slavery to Central America and the West Indies, and conquering Mexico. As a first step, they supported a series of military expeditions against Cuba organized from the American South by a Venezuelan named Narciso López.

López tried and failed in 1848 and 1849. In 1850 he landed in Matanzas province with a force of six hundred United States mercenaries (recruited for seven dollars a month and the promise of a $4000 victory bonus and a grant of Cuban land) and five Cuban exiles. The invasion received no popular support, and beat

a hasty retreat to Key West. On his last attempt, in 1851, Lopez
was captured with his men, taken to Havana, and put to death.

In 1854, the governor of Mississippi, General John A. Quitman,
a cotton and sugar planter and proslavery expansionist, took up
the banner, backed financially by George Law, the man who
owned the steamship line that carried the mail between New York
and Havana. Law provided a steamer, rifles, and cash. Quitman's
expedition was personally squashed by President Pierce before it
began. Pierce feared the invasion would upset his plans to extend
slavery into Kansas and Nebraska. He had already outraged the
Northern antislavery forces by signing the Kansas-Nebraska Bill
and could not afford to antagonize them more.

The attempts to buy or forcibly annex Cuba by invasion ended
with the American Civil War. Abolitionists of the North, on
whom the Union depended, would never agree to the annexation
of another slave state. The Confederacy, desperate to gain diplomatic support in antislavery Europe, was forced to abandon its
expansionist dreams.

When the opportunity to annex Cuba arose again in the 1890's,
slavery—by then abolished in both Cuba and the United States—
was no longer an issue.

However, as the United States plunged into the Civil War, great
changes were taking place inside the Spanish colony.

THE TEN YEARS' WAR

Do not fear a glorious death,
For to die for your country is to live.
To live in chains is to live
overwhelmed by shame and infamy.
Hark to the clarion's call!
To arms, valiant ones!

—ANTHEM OF THE TEN YEARS' WAR FOR INDEPENDENCE,
NOW THE CUBAN NATIONAL HYMN

Cuba's thirty-year struggle for independence began on October 10, 1868, on a farm in Oriente province, near the town of Yara. The entire Army of Liberation that morning was made up of thirty-eight men, including its leader, fifty-year-old Carlos Manuel de Céspedes. All were Creole plantation owners from Oriente, the province where the sugar industry was the most backward, the institution of slavery weakest, the level of rebel feeling highest, and control by the Spanish authorities least powerful.

The economic struggle that had been developing for a hundred years between the Creoles, who owned the means of producing sugar, tobacco, cattle, and coffee—Cuba's wealth—and the Spaniards, who controlled all commerce and trade, had become a struggle for political control of the country.

The men who translated Cuba's rising national spirit into war against the Spanish were landowners, but they were not the major slaveowners who feared their slaves more than they hated Spain.

Their two great leaders, Céspedes and Ignacio Agramonte, were men of scarce means. Céspedes owned about six hundred acres and fifty slaves. Agramonte was a lawyer.

In August 1868, Céspedes told a planning meeting of revolutionists: "Gentlemen, the hour is solemn and decisive. The power of Spain is decrepit and worm-eaten; if it still appears great and strong to us, it is because for more than three centuries we have contemplated it from our knees." On the afternoon of October 10, he freed his slaves, all of whom joined the rebel army.

An official Spanish newspaper in Havana thought the whole thing was laughable, and announced that "a handful of deluded, badly armed fellows have uttered a cry of rebellion in Yara." But two days after the *Grito de Yara* (the Cry of Yara), the rebel army numbered 4,000 men; toward the end of the month, 9,700; a month from its creation, 12,000. Many were blacks, free and slave, among them Antonio Maceo, who came to embody to the people of Cuba and the world the dignity, honor, and brilliance of the island's revolutionary spirit.

Maceo was the son of a free black Venezuelan dealer in agricultural products in the city of Santiago. He had little formal education and had gone to work at sixteen, delivering his father's produce by muleback. He had become interested in the political issues of the day and in 1864 joined the Masonic lodge in Santiago, a center of rebel agitation. In this he was supported by both of his parents and particularly by his mother, Mariana Grajales, an outstanding woman in Cuba's history.

It was Captain Antonio Maceo who, in the fourth month of the war, halted with a bold attack the advance of a Spanish column on the city of Bayamo, which the Army of Liberation had seized three months before. In the defense of Bayamo more than two thousand Cubans, most of them recently freed slaves, died. When the Spanish finally recovered the city, it had been burned to the ground by its inhabitants.

It was a war that pitted poorly armed and untrained *mambises,* as the revolutionary soldiers were called, against a powerful professional military force.

In a passage from his memoirs, Maceo's chief of staff recalled one battle:

> Untrained men . . . most of them equipped with machetes only, were virtually annihilated as they threw themselves on the solid rank of Spaniards. It is not an exaggeration to assert that for every fifty men, twenty-five were killed. Some even attacked the Spaniards with bare fists, without pistols, without machetes, without even knives.
>
> These men had thrown themselves against bayonets with bare hands; the clash of metal which was heard around them was the sound of their drinking cups banging against the saddle-horn.

The Army of Liberation engaged in guerrilla warfare, attempting to wear down Spanish resistance, making the war economically disastrous for the colonialists. As historian Philip Foner describes it:

> Spaniards held possession of every seaport and most of the towns on the island; the . . . insurgents often controlled the mountain ridges and forests less than a mile away. Their aim was to confine the Spanish Army to the cities, and then, by cutting the roads, isolate the units and force them to surrender. When troops were sent out to quell them, the guerrillas hid in the fastness of the interior where the enemy dared not follow them. The Spaniards shelled, strafed and fired at the unseen enemy, and returned to boast of having "cleaned up" the rebels in the area. But no sooner was the report made than resistance burst forth again. Thus the pattern continued throughout the long war.

The masters of this guerrilla strategy were Antonio Maceo and Máximo Gómez—the latter an exile from Santo Domingo who rose to generalship in the Army of Liberation and with Maceo became one of the great figures in the struggle for Cuban independence. Together they were virtually unbeatable. In a single battle, at Las Guásimas in 1874, 250 men under Maceo decimated a Spanish column twenty times their size backed by artillery. At the end of the battle, the retreating Spanish had suffered 1,037 dead and wounded; the rebels, 174.

Spain's single major victory of the war was won not in Cuba but in Washington, D.C. And if there was one man who harmed the Army of Liberation more than any Spanish general, it was the United States Secretary of State under President Ulysses S. Grant —Hamilton Fish.

Fish successfully prevented the President from recognizing the Cuban rebels and sending them aid or arms, though the United States Congress had voted 98–25 in favor of doing so.

Among those who urged the President to aid the Cuban rebels was the great black abolitionist leader Frederick Douglass, who also raised money to publish the constitution of the Cuban rebel Government-in-Arms, which declared slavery abolished. Douglass even urged young black Americans to join the Cuban cause.

The Army of Liberation fought on for ten years, winning many battles, but slowly being forced back into the easternmost province of Oriente. The rebels were never able to reach the west, where the economic power of Spain lay, and were therefore unable to deal the colonial regime a decisive blow.

Disunity began to appear in the revolutionary ranks. Though the foot soldiers of the Army of Liberation were poor peasants and freed slaves and though many military leaders, such as Maceo, Gómez, and Guillermo Moncada (after whom the Moncada garrison in Santiago was named), had risen from the ranks of the poor and working people, the chief backers of the rebellion were Creole landowners.

The landowners were true patriots, but their thinking was limited. They distrusted the blacks and the poor, and even those who came from different provinces than their own. They blocked Maceo and Gómez from launching a strong invasion at the western part of the island for fear of alienating the western plantation owners (who refused to support the war anyway, lest they lose their slaves).

They tried to prevent the Army of Liberation from freeing the slaves when it seized a plantation. Maceo did so anyway, causing some of the leaders to spread the rumor that he wanted to establish a "black republic."

Agramonte died in combat in 1873; Céspedes, the following year. The leadership of the war passed to Gómez and Maceo, who represented the interests of far poorer classes. The generals were coming closer to belonging to the same class as the foot soldiers.

When Spain, realizing it could not win the war, began to put out feelers, offering certain mild reforms in return for surrender, some of the leaders of the Army of Liberation took the bait. Suspicious of one another, unable to agree on tactics or strategy, and with their morale weakened, the majority of the leaders of the Government-in-Arms capitulated to the Spanish on February 11, 1878, at the village of Zanjón. Undefeated militarily, they had lost the will to fight.

Their collapse signified something deeper. They represented the best of the Creole landowning class. With the Treaty of Zanjón, that class lost forever the chance to lead a Cuban revolution. From now on it would be in other hands.

Antonio Maceo, however, refused to surrender. When he heard what had happened at Zanjón, he rallied fifteen hundred officers and men to the town of Baragúa in Oriente, where he had agreed to meet the Spanish commander. He denounced the dissension within the ranks, criticized the wealthy Cuban exiles who had failed to support the revolution financially and the landowners who had not supported a decisive invasion of the west, declaring his determination to continue the fight. The soldiers supported him unanimously.

When the Spanish general arrived on March 15, 1878, he was told that the Cubans rejected the Treaty of Zanjón and demanded total independence. "Then we are not in agreement?" the startled general asked.

"No," said Maceo, "we are not in agreement."

"Then hostilities will break out again?"

"Right now is all right with me," replied Maceo.

Their meeting came to be known as the "Protest of Baragúa." For those Cubans, black and white, who could not accept a peace that failed to achieve independence from Spain, it was an act that preserved their dignity and hope.

Still, the military struggle could not be won at this time. The rebels arranged for Maceo to leave Cuba uncompromised and undefeated, to rally support outside. The war had ended temporarily. It had cost the lives of 208,000 Spanish and 50,000 Cuban soldiers, but it had changed everything, marking, as José Martí later wrote, "that wonderful and sudden emergence of a people, apparently servile only a short time before, who made heroic feats a daily event, hunger a banquet, and the extraordinary a commonplace."

THE
CUBAN-SPANISH WAR

Freedom Thwarted

Once the United States is in Cuba, who will get it out?

—*JOSÉ MARTÍ, LETTER TO A FRIEND, 1889*

The years after 1878 were bitter. The country was riddled with traitors and police spies. The leaders of the revolution, unable to build a base of support and a united organization, quarreled and separated. Maceo settled on a farm in Costa Rica; Máximo Gómez returned to Santo Domingo.

One young man, twenty-six-year-old José Martí, who had organized revolutionary committees in Havana, was deported to Spain in 1879. From there he made his way to New York City. It was he, a poet, who would solve the revolutionary dilemma.

The Ten Years' War had bankrupted Spanish sugar interests in Cuba, virtually destroying the industry in Las Villas, Camagüey, and Oriente provinces. The Spanish owners sold out to North American interests, a process accelerated by the final abolition of slavery in Cuba in 1886. Once they had to pay for labor, the sugar growers began to import machinery to replace the slaves. The machinery came from the United States.

By 1890 Cuba was in the grip of "the Sugar Trust," otherwise known as the American Sugar Refining Company. The Trust supplied from 70 to 90 percent of all the sugar consumed in the United States and completely controlled the Cuban industry. "By the beginning of the year 1895, Cuba had definitely been converted into an economic colony of the United States," the National Congress of Cuban Historians declared in 1947. Of the 1,485,224 bags of sugar exported by Cuba in 1892, 1,154,193 went to the United States. Only 328,521 went to Spain, supposedly Cuba's mother country.

In 1887 Cuba's exports and imports were larger than those of Mexico, twice as great as all five Central American republics taken together, and were exceeded in South America only by Brazil and Argentina. No wonder the Detroit *Free Press* declared in 1891: "Cuba would make one of the finest states in the Union, and if American wealth, enterprise and genius once invaded the superb island, it would become a veritable hive of industry in addition to being one of the most fertile gardens of the world."

In New York, José Martí was working to bring together the shattered, divided, and demoralized Cuban revolutionary movement. He was racing against time and annexation.

Martí lived for fifteen years in the United States. Originally excited by its promises of individual freedom and opportunity, he soon became disillusioned.

"Our America [by which Martí meant "Latin" America] should know the truth about the United States," he wrote.

In the United States, the causes of unity, instead of coalescing, have become dispersed; humanity's problems, instead of being solved, have been increased; regions, instead of being incorporated into national political life, have been divided and inflamed; democracy, instead of being strong and above the hatred and poverty of the monarchies, has been corrupted and undermined and has given birth to the same menacing poverty and hatred. He who keeps his silence is not fulfilling his duty. He who speaks out, is.

Martí worked untiringly, writing, speaking, visiting the communities of Cuban revolutionary émigrés in Key West, Ocala, Tampa, and New York. Some of the older veterans of the Ten Years' War thought him a bit of a dreamer. He was, in fact, a brilliant writer. His plays, poems, songs, essays, and speeches fill some twenty-seven volumes and are considered among the greatest works in the Spanish language.

Martí knew what had foiled the older leaders: too many of them had looked on black Cubans as their inferiors; they had allowed the military men to run the movement; they had sought financial and political support only from the rich Cuban émigrés; and they had failed to argue strongly against those Cubans who wanted annexation to the United States.

Martí's first speech on arriving in New York City in 1880 dealt directly with "the Negro question," to the discomfort of the aristocratic émigrés and to the delight of the Cuban tobacco workers, black and white, who filled the rear of the hall. He was thereafter uncompromising on the issue of the equality of the races in the revolutionary struggle:

> There is no danger of war between the races in Cuba. Man means more than white man, mulatto, or black man. . . . The souls of white men and Negroes have risen together from the battlefields where they fought and died for Cuba. . . .
>
> When independence comes, every individual will be free in the sanctity of the native home. Merit, the tangible, cumulative of culture, and the inexorable play of economic forces will ultimately unite all men. There is much greatness in Cuba, in both Negroes and whites.

This antiracist spirit has been embodied in Cuba's greatest leaders—Céspedes, who freed his own slaves; Maceo, who freed the slaves on every plantation in his line of march; Martí, who wove it into his passionate democratic vision; and Fidel Castro, who finally toppled the institutions that maintained racism in Cuba.

In 1892, at a meeting of representatives of all the political groups, black and white, the Cuban Revolutionary Party was created, as set forth by Martí, "to obtain . . . the absolute independence of the island of Cuba, and to foment and aid that of Puerto Rico." The first stage of Martí's work was complete: he had knitted together, out of the diverse and demoralized exiles, a democratic organization, led by civilians, in which blacks and whites were equal.

The party was based on the truest fighters for independence— the Cuban working people. "Rich Cubans are only patriots when their purses are squeezed," Máximo Gómez had once commented. Martí knew why. "Truth," he said "is better revealed to the poor and those who suffer."

Only then did Martí involve the military leaders. He approached Maceo and Gómez; they agreed. While these preparations were going on outside Cuba, members of the Cuban Revolutionary Party inside the country were organizing feverishly for the insurrection. A planned invasion force of three ships was discovered in January 1895 and seized by the United States government, alerting the Spanish to Martí's plans. The rebel leaders inside Cuba insisted that the uprising begin immediately. Martí agreed to the date of February 24, 1895, even though he, Maceo, and Gómez would still be outside the country. On that day the insurrection broke out in the town of Baire, a village about fifty miles from Santiago. Within days, thousands of poor peasants and farm workers had joined the Army of Liberation.

Maceo arrived in Cuba on April 1. The word went from village to village: *Maceo is here. Viva Cuba Libre!*

Eleven days later, Máximo Gómez and José Martí landed on the beach of Cajobabo, the easternmost tip of Cuba. Gómez kissed the earth. From then until his death a month later, Martí kept a careful and poetic diary. This is from the entry of April 25:

Day of Combat. Straight through the woods we are drawing close.
. . . We lost our way. The thorns lacerated us. The lianas choked
and slashed us. We cross a wood of green *jigüeras.* At eleven, heavy
gunfire. Steady fire, that re-echoes, answered by concealed and
sharp counterfire. The combat is as though at our very feet: three
bullets reach us, hitting the tree trunks. . . . We make lunch on raw
eggs, a swallow of honey and chocolate. In a little while information
begins to come in from the village. They have seen one dead and
twenty five wounded. Maceo comes in to look for us, and waits
nearby; we hurry to Maceo, joyfully. I said in a letter to Carmita:
"On the very battle route, the victorious Cubans were waiting for
us; they leap from their horses, horses they have taken from the
Civil Guard; they embrace and cheer us; they mount us on their
horses, and fasten spurs on us." Why am I not horrified at the pool
of blood I saw on the road, or the half-dried blood of a head that
is already buried, with the despatch case of one of our riders for a
pillow? With the afternoon sun we began our victory march on our
way back to camp.

Martí was in camp at Dos Rios in the plains of central Oriente
on May 19, writing a letter to a friend in Mexico: "Every day I
am in danger of giving my life for my country and for my duty.
My duty is to stop the United States in time from reaching out
over the West Indies and swooping down, with its great power,
on our American lands."

He never finished the letter, for the Spanish attacked. Plunging
down a pass on horseback, riding to his first combat with the
enemy, he was shot from ambush and killed.

For three years after Martí's death, the Cuban liberating army
under Maceo and Gómez victoriously fought an occupying force
five times its size. The uprisings of 1895 created a chain reaction
across the island. "The forest thickened with insurrectees," wrote
Cuban historian José Portuondo.

In September 1895, Maceo led a force of fifteen hundred men

out of Oriente to the westernmost reaches of the island, sealing the fate of Spanish rule.

The Spanish desperately established concentration camps into which they herded entire villages that sympathized with the rebels. Thousands died there of malnutrition, malaria, and dysentery. Meanwhile the war was draining Spain of some eight hundred thousand silver pesos every ten days.

Finally even the Spanish military leaders began to lose heart. In February 1898 a Spanish admiral wrote to his commander, "I ask myself if it is fair . . . to carry out adventures . . . which will cause the ruin of Spain—and all to defend an island that *was* ours, because even in the event that we don't lose this war, we will have lost in fact."

In 1898, interventionist forces in the United States—motivated primarily by the desire for Cuban markets—pressured the McKinley administration into declaring war on Spain. United States forces joined the combat during the last two months of a war already won by the Cuban liberating army. At the cost of 266 dead, the United States took possession not only of Cuba, but of Puerto Rico, Guam, and the Philippines.

Victory was snatched from the Cuban liberating army at the moment of its success. The Spanish army in Santiago surrendered to the United States, not the Cubans. The victorious *mambises* were forced to stand outside Santiago while the United States Army occupied the city.

"I have lived inside the monster and I know its entrails," Martí had written about the United States.

Shall we bring the country dear to our hearts, virgin and fruitful, to this frenzied pack of rich against poor, Christian against Jew, white against black, peasant against businessman, Westerners and Southerners against Easterners, avid and destitute men against all which is denied their hunger and thirst. Shall we deliver it into this oven of wrath, into these sharp toothed jaws, into this smoking crater?

Delivered it was. The consistent policy of the United States, first set forth by John Quincy Adams eighty years earlier—to maintain Cuba as a Spanish possession until such time as it would fall like a ripe fruit into the lap of the United States—was a success. Martí was dead; Maceo was dead; and though most Cubans did not immediately perceive it, so were their immediate chances for independence.

Though the United States army pitched its tents on the ruins of the thirty-year struggle for independence, Martí and the movement he had led passed on to the Cubans a legacy second in value only to independence itself: an example of how to organize, a body of literature, and a political vision that would guide Cuban revolutionaries through the twentieth century. The revolutionaries of 1895 had set the moral standard for future political action.

A REPUBLIC
IN NAME ONLY

. . . Yankee troops occupied our territory. The Platt Amendment was imposed on our first Constitution as a humiliating clause granting the odious "right" of foreign intervention. Our wealth passed into their hands; they falsified our history, our administration, and molded our politics to the interests of the intruders. The nation was subjected to sixty years of political, economic and cultural asphyxiation.

—SECOND DECLARATION OF HAVANA, 1962

From 1902 to 1959, during the period Cubans now call "the Pseudo Republic," Cuba was generally ruled by men who dared not make a move until they heard from Washington, D.C., men who waited for Washington's permission, or for Washington to do it for them, or for Washington to make it unnecessary for them to do anything at all.

Martí's goal of true independence was buried without honor in 1898. When the representatives of Spain and the United States sat down to peace talks at the end of what our textbooks still call the Spanish-American War, the Cubans who had fought for thirty years and almost won were not invited, nor were they even taken seriously.

Why, they couldn't even clean up after themselves, complained General Leonard Wood, military governor of Cuba from 1900 to 1902. Wood appointed himself the task of developing in the "natives" a sense for the good American Anglo-Saxon habits: respect for authority, and next to it, cleanliness.

The missionary zeal with which General Wood cleaned up the island, bending its people to his will in matters great and small, was part of a deeper process: he was preparing Cuba for Yankeehood. He was preparing the mechanisms that would produce a subservient government, however formally independent.

Any illusions the Cuban revolutionaries might have had about their "independence" were stripped away on June 12, 1901, when the Platt Amendment—an amendment to the Cuban constitution, written and approved by the United States Congress—was passed by a convention of cowed Cuban leaders. Only a few opposed it. The majority bent under the threat of the permanent occupation of Cuba by United States troops.

The Platt Amendment proclaimed that the United States had the right to intervene in Cuba at any time. No one explained it better than General Wood himself:

> Of course, Cuba has been left with little or no independence by the Platt Amendment. . . . The Cuban Government cannot enter into certain treaties without our consent, nor secure loans above certain limits, and it must maintain the sanitary conditions that have been indicated.
>
> With the control that we have over Cuba, a control which, without doubt, will soon turn her into our possession, soon we will practically control the sugar market in the world. I believe that it is a very desirable acquisition for the United States. The island will gradually be "Americanized," and in the due course we will have one of the most rich and desirable possessions existing in the world. . . .

Article 7 of the amendment provided that "the Government of Cuba will sell or lease to the United States the lands necessary for coaling or naval stations at certain specified points." This clause begat the Guantánamo naval base, a strip of Cuban territory surrounding the Bay of Guantánamo, fifty miles east of Santiago on the southeast Cuban coast. It was leased "in perpetuity," meaning forever. It was a foreign garrison—a thorn in perpetuity between the two nations.

The following year a reciprocity treaty was signed allowing Cuba and the United States to export goods to each other at lower tariffs than those enjoyed by any other nation. Cuba, poor and underdeveloped, exported little besides sugar and coffee. Her products paid a 20 percent lower tariff on entering the United States. The United States, on its way to becoming the richest nation in the world, exported practically everything. Its goods entered Cuba at a 40 percent lower rate. It was not an equal relationship.

The effect was to lock up the Cuban market for American goods. Within fifteen years, 74 percent of all Cuba's imports came from the United States. Economically Cuba was tied closer to its northern neighbor than it had been to Spain.

The United States military occupation ended in 1902 when Tomás Estrada Palma became Cuba's first president. Three times in the next fifteen years United States military returned to Cuba to quell revolts and insure Cuba's loyalty.

Cuba's enforced subservience to the United States continued until 1960. During those years the main enforcer, however, was not the U.S. Army but the U.S. dollar. As U. S. historian Lester D. Langley put it, "Economically, Cuba remained as much a colony in the twentieth century as it had been under four centuries of Spanish rule."

Cubans call the period surrounding World War I "the dance of the millions." The price of sugar climbed steadily during those years, stimulated by protective tariffs and the war, producing a bonanza of profits, not for the Cuban people but for those who owned 51 percent of the Cuban sugar harvest (1923 figures): the House of Morgan financial group, the National City Bank, the Chase Bank (now Chase Manhattan), Brown Brothers, United Fruit Company, and the Rockefeller family.

Capital investment by U.S. financial interests in Cuban sugar and other holdings had increased from around $50,000,000 in 1898 to $1,500,000,000 in 1925! This produced two fundamental distortions in the economy from which Cuba is still recovering: (1) the massive sugar plantations *(latifundia),* formed by squeezing out the small growers; and (2) a single-crop economy: sugar.

Some 80 percent of the exported mineral wealth of Cuba was owned in those years by the Bethlehem Steel Company. U.S. citizens owned the railroads, the tobacco industry, the electrical industry. Cubans spoke to one another over the ITT-owned Cuban Telephone Company—even its name was in English—but sugar was king, and when the price of sugar, totally dependent on the U.S. market, fell, "the dance of the millions" flew to pieces, like a merry-go-round out of control.

In the summer and fall of 1920, the price of sugar dropped from twenty-two cents to three cents a pound and stayed at that price, or lower, for twenty years.

When the Great Depression hit the United States in 1929, the United States slashed its imports from Cuba, eliminating the only benefit Cuba received from her dependency—a market she could count on. By 1932 Cuba exported to the United States only 18 percent of what she had exported ten years before. As a result, it is estimated that by 1935 one million Cubans—one in four—were living in extreme poverty.

Sugar workers were laboring for lower wages than they had received twenty-five years before—when they could find work. The period when they could not work, the *tiempo muerto* (dead time) between harvests, was stretched by the sugar-mill owners to almost nine months. Older sugar workers in Cuba today remember what that meant. During the *tiempo muerto,* families ate roots and bark to stay alive, hunted locusts, lived in woods, in caves. Sugar, under foreign control, was a pitiless tyrant.

The generation of students at the University of Havana in 1923 was the first born after the death of Martí. They were the generation of pseudo independence under the pseudo republic. They had been made worldly by World War I and were intrigued by the Russian Revolution of 1917, which held out the hope of a society free of exploitation. Their own world was in ashes—the "dance of the millions" had just collapsed—and the possibility of change stirred them deeply, though most were fired more by the visions of Martí than the polemics of Lenin.

They were repelled by the political corruption around them and encouraged by the rising militancy of the Cuban working class.

In 1921, the university administration decided to award an honorary rectorship to General Enoch Crowder. Crowder, who had arrived two years earlier aboard the battleship U.S.S. *Minnesota,* had been ordered by President Woodrow Wilson to straighten out Cuba's bookkeeping, banking system, and electoral laws, which were not in line with U.S. business interests. In the process, he personally picked who would be elected president of Cuba in the 1920 election, recommending at one point that the United States land troops to make sure things came out right.

A protest manifesto was circulated among the students, and the uproar brought about the cancellation of the award. One of the signers of the manifesto was Julio Antonio Mella, eighteen, star of the university basketball team.

Under Mella's leadership, the students seized the university in January 1923, demanding the dismissal of corrupt and incompetent professors, the modernization of textbooks, the granting of university autonomy, and free education. The students won many of their demands.

So powerful was the wave of protest awakened by the students that the following year Gerardo Machado, Liberal politician and electric-power businessman, rode it to the presidency in a landslide election.

Machado's campaign slogan was "Water, roads, and schools." When his Conservative opponent, General Mendieta, published a photo of himself on horseback, Machado's backers pasted up posters of Machado in a crowd, entitled "With the People and on Foot." Machado called for "regeneration" and "honesty in government," but within a few years he had installed one of the most brutal dictatorships in Cuba's history.

He forced an abject congress to extend his term until 1935, tied up the opposition in repressive legislation, and forbade new political parties, public meetings, or unkind criticism in the press.

Some had seen it coming. A few days after the election, Julio Mella wrote in a student magazine, "In a democratic carnival, the people have gained another master. . . . Soon we shall see that he acts as his predecessors have acted." Several months later he was calling Machado "a tropical Mussolini."

One of Machado's first acts as President of Cuba was to reinstate all the faculty members ousted by the students the previous year, which only served to further radicalize the student body.

In mid-August, 1925, a group of people around Mella and Carlos Baliño, a veteran socialist and comrade of José Martí, founded the Cuban Communist Party. Only thirteen delegates attended the meeting, but in the climate of labor unrest and radicalization, it rapidly developed an influence far beyond its actual numbers.

The following month, Mella was expelled from the university and arrested on a charge of terrorism. His twenty-three-day hunger strike rallied support across the country, forcing Machado to free him. Mella went into exile in Mexico.

Machado's thugs beat up opposition professors, students, lawyers, and doctors. Labor leaders, Communists, and newspaper editors mysteriously disappeared, their corpses turning up later. But nothing could stop the avalanche of events in Cuba, not even the death of Mella himself. In 1929, while walking along a Mexico City street, he was shot in the back and killed by a Machado gunman. He was twenty-six years old.

The time was right for the introduction of Marxist ideas into Cuba.

Mella's newly formed Communist Party threw itself into organizing the sugar workers. Sugar was Cuba's most important industry; its workers, the most oppressed.

A forty-eight-hour general strike in 1930, organized by Communist leader Rubén Martinez Villena, was a partial success, though he himself was forced into exile. In May of that year, a mass meeting of the Nationalists, (the upper-class opposition to Machado) was fired on by the police; eight persons were killed. On the day classes opened at the university, students found the buildings guarded by the police; they refused to enter and began to march through the streets. The police attacked the demonstration, killing one student.

These three forces—the labor movement, led by the Communists, the old-guard Nationalists, and the students—together formed the opposition to Machado and together would overthrow him.

THE REVOLUTION
OF 1933

*The red flags hoisted stealthily in the night over the chimneys of the
Armour Company herald the raising of those other flags which will
float in plain day over all the factories of the sugar industry.*

*Eyes that are young today will not be old when they behold this
marvel.*

—*RUBÉN MARTINEZ VILLENA, May 1933*

In 1933 the newly elected government of Franklin Delano Roosevelt found the situation in Cuba to be entirely out of hand. It
greatly alarmed Roosevelt's "Brain Trust," three of whose members were officers of the American Molasses Company, which
owned the Sucrest Corporation, which depended on Cuban sugar.

The "tranquility of the government and the country," promised
by Machado in 1925, had not been delivered, and now Cuba was
a political whirlpool in which an estimated $1,500,000,000 in U.S.
investments was likely to drown. Assuming that Machado had
lost the ability to govern, Roosevelt sent his Assistant Secretary
of State, Sumner Welles, as ambassador to Cuba to find some way
to replace him.

From the day he arrived in Havana in May 1933, Welles became the center of the whirlpool. Every "respectable" political faction—except the students, the Communists, and the labor movement—wheeled about him, seeking the approval of the "good neighbor" from the north.

Welles maneuvered between Machado and the upper-class opposition, seeking a way to replace the President with an acceptably pro-U.S. substitute. In the end, however, it was not he who forced Machado out. On August 4, 1933, a general strike closed the city of Havana; by August 9 the whole island was affected. Machado resigned and fled to Nassau with his family.

Sumner Welles then proposed to the army officers and the Nationalist opposition that Carlos Manuel de Céspedes, one-time Cuban ambassador to Washington, only son of the leader of the Ten Years' War, and "a most sincere friend of the United States," replace Machado. They accepted. That night Welles received a telegram from Washington: "The President and Secretary [of State] have asked me to express their warm congratulations to you and their appreciation of what you have done."

The "government of Sumner Welles" lasted twenty-three days. It was made up of indecisive conservative men who agreed with Welles that "for Cuba the essential thing now is to keep public order." But once released, the revolutionary impulse could not now be sung to sleep. The Cuban people identified their aspirations for a new society with those of the revolutionary labor movement, the Communists, the students, and a new organization —the Columbia Military Union—formed by a group of dissatisfied army sergeants, among them Sergeant Fulgencio Batista y Zaldívar. None were represented in the "Welles government."

In the name of better conditions for the soldiers and more open promotion opportunities, a group of the Cuban army sergeants seized the Columbia garrison on September 4, 1933. The rest of the garrisons in the country joined quickly.

Rushing to the camp as soon as they heard of the revolt, the leaders of the radical student organization talked the sergeants into transforming their rebellion into a revolution. Together they chose a ruling body, and at one o'clock the next afternoon informed President Céspedes that he had been deposed. Céspedes abandoned the presidential palace as inconspicuously as he had arrived.

Not much is known about Antonio Guiteras before 1930, except that he was a militant student and had been expelled from the university in 1927. But from 1930 to 1935 he pursued a revolutionary path that placed him firmly in Cuban history.

In 1931 he had helped to organize an unsuccessful uprising against Machado in Oriente province. After four months in prison he was released, and making use of the travel involved in his line of work, selling pharmaceutical products, he again began organizing an insurrection in Oriente. By April 1932 his movement was ready for another military assault on the dictatorship; Guiteras's plans called for simultaneous attacks on several military posts and the bombing of the Moncada garrison by plane. Again his plans failed.

Undaunted, he kept on organizing and was planning an assault on the Bayamo garrison when the Machado government fell. He was still in Oriente when the sergeants' revolt of September 4 overthrew President Céspedes, and there he heard that he had been appointed to the Cabinet of the new government.

Today Cuban historians refer to the government he joined as the "Grau-Guiteras" government, though Grau San Martín was its president, for it was twenty-seven-year-old Guiteras—not Grau —who held it together.

It was a government *for* the people, but not *by* the people or *of* the people. It rested on a shaky alliance between the militant students, full of nationalistic fervor but with no experience at governing, and the rebel sergeants who originally had only intended to oust their superiors, not create a revolution. It floated on the surface of the mass strikes and revolts that had overthrown Machado, like a rowboat in a gale; it was beset by friends who acted like enemies and enemies who acted like friends.

The members of the new government were united by their opposition to United States intervention and control of their country, but as soon as they had formed the government, they began to fall out. "Our program could not rest simply on the principle of nonintervention," Guiteras wrote later. "It had to go ferociously toward the root of our ills—economic imperialism—which made many back out, dividing our ranks."

Guiteras knew that he had achieved "power without revolution" and that the government had to be anchored in public support in order to survive. The reforms he carried out, however, succeeded more in antagonizing the United States than in winning over the radicals.

These reforms do not seem so radical now, but in 1933 they were deeply threatening to the United States. The Grau-Guiteras government renounced the Platt Amendment and established an eight-hour working day. It set up a Department of Labor, opened the university to the poor, granted peasants the right to the land they were farming, gave women the right to vote, and reduced the electric rates by 40 percent. In the eyes of Roosevelt's trusted adviser, Sumner Welles, this made it "communistic" and "irresponsible."

Far from being a tyranny, the Grau-Guiteras government had little control over its own military, which was rapidly being shaped by ex-Sergeant, now Colonel Batista into his private political instrument. Batista's army, supposedly the mainstay of the government, was arresting and killing the very people whose support the government needed to stay in power.

Batista was meeting secretly with Sumner Welles, who was

pursuing a clever strategy of "destabilization." By refusing U.S. recognition of the Grau-Guiteras government, Welles denied it legitimacy and encouraged the opposition to overthrow it. This in turn maintained the very instability that was the excuse for withholding recognition. It was an effective circular strategy, and it worked.

Guiteras urgently appealed to the revolutionary left to support his besieged government. The left, however, blamed the government for the brutality of Batista's army, attacked it as "Fascist," and concentrated on encouraging the workers to seize the sugar mills. The sugar workers set up "soviets"—organizations of workers' power modeled on those of the Russian Revolution—in more than thirty mills.

Guiteras, on the other hand, failed to see what ruin was being carried out in his name by Batista. He opposed the seizures and the strikes and could not prevent the army from attacking the workers.

Batista, the only leader to benefit from these clashes of interest, was becoming enticed with visions of himself as the Cuban "strong man," and was encouraged in this by Welles.

On January 14, 1934, Guiteras announced the nationalization of the American-owned Electric Bond and Share Company. It was his last governmental act. The next day Batista, with the U.S. ambassador's blessing, demanded and received President Grau's resignation. Guiteras desperately tried to rally the revolutionary groups to stop the coup, but they were too dispersed, mutually suspicious, and exhausted. Five days later the United States Department of State recognized the Batista-installed government.

Guiteras could not be deterred. He returned to Oriente, this time to build a new organization with a defined radical program —the last coherent attempt during that decade to continue the revolution.

Despite the defeat of the revolution by Batista, the spirit that had lain dormant since the United States invasion of 1898 had been reawakened and given new form—by the Marxism of Julio Antonio Mella and the antiimperialism of Antonio Guiteras. Opposed to each other in the thirties, these political currents merged two decades later in the Cuban Revolution.

On May 8, 1935, Guiteras was preparing to leave Cuba to organize an armed invasion like that of Martí, forty years earlier, and of Fidel Castro, twenty years later, when he was betrayed to the army by an informer and killed.

Fidel was nine years old that year.

FIDEL CASTRO

The Making of a Revolutionary

When there are many without honor, there are always some who have within themselves the dignity of many men. They are the ones who revolt with terrible force against those who steal the people's freedom.

—JOSÉ MARTÍ, *Age of Gold*

Fidel Castro Ruz, fifth of the seven children of Angel Castro y Argiz, plantation owner, and his wife, Lina Ruz Gonzales, spent a normal rural childhood, running barefoot, growing up sturdy and large. His father, an immigrant laborer from Galicia, Spain, had risen through shrewdness, thrift, and hard work to own sugar lands that ran along the northern coast of Oriente in the district of Mayarí.

It seems that from an early age Fidel (no one in Cuba refers to him any other way) identified more with those who labored for his father than with that innately conservative man.

Fidel was attending a parochial grade school in Santiago run by the Christian Brothers when Fulgencio Batista crushed the gen-

eral strike of March 1935, assassinated Antonio Guiteras, and
stilled the final tremors of the revolutionary movement of the
thirties.

Though Batista rode to power over the wreck of the 1933
revolution, the energies it had released lived on. The students,
sugar workers, small planters, professionals, and the growing industrial working class were further strengthened by the worldwide
democratic movement that rose to meet fascism and Nazism in the
late 1930s.

The outbreak of the Spanish Civil War in 1936 stirred Cuba
deeply. Hundreds of thousands attended rallies in support of those
fighting to defend the Spanish Republic against the fascist rebels
led by General Francisco Franco. Almost a thousand Cubans
fought in Spain with the International Brigades, who came from
many countries to defend Spanish democracy.

During this period, democrats, socialists, and Communists
cooperated more closely together in the face of the rising fascist
threat. In Cuba, General Batista found it expedient to cooperate
with the antifascist movement and to make peace with the left. In
1938 he legalized the Cuban Communist Party and freed thousands of political prisoners.

The Communist Party was led at that time by the great-grand-
son of an African slave, a young shoemaker named Blas Roca,
who had helped organize the seizure of the Mabay sugar mill
during the revolution of 1933. Under Roca, the party moved into
the stormy center of Cuban political life, and Roca himself became
one of Cuba's undisputed, though controversial, national figures.

With the legalization of the Communist Party, new life returned
to the labor movement. A unified national labor organization was
formed, the *Confederación de Trabajadores de Cuba* (Confederation of Cuban Workers, or CTC), under the leadership of a

twenty-eight-year-old black Communist, Lázaro Peña.

At the head of the sugar workers' union was one of Cuba's most respected labor leaders, a black man and a Communist, Jesús Menéndez. Menéndez, who had been forced by poverty to leave home at the age of thirteen to cut sugarcane, was a tireless union organizer, risking his life against the hired thugs of the sugar-mill owners. Protected by the workers when he visited the mills, Menéndez organized local unions, investigated ways of keeping employment high, solved health and safety problems. He was instrumental in establishing a retirement fund for sugar workers and in quadrupling their wages in the years 1942–47. Menéndez personally negotiated the escalator clause with the United States government that gave sugar workers a yearly bonus proportional to the rise in sugar prices.

Blas Roca was elected to serve in the national assembly that drafted a new constitution for Cuba, known as the Constitution of 1940. This document struck a balance between the rich and the working class. It protected individual and social rights, supported full employment and a minimum wage, extended social security, called for equal pay for equal work, and outlawed the huge plantations, the *latifundia*.

As the new constitution was being passed, Fidel was about to enter a Jesuit high school in Havana. He was proclaimed the best high school athlete in Cuba for the year 1943–44, and when he graduated, his high school year book said of him:

> Fidel distinguished himself always in all the subjects related to letters. His record was one of excellence, he was a true athlete, always defending with bravery and pride the flag of the school. He has known how to win the admiration and the affection of all. He will make law his career and we do not doubt that he will fill with brilliant pages the book of his life. He has good timber and the actor in him will not be lacking.

Equally significant were the words of a close friend:

When his teachers could not find him and wanted to talk to him, they knew that the best thing to do was to go to the kitchen where he would probably be found talking to the cook or some other humble employee about their problems and agonies.

Fulgencio Batista was certain that his antifascist positions and wartime leadership would win the 1944 presidential election for his handpicked candidate, but he was beaten by Grau San Martín, who based his campaign on his revolutionary reputation from the Grau-Guiteras government of 1933 and against governmental corruption. Batista was stunned, but under pressure to preserve national unity, he stepped down. A short time later he went into "voluntary exile" in Daytona Beach, Florida.

Grau, however, was not the revolutionary he had appeared to be eleven years earlier. He won the election with the support of conservatives and big business and paid off his backers by setting out immediately to crush the growing Communist and labor movement. When some 90 percent of the workers voted for Communist and noncorrupt leaders in the trade-union elections of 1946, Grau began to employ overt terror. The rights promised by the new constitution would not be enforced during the next twenty years.

Fidel's college years were spent during the second Grau administration. The University of Havana, which Fidel entered in 1945, was a major power center in Cuba, the stepping-stone to a political career, since those other normal centers of power—commerce and industry—were controlled by North Americans. Among the refuse of the revolution of the thirties were several armed groups, called *bonches* (from the English word "bunch"), made up in part of men who had fought against Machado, now soured into gangsters who terrorized students and teachers into supporting them.

Fidel later said that his four years at the university were far more dangerous than the battles he fought against Batista in the mountains. A fine speaker and rising as a student leader, Fidel was opposed to the *bonches*, which put him in danger of being beaten or killed. He had several narrow escapes.

By 1947, Fidel's study of the writings of José Martí, his sympathy for the poor, his humanism, and his contacts at the university had made him a conscious but unformed revolutionary. That year in July, he joined an abortive expedition led by Dominican exiles to invade the Dominican Republic and overthrow its dictator, Generalissimo Rafael Trujillo. The expedition never got beyond a mosquito-ridden key off the coast of Cuba.

In January 1948, labor leader Jesús Menéndez was touring the sugar mills, rallying the men against the reign of antiunion terror. The next-to-last mill he visited that month was the Mabay mill, scene of the workers' takeover during the revolution of 1933. As he stepped down from the train at Manzanillo, an army captain shot him to death.

Along the route of the train that carried Menéndez's body to Havana, the sugar workers to whom he had devoted his life massed to pay him tribute. Among the crowd that awaited the train in Havana was twenty-year-old Fidel Castro.

That same year Fidel was elected president of the Law Students' Association. He began organizing the "First Latin American Congress of University Students," a meeting that would gather students who supported the independence movements in the colonial countries of Asia, Africa, and Latin America. It was agreed to hold a planning meeting of the congress in Bogotá, capital city of Colombia.

On April 9, 1948, Fidel was waiting in the Bogotá offices of the newspaper *El Tiempo* for an interview with the popular leader of the Colombian Liberal Party, Jorge Eliecer Gaitán. As Gaitán was walking to the newspaper office, a gunman emptied a revolver into him, killing him instantly. An infuriated crowd beat the assassin to death, and the rage spilled over into the population. A popular insurrection known as the *Bogotazo* erupted.

At a nearby police station, sympathetic police were handing out rifles to the crowd marching on the presidential palace. Fidel took one of the guns, but could find no signs of anyone leading or directing the rebellion, and was appalled at the looting that spontaneously broke out. Bogotá was on fire; sporadic fighting between the army and groups of citizens and rebel police continued throughout the night.

At dawn the Liberal leaders and the government came to an agreement that halted the fighting. Fidel took refuge in the Cuban embassy and three days later returned home. He had not fired a shot, but he had experienced a popular rebellion in its most chaotic and spontaneous form.

That fall, Carlos Prío Socarrás—who had been Grau's repressive Minister of Labor—was elected President. Under his administration, brutality and corruption reached new heights. Prío took advantage of the cold-war anti-Communist hysteria of the times to divide the labor movement and purge many Communist labor leaders. The leader of the Havana dockworkers was shot down. By threats and blackjacks and back-street beatings, the workers' organizations were seized by gangsters. The Communist Party newspaper *Hoy* was attacked and closed; the party passed into semilegality—legal on paper but heavily persecuted.

The corruption and violence of the years after World War II resulted from economic and social pressures that squeezed Cuban society almost to the breaking point. A Brookings Institute study describes the Cuban economy at that time:

Before the Castro regime, over 90% of the telephone and electric services, one-half of the public service railways, one-fourth of all bank deposits, about 40% of sugar production and much of the mining, oil production, and cattle ranching was in the hands of United States businessmen. . . .

As these businessmen drained money out of Cuba, American postwar prosperity brought an avalanche of tourism down upon Havana, the immediate by-products of which were gambling, prostitution, and organized crime.

Cuban per-capita income from the production of sugar actually *fell* between 1925 and 1953—from eighty-two to sixty-four dollars. Except for a thin layer of wealth floating at the top, the Cuban people were growing poorer. They were being drained as surely as if they had cut their wrists.

The glitter and erotic allure of prerevolutionary Havana was powered by the massive exploitation of sugar workers, farmers, and women. There were two careers that a working woman in Havana could follow in those years—as a domestic servant or as a prostitute.

It was not long before a wave of revulsion against the payoffs, gangsterism, and corruption took hold of the people of Cuba. The man who gave that revulsion a national voice was Eduardo R. Chibás. He had been a student leader in 1927, was sent to prison twice by the Machado dictatorship, had been a constant critic of Batista, and was elected senator in 1944. In 1947, sickened by the compromises and bad faith of Grau and Prío, Chibás formed a new political party, the *Partido del Pueblo Cubano* (Cuban People's Party), commonly referred to as the Orthodox Party.

Chibás's Sunday-evening radio programs were searing and passionate. He named names—all the way to the top of the government. He told what they took, whom they bribed, what was wrong with the health system, banking, international finance. Hundreds of thousands of Cubans listened.

In five years Chibás built the Orthodox Party from a tiny splinter group in 1947 to the top contender for presidential power in 1952. His campaign had the full support of the Communists, though the feeling was not mutual: Chibás and many of the *Ortodoxos* were strongly anti-Communist.

One of his staunchest young followers was Fidel Castro. Fidel was graduated from law school in 1951 and joined a law firm. He spent most of his time taking the cases of student demonstrators, coal workers, and vegetable vendors at the central market—usually for free. He was married to Mirtha Diaz Balart and had a two-year-old son, Fidel, Jr. The Orthodox Party was running Chibás for president; Fidel was a candidate for Congress.

On August 5, 1951, Fidel accompanied Chibás to the CMQ radio station for the evening broadcast. Chibás was depressed; he had been unable to back up with hard facts some accusations he had made earlier against the Minister of Education. He knew he was right, but unable to come up with proof, he found himself being ridiculed by the government party. Nevertheless, his denunciations that night were no less hard-hitting:

Today I accuse the government of Carlos Prío Socarrás of being the most corrupt in our Republic up to today, and his Minister of Education of robbing money from material and from the school breakfast program and of making vast investments in Guatemala and other Central American republics.

At the end of his speech he cried:

Comrades of the Orthodox Party, move forward! For economic independence, political liberty and social justice! Sweep the thieves out of government. People of Cuba, rise and move forward! People of Cuba, awake! *This is my last knock at the door!*

Then with the microphone still on, and before a stunned Fidel, he took a gun from his pocket and fatally shot himself.

Chibás's death did not halt the momentum of the reform movement. Running its vice-presidential candidate in Chibás's place, the Orthodox Party was far out in front, supported by a clear majority of the Cuban people and expected to win.

Running a slow third in the race for president that year was Fulgencio Batista, recently returned from his self-imposed exile in Florida. With no chance of winning a fair election, his influence in the army eroding, and threatened with a left-of-center government, Batista reverted to his 1933 style and began meeting with a group of dissatisfied officers to plan a coup.

On March 10, 1952, Batista and his coconspirators took control of most of the military garrisons and posts in Cuba. Students, Fidel among them, crowded into the university, clamoring for guns to defend the government, only to find that President Prío had already packed his bags and left the country.

In the shock that followed the coup, one of the first voices to speak out was that of twenty-four-year-old Fidel, in a mimeographed paper that appeared on the streets three days later:

> It is not a revolution, but a brutal snatching of power! They are not patriots, but destroyers of freedom, usurpers, adventurers thirsty for gold and power. The coup was not against Prío but against the people. . . .
>
> It was right to remove from office a government of murderers and thieves, and we were trying to do so peacefully with the support of public opinion and the aid of the people. But by what right do the military do so, they who have murdered and stolen without limit in the past?

Fidel even took his case to court, asking that the coup be declared illegal and Batista sent to jail. When the court refused, all legal means for Fidel and his generation were closed. Only revolution remained.

On the 16th of March [1952], the *Ortodoxos* called the citizens to the cemetery of Colón [in Havana] to pay homage to the memory of their unforgettable founder. An ominous blue stain surrounded the tomb like a threat: the police.

At the end, when the crowd began to disperse, a young vigorous man leaped up on the marble and began to speak in a strong, clear voice. He was not on the program and no one announced his name. However, as he began to talk, the people, who were searching desperately for a leader, more by intuition than reason, understood that they were in the presence of a person with a driving message.

"Eduardo Chibás, we come to tell you that your people will not fail you. . . . Eduardo Chibás, we come to tell you that we shall never turn away from your ideals. . . . Eduardo Chibás, we come to tell you that we will be worthy of your sacrifice and that we will not slacken in our effort to see a free nation."

The emotion broke out in applause. Salas Canizares [the Havana police chief], immobilized by such audacity, decided not to intervene. From his marble platform the fiery speaker looked him straight in the eyes and threw the words in his face. When he finished, a youthful voice rose above the noisy applause:

"Viva Fidel Castro!" it said.

—Edmundo Desnoes, *La Sierra y el llano*

From that moment, Fidel began to organize secretly to over-throw the Batista dictatorship. As a leader of the younger members of the Orthodox Party he was widely respected. While the traditional politicians cowered before the coup, Fidel gathered a group of young men and women around him who were willing to die to restore democracy to Cuba:

Juan Almeida, a young black bricklayer, had gone to the university the day of the coup to see if the students were organizing any resistance, but there were no guns. "I met Fidel there, and he began to talk about revolution, what a revolution was, how the coup was holding it back, that the young people had to unite, and that there were forces existing that had no complicity with the past." That's what Almeida had been wanting to hear, so he joined Fidel.

José Ponce had a little print shop in Artemisa, in Pinar del Río province. The day after the coup, students brought an anti-Batista manifesto to him; he printed it, and the next day the police arrested him and beat him up. Then one night he met a friend in the park: "It was he who told me something was going on. He told me about Fidel, that he was a young man who had new ideas and that his movement had no relation to the past or to the old politicians. So I told him, 'Good, that's for me. Tell me what to do.' "

Melba Hernández had studied law "with only one objective: to transform society." Her view of what her profession could accomplish changed quickly after she graduated.

"As soon as I faced reality with my law degree in my hand, with a law that was supposed to back me up, I couldn't get anywhere. It was all a lie. As lawyers, we were all frustrated. We were always defending the most difficult cases. We came before the judges, the great gentlemen, and we came out of the courtrooms sick inside. We came to the conclusion that we couldn't achieve what we thought we could achieve by being lawyers."

She met Abel Santamaría and his sister Haydée (her friends called her 'Yeye') through a common friend, and one night she visited them in their Havana apartment.

"Abel, Yeye and I talked a great deal. . . . We agreed that the solution for the problems of the nation was to be found in revolutionary violence. . . . On that occasion Abel said that there was a young man in our ranks who, in his opinion, was capable of leading such a future action.

"One afternoon Abel summoned us . . . and Fidel came in unannounced. We started to talk, and Fidel sat on the edge of the chair and started to talk about how it was our duty—not one we could leave to another generation—to liberate our homeland.

"He told us that it wasn't a case of replacing the existing government with an honest one; it was necessary to take much more radical action. . . . I remember that Fidel would say, 'This must be done with anonymous young people who can understand every-thing that has to be done.' In order to do this we would have to search among the ranks of the workers."

Abel Santamaría was the same age as Fidel. His father was the head of the carpentry shop at the Constancia sugar mill in Las Villas province. Abel was studying in commercial school in Havana at the age of twenty, hoping to go on to the university, when he was drawn to the Orthodox Party by its call for honesty in politics. His apartment, which he shared with his sister Haydée, was a center for young radicals who spent the evenings discussing the country's problems. Most of them were also *Ortodoxos*.

One night at a political meeting at the university, he met Fidel Castro.

"Fidel lost an extraordinary friend when he lost Abel," Haydée Santamaría recalled years later. "Abel wasn't just Fidel's comrade and second-in-command. Abel was the most loyal of Fidel's friends. He was probably the first person in this country to realize Fidel's extraordinary merits. The other comrades that were with Fidel respected him and had great faith in him, but I think I can safely say that none of them realized the importance of Fidel's role as clearly as Abel did."

The preparations for the attack on the Moncada garrison in Santiago were carried out in total secrecy. In a country rich in clandestine plots, it was one of the few popular ones—involving some fifteen hundred people—that was never suspected or be-trayed. Almost all its participants were under thirty and followers of Eduardo Chibás. They financed it from their own pockets: one sold his job for three hundred dollars; another, the photographic equipment with which he made his living; another contributed three months' salary; another, his life savings.

"It was never our intention to engage the soldiers in combat," Fidel said afterward, "but to seize control and weapons by surprise, to arouse the people and then call the soldiers together. We would have invited them to abandon the odious flag of tyranny and to embrace the banner of liberty; to defend the supreme interests of the nation and not the petty interests of a small group; to turn their guns around and fire on the enemies of the people and not the people."

Once having seized the garrison, a group of rebels was then to take control of a nearby radio station where they would play a recording of Chibás's last speech and call on the people of Santiago to rise against Batista.

"We were convinced," Raúl Castro has said, "that it would be the spark that would loose a revolutionary tempest over the entire country."

The small farmhouse in Siboney on the outskirts of Santiago, where they stored the guns and where they met the night before the attack, is now a museum. The photographs on the walls brutally recall the carnage after the battle: barefoot men clotted with blood, their features smashed, their bodies strewn in the halls and on the lawn before the garrison. Brown uniforms hang in glass cases, the khaki brown caked with a darker brown, next to letters written home by men before they died, and poems.

Abel Santamaría came to Haydée in the hospital when the retreat began and said, "Now they are going to kill us, but Fidel is the one who must not die." A few hours later, Abel was dead, machine-gunned, after having been tortured.

To his followers, Fidel embodied the goals for which they were struggling. It was this quality that made him already a great leader at the age of twenty-six, and that placed its stamp on the Cuban Revolution as a whole.

Orders were given not to take Fidel alive. More than half the revolutionaries were murdered within hours after their capture or surrender. Fidel and a small group, including Juan Almeida (now the head of the Cuban Communist Party in Oriente province), attempted to reach the Sierra Maestra mountain range. The Archbishop of Santiago publicly appealed to the army for mercy. Public opinion rose against the murders.

On August 1, a Rural Guard patrol under the command of a Lieutenant Sarría surrounded Fidel and his exhausted and almost defenseless group and captured them.

Sarría, a humane man who knew Fidel from his university days, refused a direct order to take him to military headquarters, where Fidel was certain to be executed, escorting him instead—in public —to the civil jail.

The outrage expressed by the people of Santiago and the sympathetic responses of the archbishop and of the very soldier who had captured him show that though Fidel's plan failed militarily, it was succeeding politically. Eduardo Chibás had died believing he was not heard, but his young followers had now pounded a "knock on the door" that was noticed from one end of the island to the other.

FIDEL CASTRO

The Making of a Revolution

Look, the Cuban people want something more than a simple change of command. Cuba longs for a radical change in every aspect of its political and social life. The people must be given something more than liberty and democracy in the abstract; decent living must be given to every Cuban.

—FIDEL CASTRO, NEW YORK CITY, 1955

Freedom is not to be begged for, but conquered with the edge of the machete.

—ANTONIO MACEO

The trial of the surviving Moncada attackers began on September 21, 1953, in the Santiago courthouse. The route between the prison where they were held and the courthouse was guarded by a thousand soldiers carrying automatic weapons. Fidel, as a lawyer, was allowed to defend himself, but his courtroom cross-examinations on behalf of his codefendants became more than the prosecution could bear. His case was severed from the rest, and he was brought to trial alone two weeks later.

Fidel's speech in his defense at the trial gave the movement against the Batista dictatorship a program around which to unite, as well as a moral tone and a testimonial of faith in the Cuban people. Reprinted afterward as *History Will Absolve Me* and distributed throughout Cuba, this lengthy speech became a major document of the Cuban Revolution.

> When we speak of the people we do not mean the comfortable ones, the conservative elements of the nation, who welcome any despotism, prostrating themselves before the master of the moment until they grind their foreheads into the ground.
>
> When we speak of struggle, the *people* means the vast unredeemed masses, to whom all make promises and whom all deceive; we mean the people who yearn for a better, more dignified and more just nation. . . .
>
> To the people whose desperate roads through life have been paved with the bricks of betrayals and false promises, we were not going to say: "We will eventually give you what you need," but rather— "Here you have it, fight for it with all your might, so that liberty and happiness may be yours!"

The military court sentenced Fidel and his followers to fifteen years in prison. They were sent to a penitentiary on the Isle of Pines, off Cuba's southwestern coast. There the prisoners maintained a tight discipline, reading and studying. Fidel concentrated on history, particularly books by and about José Martí and the war of independence.

The Moncada attackers were not seen by the Cuban people as extremists or radicals. They were, after all, members of the majority party, who had done what no one else dared to do. Fidel was visited in prison by members of Batista's Cabinet and even an army colonel, who expressed their sympathy. A national movement demanding amnesty grew up rapidly, too powerful for the government to ignore. Fidel demanded that it be an amnesty without conditions. On May 13, 1955, Batista signed a bill granting the Moncada defendants unconditional amnesty. They had spent not quite two years in prison.

They returned to Havana as heroes. The entire leadership of the Orthodox Party was at the railroad station to greet them, together with most of the members of the University Student Federation. The crowd pushed into the coach, hoisted Fidel's large frame onto their shoulders, and carried him off through the streets to his sister's apartment, which was crowded with reporters, photographers, and friends. He sat down and took his shoes off. He told the press that unity against Batista was the most important element in the political struggle to come.

Within a few weeks, it became apparent that the amnesty, in Fidel's words, was a "bloody hoax." Some of the released prisoners were rearrested; others threatened with death. Fidel was prohibited from making any public speeches. *Ortodoxo* radio and TV programs were suspended by decree; mysterious bombings occurred throughout the city.

Though Batista dangled the possibility of elections before the politicians to keep them eager to please, his dictatorship had no end in sight—nor had its brutality slackened. Eusebio Mujal, the racketeering labor boss who had replaced Lázaro Peña, had turned his union-busting services over to Batista. CIA director Allen Dulles visited Cuba that year to help Batista organize a Bureau to Repress Communist Activities, which became one of the regime's most hated instruments of terror.

On July 7, 1955, Fidel wrote an open letter to prominent political leaders: "I am leaving Cuba because all doors of peaceful struggle have been closed to me. . . . As a follower of Martí, I believe the hour has come to take rights and not to beg for them, to fight instead of pleading for them." He flew to Mexico City.

The Communist Party of Cuba—at this time called the *Partido Socialista Popular* (Popular Socialist Party) or PSP—did not agree with Fidel's call for immediate armed struggle. Blas Roca wrote in *Hoy* (published underground) that the party planned to prepare for a future insurrection by organizing "fighting committees" in the factories and communities. Roca also called for the formation of a "national democratic front" uniting all political groups opposed to Batista. This careful preparation would turn out later to be crucial for the success of the Revolution.

From Mexico, Fidel announced the formation of "the July 26 Movement" (or *M-26-7* as it appeared on armbands and painted slogans on walls), named for the date of the attack on the Moncada garrison:

> It is not a political party but a revolutionary movement. Its ranks are open to all Cubans who sincerely desire to see political democracy reestablished and social justice introduced in Cuba. Its leadership is collective and secret, formed by new men of strong will who are not accomplices of the past. . . . Young and old, men and women, workers and peasants, students and professionals, can join its fighting groups, its youth cadres, its secret workers' cells, its women's organizations, its economic sections, and its underground distribution apparatus throughout the country. . . . Above all, this must be a revolution of the people, with the blood of the people and the sweat of the people.

Fidel concluded, as Martí had before him, that an invasion must be organized from outside the country, drawing on the resources of those who had been forced to emigrate.

November 1955 found Fidel traveling up and down the East Coast of the United States to cities where groups of Cuban émigrés were living—Bridgeport, Union City, New York, Tampa, Miami, and Key West—recreating Martí's base of support among those who had fled starvation, unemployment, or repression in Cuba. It was tiring and often frustrating; like Martí and Maceo, Fidel found that those who had least were often willing to give most. He asked for a dollar from every Cuban and a day's wages from every worker. The émigré clubs in the United States were crucial during the revolutionary war, financially, politically, and militarily.

When Fidel first arrived in Mexico, with neither money nor an army, he approached Alberto Bayo, a Cuban instructor at the School of Military Aviation in Mexico, asking him to train an invasion force.

"A young man only twenty-nine?" asked Bayo, who had commanded an air combat wing against the fascists in the Spanish Civil War.

"I will be successful," Fidel replied.

Half a year later, Fidel had the money, contributed by thousands of Cubans in Cuba and the United States. Bayo rented a ranch a few miles from the Mexican capital and organized a school of guerrilla warfare.

By this time the nucleus of a revolutionary army was gathering in Mexico City. Men who had escaped from Cuba, or been exiled, or worked their way through a dozen countries, sleeping on park benches, hitchhiking, taking odd jobs to make their way, gathered under the volcano Popacateptl.

Camilo Cienfuegos, twenty-three, had emigrated illegally to the United States to find work shortly before the Moncada attack. One of his many jobs was as a waiter at the Waldorf-Astoria Hotel in New York City. He was deported back to Cuba just as Fidel was leaving for Mexico.

The police were harassing the Cienfuegos family, who supported the anti-Batista movement. One afternoon Camilo joined a student demonstration in honor of Antonio Maceo. As the crowd marched through the streets chanting, "Revolution! Revolution!" they were fired on by the police and attacked by thugs carrying steel bars in rolled-up newspapers.

Camilo was hit in the leg with a bullet. At the hospital, his father held up the jacket that had been wrapped around his son's wound, crying, "This is the blood of my son, but it is blood of the Revolution!"

"They carried me to the student clinic," Camilo later recalled, "where I experienced one of the greatest emotions of my life, when more than a hundred people gathered there in the entrance broke into cheers and applause when they carried me up, and I felt such an emotion, I felt about to cry, and I yelled out, *'Viva Cuba!'* I was most sure then that, whatever the cost, Cuba had to be free."

That summer Camilo returned to the United States, this time on his way to Mexico. From San Francisco he wrote, "In my way of thinking there is only one dignified road toward ending the present situation . . . to follow the cause of Fidel. To carry things to the point where the Government is obliged to hold general elections. . . . If not, blood will be shed. Fidel affirms that this year we will be free or he will be dead."

He arrived in Mexico City in September 1956. He was spontaneous and undisciplined and didn't get along too well at first with some of the others, like the young Argentine doctor who had earlier joined the group—the one everyone called Che.

Ernesto Guevara, twenty-six, also arrived in Mexico City at the end of a personal odyssey. Born in Rosario, Argentina, in 1928, Guevara was a brilliant student, though subject to crippling asthma attacks. "We would listen to him gasping, studying lying on the floor to ease his breathing, but he never complained," his aunt recalled. "For him it was a challenge."

"Like everyone, I wanted to succeed," Guevara wrote later. "I dreamed of becoming a famous medical research scientist; I dreamed of working indefatigably to discover something which would be used to help humanity, but which signified a personal triumph for me. I was, as we all are, a child of my environment."

After graduation, Guevara traveled through Latin America. During his travels, he said, "I came into close contact with poverty, hunger, and disease; with the inability to treat a child because of lack of money; with the stupefaction provoked by continual hunger and punishment. . . . And I began to realize . . . that there were things that were almost as important to me as becoming a famous scientist or making a significant contribution to medical science: I wanted to help those people."

On Christmas Eve 1953, he arrived in Guatemala City, where he lived in a fifty-cents-a-day flophouse and peddled encyclopedias, spending most of his time reading and talking with other young exiles and travelers. There he met supporters of Fidel Castro, who was then in jail in Cuba.

In 1954, a CIA-backed coup by a right-wing general overthrew the progressive government of Guatemala. Guevara joined in the defense of the government, but when it collapsed, he left the country, making his way to Mexico City.

When Fidel arrived in Mexico the next summer, Guevara met him. "I talked with Fidel all night, and by dawn I had become the doctor of the future expedition. In reality, after my experiences all over Latin America, and the coup in Guatemala, it didn't take much to arouse my interest in joining any revolution against tyranny. But my overall impression of Fidel was that he was an extraordinary man. He confronted and solved the most impossible problems. He had an unshakable faith that once he left Mexico and arrived in Cuba he would fight, and that fighting, he was going to win. I shared his optimism. . . . It was imperative to stop crying and fight."

In Argentina everyone calls everyone else *Che,* which means "pal" or "buddy." The Cubans in Mexico City bestowed "Che" on Ernesto as a nickname.

Frank País, twenty-one, teacher at a Baptist high school in Santiago, poet, musician, and admirer of José Martí, also came to Mexico City in 1956, but only to confer with Fidel and return home.

País was the national coordinator of the other half of the revolutionary war-to-be: the underground movement in the cities. He was carefully building revolutionary organizations in the major cities, particularly Santiago, that would supply Fidel's mountain guerrillas with recruits, food, clothing, guns, and money. País's clandestine groups would also organize public support for the rebels, carry out armed attacks on the dictatorship in the cities, and serve as the link between the Cuban people and the guerrilla army.

País agreed to lead an armed uprising in Santiago timed to coincide with Fidel's landing on the coast. It would draw the army away from the landing party and would dramatize the national struggle against Batista. The uprising and landing were scheduled for November 30, 1956.

País was one of the most brilliant and at the same time most typical members of the July 26 Movement. Visionary and idealistic, he was also precise, disciplined, and tenacious, pouring all his energies into the movement.

Another young leader who met with Fidel in Mexico was José Antonio Echeverría, the twenty-four-year-old president of the University Student Federation in Havana, and leader of the militant student group, the Revolutionary Directorate. Echeverría told Fidel that his group was planning an armed attack on Batista at the presidential palace, early in 1957.

Batista twice sent paid assassins to Mexico to kill Fidel, but when they failed he changed his tactics. On a June night in 1956, Fidel and Ramiro Valdés (who had fought at the Moncada garrison and is today a leader of the Cuban Communist Party) were arrested in Mexico City by the Mexican federal police, at the request of Batista.

Forty others were arrested a few days later, beaten, and threatened with deportation, to which they responded, "Great! Send us back; that's where we want to go." Former Mexican President Lázaro Cárdenas used his influence to get them released after a month.

Now the hounds were on their trail. An informer inside their ranks led Mexican police to seize $56,000 worth of weapons, the loss made more bitter by the revelation that the spy was a long-time friend of Fidel's.

Fidel decided to go ahead with the invasion, though they were not fully prepared. On a stormy night in late November 1956, he and the eighty-one other revolutionaries set out from the Mexican harbor town of Tuxpán in a little yacht, the *Granma,* recently purchased and badly in need of repairs.

The engines malfunctioned and the boat, built to hold only eight, shipped water. The men, seasick in a freezing rain, bailed with their hands. But as the lights of Tuxpán faded behind them, they broke into song—the Cuban national anthem.

They were still at sea, making slow way against headwinds on November 30, the day they were scheduled to land, and had to follow by radio the news of the uprising in Santiago, which was to have coincided with their landing.

Two days from shore they heard of the brave and futile attacks by Frank País's troops—wearing for the first time the uniforms of the July 26 Movement—against the police station, the naval military headquarters, and the Moncada garrison. The M-26-7 rebels took the naval station, but though the police were forced to abandon their cental office, the revolutionaries were repulsed. Retreating, the attackers cut their losses, retired successfully, hid their weapons, and prepared to strike again, unaware that the *Granma* had not landed.

As Fidel's boat approached Cuba, Celia Sánchez, one of the founders of the July 26 Movement, was waiting at the intended landing point with a force of about fifty men, trucks, jeeps, food, and arms. Instead the *Granma* was forced to land some thirty miles to the south, among mangrove swamps near the village of Las Coloradas. Fidel and his men had to wade ashore and without transportation or reinforcements find their way to the mountains.

To the charcoal makers of Las Coloradas, Sunday December 2, 1956, started off no differently from most others. They awoke at 2 A.M. and went into the woods to cut branches for the charcoal ovens.

When they heard the sound of a boat offshore, they took it for the one that carried wood and coal up the coast to Niquero. Later they heard shots. "We still didn't pay much attention," Pedro Luis Sánchez recalled in a newspaper interview years later. "No we didn't," added his friend Angel Pérez Rosabal. Pérez was walking back to his charcoal oven along a narrow path through the trees, when a young man carrying a rifle stepped in front of him. "Don't be afraid. I won't hurt you," he told Pérez, and took him off the path to where another man was standing.

"My name is Fidel Castro," the second man told the astonished charcoal maker. "We've come to fight for Cuba's freedom."

"Well," Pérez recalled, "I had heard about the story of Fidel's attack on the Moncada from a friend of mine who knew how to read and write and often got newspapers and magazines from Niquero."

Fidel asked for advice on how to get to the Sierra Maestra, and the charcoal maker invited him to come up to his house and have something to eat. Meanwhile another detachment had entered the woods and come to the house of Lilia Alcala Torres.

"These men were so young and their smiles were so sincere that, almost immediately, I felt as if I were among members of my own family," she remembered. "One of them threw his arms around me, just like my own son, and said, 'Don't be afraid, Ma'am, we're revolutionaries and we've come to fight the tyrant.' I told them that even though our house was a humble one, they should feel right at home."

THE BATTLE OF ALEGRÍA DE PIO

Much later, after they had won the war, they could recall vividly their first terrible battle:

CHE GUEVARA: Alegría de Pio is a place in Oriente province. At this very spot, on December 5, 1956, Batista's forces discovered our hiding place.

We were exhausted from a long, painful trek; more painful than long, to tell the truth. We had landed on December 2 at a place known as Playa de las Coloradas. We had lost all our equipment and had trudged for endless hours through marshlands and swamps.

By daybreak of the fifth we could hardly walk. On the verge of collapse, we would walk a short distance and then beg for a long rest period. Orders were given to halt at the edge of a cane field, in a thicket close to the dense woods. Most of us slept throughout the morning hours.

JOSÉ PONCE: There was a first shot and then there was a terrible barrage; some returned the fire and others didn't, the ones crawling on the ground, and then I was hit. I was crawling, trying to drag myself into the field of sugar cane. I couldn't get over there because the firing was too heavy, so I turned around. Then everyone began to scatter.

CHE: Perhaps this was the first time I was faced with the dilemma of choosing between my devotion to medicine and my duty as a revolutionary soldier. There, at my feet, were a knapsack full of medicine and a box of ammunition. I couldn't possibly carry them both; they were too heavy. I picked up the box of ammunition. . . .

I felt a sharp blow on my chest and a wound on my neck and I thought for certain I was dead. . . . Flat on the ground, I turned to Faustino [Pérez, now a leader of the Cuban Communist Party], saying, "I've been hit"—what I really said is unprintable—and Faustino, still firing away, looked at me and said, "Oh, it's nothing," but I could see by the look in his eyes that he considered me as good as dead.

I heard someone on his knees say that we had better surrender, and then a voice—later I found out it was Camilo's—shouting, "No! Nobody surrenders here!" followed by a four-letter word.

For a moment I was left alone, just lying there waiting to die. [Juan] Almeida approached, urging me to go on, and despite the intense pain I dragged myself into the cane field.

PONCE: I spent two days in the cane. I lost my mind for one day. There comes a moment when you give up and you say: Very well, this is it. . . . I was wounded here, in the chest. I lay there, just listening to some roosters crow.

CHE: With Almeida leading, we reached the safety of the woods. The first shouts of "Fire!" were heard in the cane field, and tongues of flame and columns of smoke began to rise. I cannot remember exactly what happened. I felt the bitterness of defeat, and I was sure I was going to die. We walked until darkness made it impossible to go on. . . .

THE
REVOLUTIONARY WAR
BEGUN

Twelve Men Lost in the Mountains

*What matters is not the number of weapons in one's hand, but the
number of stars on one's forehead.*

—JOSÉ MARTÍ

At a given moment, a country is either ripe for revolution or it is
not. Its people are either prepared for and willing to endure the
pain of an upheaval or they are not. The Cuban people were ready
in the last days of 1956. The outcome depended on their strength,
the wisdom of their leaders, the balance of political and military
forces—and luck.

Guillermo Garcia, a peasant organizer of the July 26 Movement
in the Sierra Maestra mountains, remembers the terrified men
streaming into the hills from the disaster at Alegría de Pio: "They
came like 'a soul carried away by the Devil.' Why hide it? Why
hide the fact that they told me in the mountains that it was the
worst barbarity they had ever seen? One said he had fought in the
[Second World] War, and how were we who were so few ever
going to defeat Batista? And that's the truth, why hide it?"

Fidel had stayed near the cane field for as long as he could, trying to find his men. He found only two. They headed into the mountains, walking by night, sleeping by day, under torrential rains.

Camping one day in the tall grass they saw vultures wheeling overhead. "They've gotten used to eating our dead comrades," Fidel said bitterly.

All the survivors were moving east toward Pico Turquino, Cuba's highest mountain, according to plan. By December 24, they had found each other and arrived at the mountain. They were twelve: Fidel, Raúl, Che Guevara, Camilo Cienfuegos, Calixto García, Juan Almeida, Calixto Morales, Faustino Pérez, Universo Sánchez, Efigenio Amejeiras, Ciro Redondo, and Rene Rodriguez. Ten others had survived the slaughter and were in jail. Of those who arrived at the mountain, none had more than ten bullets.

Elated at having arrived at the mountain, Fidel advised them not to lose hope. "We have already won the war," he declared to the astonished band. "Batista is beaten."

Fidel was optimistic because his plan did not depend on having men and arms equal to those of the dictatorship. He had chosen the Sierra Maestra for the field of war because it was favorable to the guerrillas. Batista's airplanes and artillery were almost useless in the mountains; his larger forces could be pinned down and destroyed by much smaller ones. The guerrillas would even outnumber the enemy in attacks against outlying mountain garrisons.

Once Batista's forces had been driven from the Sierra (and Fidel knew he could depend on the peasants of the area, who had long opposed the government), the rebel army would have a "liberated zone" from which to open up new fronts in neighboring mountain ranges near the big cities. As the dictatorship became more desperate, the Cuban people would turn to the rebels as a practical alternative. Soon an enlarged and trained rebel army, supported by strikes and uprisings in the cities, would be able to leave the mountains and drive the demoralized army of the dictatorship out of the cities of the plain.

That was the plan, but first they had to endure the nomadic phase of the war. For six months their objective was basically to stay alive, win the confidence of the peasants in the mountains, and make contact with their supporters in the cities, principally in Santiago, some seventy miles to the east.

On January 14, 1957, they opened the war with an attack on a small army garrison at the mouth of the La Plata River. "The effect was electrifying," Che wrote in his diary, "proving that the rebel army really existed and was ready to fight." A few days later they won another skirmish. But for months that was not the war. The war was walking endlessly and trying to find something to eat.

Efigenio Amejeiras recalled it vividly:

Floundering through muddy fields and paths, pushing on beneath the low-hanging branches of the forest through brush, crossing grass pastures, climbing up and down mountains, we marched without a guide and had to depend on our own vague topographical knowledge. Fidel was leading us toward Mount Caracas, a great long mountain well over 3,000 feet high, famous for its lush vegetation, filled with wild bees and teeming with flocks of trilling nightingales.

We advanced with difficulty and our boots kept sinking in over our ankles. If the climbs were hard, the descents were no less so. The one big difference being, if your foot slipped while climbing, the fall set you back a few yards; the opposite is true going down, you're thrown forward a few. That's why the peasants say, "Going down, the saints help you."

One painful day, after a long march in the rain, they captured three old chickens and a duck and cooked a meal. In the blissful after-dinner atmosphere they began to daydream aloud about what they were going to do after the Revolution. One of them objected, saying, "Look, we've almost been wiped out three times. Two days ago we nearly fell into an ambush. Now here we are, practically surrounded, with twelve guns and scarcely forty bullets!"

Fidel broke in:

Comrades, it's true . . . but it's also true that we have fulfilled our promise to the Cuban people.

It's true as well that Frank País will keep his word and should be arriving from Santiago with an armed contingent. It's also true that not long ago instead of twelve guns and one victory to our credit, we had only seven guns and no victory at all.

The terrain here lends itself to the defeat of the tyranny's best forces, and soon we will encircle and annihilate their best battalions and then will go on to defeat them on the plains and in the cities.

And if despite everything, if despite all this, we still must die in combat . . . even the children of our enemies will have to take off their hats before the peaks of our Sierra Maestra.

"Silence gripped our hearts," recalled Amejeiras.

It continued to rain. The wet wind beat at the cracks in the abandoned shack in the heights of the Sierra Maestra.

On March 13, 1957, they were drawing close to Mount Caracas, picking their way through an old camp site where a B-24 had bombed them two months earlier. Fidel was listening to a portable radio, playing nervously with the dial, holding it close to his ear because the batteries were half dead, when suddenly he said, "Something great is happening in Havana!"

In Havana, the Revolutionary Directorate was carrying out the attack José Echeverría had promised in Mexico.

At three that afternoon, a panel truck and two cars pulled up at the rear entrance of the presidential palace, the office and residence of Batista. A commando group of fifty students shot their way through the gates and ran for the marble stairs that spiral upward at the corners of the inner patio.

Under machine-gun fire from Batista's guards on the second floor, the attackers fought their way into the dainty salons, gunfire shredding the crystal chandeliers, thudding into the art works and colonial furniture.

But when they shot open the door to Batista's office on the second floor, it was empty. Batista had escaped by the roof.

The students were also aware at that moment that the two backup assault groups, numbering one hundred men, had not arrived, making retreat practically impossible. One by one, they were cut down as they made their way back to the ground floor.

Meanwhile, José Echeverría and a small group had seized a radio station and read over the air an announcement of the attack. Retreating back to the campus, their car met a patrol car at the university wall. Echeverría jumped from the car, firing, and was machine-gunned to death.

The assault on the palace almost eliminated the Revolutionary Directorate as a force against the dictatorship. Most of its leaders were killed either that day or in the repression that followed. On the other hand, it shook public opinion in Havana, in Cuba, and throughout the world. It was the first assault against the government in the capital city, demonstrating the willingness of young revolutionaries to die for their cause.

The garrison of El Uvero was an important military post of the Cuban army, located in a small town on the narrow coastal strip to the south of the Sierra Maestra range. Fidel chose it for the first major battle of the war—May 28, 1957.

It was a reckless, all-out attack by the rebel force now numbering eighty (Frank País's reinforcements had arrived from Santiago two months earlier). After two and a half hours of fighting, the rebels won, with high casualties on both sides.

The battle of El Uvero marked the end of the first period of the war. "For us," wrote Che Guevara, "it was a victory that meant that our guerrillas had reached full maturity. From this moment on, our morale increased enormously, our determination and hope for victory also increased, and though the months that followed were a hard test, we now had the key to the secret of how to beat the enemy. This battle sealed the fate of every garrison located far from larger concentrations of troops, and every small army post was soon dismantled." The Rebel Army now controlled the Sierra Maestra.

After the battle of El Uvero to the spring of 1958, a military stalemate existed between the guerrilla forces and the army of Batista. The rebels did not come down into the plains; the soldiers of the government made sporadic ventures into the mountains but were always driven back.

The Rebel Army no longer had to run and hide. The revolutionaries built primitive hospitals for the peasants and equally primitive small factories that turned out bullets, shoes, knapsacks, cartridge belts. There was an armory that repaired damaged rifles and made mines from Cuban air-force bombs that had landed unexploded. They began to mimeograph a newspaper, *El Cubano Libre.* An information network among the peasants advised them immediately of the presence of any stranger.

A popular revolutionary war is above all a political struggle in which the military aspects, though decisive, are often secondary. From the summer of 1957 to the spring of the following year, a vast political struggle shook the entire island—involving every institution in Cuban society, altering people's lives, creating and tearing apart organizations, and intimately involving the United States.

At the heart of it, standing like a rock over a stormy sea, was the "Free Territory of Cuba" (marked with handmade signs): the mountain range of the Sierra Maestra, under the administration of the Rebel Army.

The Batista dictatorship was no longer strong enough to defeat the Revolution, nor was the Revolution yet strong enough to bring the war out of the mountains and into the cities. This balance between two opposing forces threw the government into confusion. One month Batista would lift censorship, and news articles about the rebels would flood the papers. The next month he would shut down the media and throw the reporters into jail. One month, Batista would dangle before the opposition the possibility of partial elections; the next, he would have his most vocal opponents arrested.

Even within the July 26 Movement, many did not understand or agree with what Fidel was trying to do. Most of the M-26-7 leaders worked underground in the cities and felt that the urban areas should be the focus for revolutionary work, not the relatively unpopulated mountains, far from the centers of power. Militarily it seemed absurd to them; two hundred men armed with rifles against an army of tens of thousands.

But Fidel was developing a strategy far more complex than a test of arms. The Sierra Maestra was not only a military stronghold against which Batista's army uselessly battered itself. The "Free Territory of Cuba" was a political magnet that slowly drew toward itself all the anti-Batista forces in the country, offering them an alternative to dictatorship and corruption. The longer it endured, the more appealing it became. As the Batista regime in its desperation became more lawless, the Rebel Army came to stand not only for liberation, but for justice, stability, and order.

Most accounts of the Cuban Revolution logically focus on the guerrillas in the mountains. Little written about even today is the struggle that took place in the plains, the broad movement against Batista that unfolded in the major cities and towns of Cuba, a movement that was both open and clandestine. It was in the cities that the outcome of the revolution would, in great part, be determined. There, in every organization, plans were debated, actions carried out: in the labor unions, where the Communists were organizing "fighting committees"; in the universities and high schools, where the Revolutionary Directorate and the M-26-7 had influence, even in the professional and business organizations of the middle and upper classes.

The underground movement against Batista was everywhere, but nowhere was it stronger than in Santiago, the home of Frank País. Shortly after the attack on the Moncada garrison in 1953, País had begun talking with students and young working people, men and women he knew personally, drawing them around him in an embryonic revolutionary group.

"Frank had a tremendous presence," one of those who joined the underground said. "He had a sense of the moment we were living through. He created respect by the way he acted. Even though he was disciplined, he had a real human personality. He was one of us, a youth."

País asked each person to organize a cell, to prepare a list of their friends and close associates, people they could trust. There were both blacks and whites among those selected. Some worked; others were in school. Their average age was seventeen.

They prepared carefully, finding, repairing, and hiding weapons, participating in mass demonstrations against the dictatorship, raising money, collecting medical supplies. They published a little mimeographed bulletin which sold for ten cents, reporting news and criticizing the government, countering the censorship with which Batista periodically blanketed the island.

In the summer of 1955, País's organization merged with the July 26 Movement of Fidel. Frank became the leader of the new organization in Oriente province.

Up to this moment neither the police in Santiago nor the members of the group themselves knew the extent of the organization Frank had so painstakingly built. Then one day in early 1956 each cell was given the order to paint the name of the movement and slogans against the tyranny on all the walls and buildings in their neighborhood.

The next morning, the army, the police, and the people of Santiago awoke to the magnitude of the resistance. Every block in the city was covered with writing splashed in paint: *"Down with Batista! M-26-7."* No one had been arrested.

Toward the end of that year, the movement began to prepare the armed uprising that would cover Fidel's landing and entrance into the mountains.

M-26-7 uniforms were sewn by women who worked in the garment factories, working from a list of the sizes of each man in the cell, sewing at night in their homes. Those who cut the patterns did not know those who sewed them. Those who sewed were not told their final destination or the names of those who picked them up. The movement in Santiago by that time counted on about three hundred members, one hundred and fifty of whom had participated in the failed November 30 uprising. Hundreds more were close collaborators.

December 1956 was a cruel month. In retreat, after the uprising had been crushed, the movement had to find hiding places for its members. Though many members and sympathizers had been killed, support for the M-26-7 increased.

When a person inside or outside the movement was killed or tortured, people would spontaneously go to the house of the family to express their indignation and support. Sometimes they would intercede when the police were trying to make an arrest.

The movement was soon able to use factories rather than homes to hide arms and sew uniforms.

After the November uprising, the police were given the power to enter homes and to arrest at will. Some became notorious for their treatment of prisoners, tearing the names of sympathizers out of them in police-station basements. They entered restaurants, eating without paying, killing rivals in love and business, raping women with no fear of investigation.

The movement organized to strike back, assassinating some of the worst torturers, taking reprisals against the police whenever a revolutionary was killed. These retaliatory measures made the M-26-7 even more popular.

Most hated were "the Tigers of Masferrer," the private army organized by Senator Rolando Masferrer from the dregs of society, whose purpose was to attack and neutralize the revolutionary movement. The Tigers patrolled in private cars, stopping people, arresting, beating, and killing at whim. This was even more of a shock to the people than the actions of the police and army. The leaders of the movement issued an order to shoot known Tigers on sight, and launched attacks against their meeting places. This also increased the popularity of the movement among the people of Santiago.

Workers in a factory or sugar mill would tell the underground which were the best places to sabotage and burn. The movement would carry out the act and then publicly claim credit to draw suspicion away from those who worked there.

By mid-1957, the time was at hand for every Cuban to make a choice: Batista or Fidel; the presidential palace or the Sierra Maestra; a corrupt and bloody dictatorship or a popular movement with a program of land reform, workers' rights, democratic elections, and social justice.

Tens of thousands chose the Revolution. They did not know exactly where it would lead them; but the poverty and brutality, the prostitutes and the casinos, gangsterism, and the nightly murders, reminded them every day of the alternative if they did not.

"Without the struggle in the cities there would have been no guerrilla army," said a man who had fought in Santiago with the underground movement of Frank País. "And without the guerrillas we would have had no movement in the cities. They were two fronts of the same war."

On July 30, 1957, while Frank País was moving from one hiding place to another, an informer pointed him out to police, who shot him to death in the street.

Almost the entire city of Santiago came out for País's funeral. A spontaneous general strike was called. The crowds were too large for the police to control. The funeral was held openly; Frank was buried wearing the olive-green uniform of the July 26 Movement, his coffin draped with the Cuban flag. A riot erupted at the cemetery.

For three days the city closed down. The police went into the streets, kicking in doors, breaking windows, trying to beat the shopkeepers into opening their stores.

In early September 1957, as the remnants of the government's mountain garrison troops were being withdrawn from the Sierra Maestra, a conspiracy emerged inside the military. A group of young naval officers in the important port city of Cienfuegos, on the southern coast of Las Villas province, a few miles from the Escambray Mountains, had been organizing against Batista from the moment of the 1952 coup. The conspiracy was part of a larger underground military movement led by a group of officers in Havana called "the pure ones" because they had not participated in the crimes of the Batista regime.

At the last minute and for unclear reasons, the plan for an uprising to take place simultaneously in Havana, Santiago, Cienfuegos, and a number of other towns was postponed by its leaders, who failed to notify the rebels in Cienfuegos.

On September 5, members of the July 26 Movement in Cienfuegos and their allies in the navy launched attacks on the naval police headquarters, the national police headquarters, and the garrison of the Rural Guards. The naval police surrendered first; most of them joined the uprising.

When the national police surrendered, a Cuban city for the first time was in the hands of the people. For two hours the revolutionaries rejoiced, believing the same success had been achieved across the land. They did not know that an armored troop train was rushing toward them to crush the uprising.

The following day, when the last group of rebels surrendered after they had run out of ammunition, the regime vented its rage on the rebel city. "There were bodies strewn everywhere, of men drilled by machine-gun fire, hanged or tortured to death," Major Julio Camacho, head of the July 26 guerrillas in Las Villas province, recalled. "The killer forces of the regime took the wounded from the hospitals, without the doctors being able to protect them."

It was the most powerful uprising to occur in the cities during the war. Its failure proved to the guerrillas that their strategy of wearing away the dictatorship from the mountains was correct. The uprising showed, however, that the revolutionary feeling in the country had grown incredibly since the landing of the *Granma*. The unity within the armed forces was shattered. A year later, when Batista needed a disciplined military machine, it was not there.

On the night of February 24, 1958, the sixty-third anniversary of the beginning of the war of independence, in 1895, the people of Cuba heard over their radios a voice announce: *"Aquí Radio Rebelde! Transmitiendo desde la Sierra Maestra, en Territorio Libre de Cuba!"* ("This is Rebel Radio! Transmitting from the Sierra Maestra, in the Free Territory of Cuba!")

Radio Rebelde broadcast nightly from Fidel's mountain headquarters and could be heard over almost the entire island. It soon had the highest "rating" of any of Cuba's stations, despite Batista's attempts to jam it from Havana. Fidel later said that *Radio Rebelde* was "worth ten columns of troops" in the political-military struggle that was the Revolution.

Radio Rebelde told the plain truth in a country blanketed with lies and censorship. It reported on the revolutionists' mistakes and losses as well as their victories, and contributed greatly to the reputation of the guerrillas.

A reporter from *Look* magazine who came to the mountains in February 1958 asked Fidel what support he thought he had among the people. Fidel replied, "Our Cuban support comes from all classes of society. The middle class is strongly united in its support of our movement. We even have many wealthy sympathizers. Merchants, industrial executives, young people, workers are sick of the gangsterism that rules Cuba."

In March of that year, forty-five civic institutions signed an open letter supporting the July 26 Movement. Among those represented were the national organizations of lawyers, architects, public accountants, dentists, electrical engineers, social workers, English professors, and veterinarians. Even the Lyceum Lawn Tennis Club in Havana supported the rebels.

This was a new situation. The various revolutionary groups were not at odds as they had been in 1933. Though most of the revolutionary leaders came from student or middle-class backgrounds, they had turned to the workers and peasants to make the revolution. Thanks to the mass media, Fidel was able to communicate his program to most of the population. The poor, who were mostly illiterate, were not isolated from revolutionary ideas as they had been in the days before radio.

These factors enabled Fidel Castro to win broader support than any previous revolutionary movement in Cuba's history. The United States Ambassador to Cuba, Earl T. Smith, unfortunately refused to acknowledge this fact, however. When he was shown the statement of the forty-five organizations, he ridiculed it as anonymous and unofficial because it contained no personal signatures.

The mass support, a wave of armed actions across the country, the opening of a new guerrilla front in the central Escambray Mountains by surviving members of the Revolutionary Directorate, created among the rebels in the spring of 1958 an almost giddy feeling of imminent victory.

In the Sierras, the guerrilla army was on the offensive again. Fidel had divided his forces into five columns. On March 1, Raúl Castro left the Sierra Maestra with a column of sixty-seven men to open a second front in the mountains north of Santiago—the Sierra Cristal.

Juan Almeida was given command of a column that moved to the eastern end of the Sierra Maestra to command the heights near Santiago. Camilo Cienfuegos, who had risen from an undisciplined fighter to a brilliant, disciplined, but still incautious captain of the point platoon—the most dangerous position—was sent at the head of a column to the plains of Bayamo, north of the Sierras, for the first emergence of the Rebel Army into the plains.

Che Guevara led a column that operated on the northern slopes of the Sierra Maestra. Each leader had proved himself in battle, taking on dangerous assignments and earning the respect of his comrades. A guerrilla army is perhaps the purest arena for the "natural selection" of leaders. Failure cannot be covered up, nor abilities ignored.

The leaders of the July 26 Movement in the cities now believed that the war could be won by a general strike across the island. Fidel was not convinced, but agreed to give the strike all possible military support, moving his columns near the major towns of Oriente.

When the strike was called—on the morning of April 9, 1958 —the movement was almost crushed. It had been called too hurriedly, while rebel organizations in the cities were still too weak. Though thousands walked off their jobs in the interior cities, the strike failed in Havana, where ninety-two people were killed by Batista's police.

But though the cities bled, the strike proved that the rebels had won the allegiance of the majority of the Cuban people. Once the city dwellers of all classes, from longshoremen to factory owners, turned their faces from Batista, he could no longer govern; he could only rule.

The defeat of the general strike forced the movement to change its strategy. It had been a mistake, the urban leaders realized, to concentrate so much on overthrowing Batista in the cities, where his military, psychological, economic, and political power was the greatest.

From then on, all attention turned to the mountains of Oriente. "The country understood that it was necessary to support the guerrilla, that it was only the guerrilla that could break the military apparatus of the tyranny," said Carlos Franqui, director of *Radio Rebelde.*

Batista, too, turned his attention to the Sierra Maestra, knowing that two opposing centers of military and political power cannot exist in the same nation. The time had come for the final struggle.

THE WAR WON

A Joyful Nation in Arms

The history of 1895 will not be repeated. Today the Mambises *will enter Santiago de Cuba!*

—*FIDEL CASTRO TO THE PEOPLE OF SANTIAGO*
ON THE EVE OF VICTORY

During May 1958, Fulgencio Batista began to mass an army of ten thousand men in the foothills of the Sierra Maestra, north and south of the rebel headquarters near Turquino Peak. Fidel called back all his columns—there were now six—except that of Raúl in the mountains north of Santiago, to form a compact defensive front eighteen miles long around the high ground of the mountain range. For this defense, Fidel had three hundred troops.

For seventy-six days in all, from late May to early August, Fidel Castro orchestrated a brilliant series of offensive and defensive battles, combined with psychological warfare and political moves. This was no longer guerrilla war, but a war between two armies fighting for position and advantage; Batista's forces desperately trying to thrust through from north and south to cut the Sierras in half and annihilate the rebel headquarters; the Rebel Army moving rapidly from north to south, east to west, throwing back the advance forces of the dictatorship.

For thirty-five days Batista's troops slowly gained ground. By mid-June barely four miles separated the attackers from north and south.

The battle of Jigüe, which lasted for ten days in mid-July, was probably the most important and certainly one of the most interesting, revealing the complex nature of the war. During it, letters were exchanged, troops on opposite sides shared their food, and a commander changed his allegiance.

Battalion 18 of the government forces was camped at a river fork close to the rebel headquarters. Rebel units took up positions surrounding it. Seventy-two hours passed in silence, during which the government troops ran out of food. They made several attempts to break out and were beaten back.

"On the morning of the fifteenth, the air force appeared," Fidel reported over *Radio Rebelde.* "The aerial attack against our positions, with machine-gun strafing and 500-pound explosive bombs as well as napalm, lasted uninterrupted from six in the morning until one in the afternoon. The pasture and forest . . . were left scorched, but not one of the rebel combatants moved from his position."

That same day Fidel learned that the commanding officer of the besieged battalion was Major José Quevedo, a former classmate of Fidel's at the University of Havana. Fidel wrote his opponent a letter, which was delivered by one of the government soldiers who had been taken prisoner.

"With great sorrow I have learned . . . that you are in command of the surrounded troops," Fidel wrote. "We know that you are a learned and honorable military officer of the Academy, with a law degree. You know that the cause for which your soldiers, as well as yourself, sacrifice and die is an unjust cause."

Fidel offered Quevedo "a dignified and honorable surrender."

Accept this offer; you will not surrender to an enemy of the fatherland but to a sincere revolutionary, a man who fights for the welfare of all Cubans, including that of the soldiers who fight us. You will surrender to a university classmate who wants the same things that you want for Cuba.

Still believing that reinforcements could break through, Quevedo refused. Four days later, the rebels beat back the last reinforcements advancing from the coast.

"On the morning of the twentieth, we ordered a cease-fire from six in the morning until ten," Fidel reported. "The enemy soldiers, who were weary in the trenches, accepted the cease-fire. Little by little several of those who still could walk laboriously came close to our trenches and asked for water, food, and cigarettes. On seeing that our men did not shoot and shared the food they had in their hands, they embraced our soldiers and cried with emotion. How different was the treatment from that which they expected perhaps, fooled by the dictatorship's false propaganda! The sight was an emotional one for all."

The next day, the battalion surrendered.

Major Quevedo, who remained at the Rebel Army headquarters, deeply influenced by what he had experienced and by his discussions with Fidel, joined the revolutionary forces and convinced several other military units to surrender or defect to the rebel side.

By August 18, Fidel was able to report that after seventy six days of battle, the Rebel Army had "repelled and virtually destroyed the cream of the tyranny's forces, inflicting on them one of the greatest disasters a modern army, trained and equipped with all the military resources, could suffer before nonprofessional forces, enclosed in a territory surrounded by enemy troops, without aviation, without artillery, and without supply routes for ammunition and food."

The shambles of the Batista army fled from the mountains. They had lost a thousand men, either dead or wounded; four hundred had been taken prisoner. The Rebel Army suffered a total of twenty-seven dead and fifty wounded. No rebel had been taken prisoner or deserted.

Throughout the war, the United States government pursued a divided policy toward the rebellion. Popular feeling in the United States ran strongly toward the insurgents, and there were those in the State Department who looked favorably on the overthrow of Batista, whose monstrosities shocked even hardened diplomats.

Nevertheless, in early 1958, Batista had received $1,000,000 in military aid from the United States. United States diplomatic personnel wined and dined Batista and appeared publicly with him during the war, which the dictator used to best advantage. All of Batista's arms, planes, tanks, ships, and military supplies came from the United States. His army was trained by a joint mission of the three branches of the U.S. armed forces.

On the other hand, the United States did not send in the marines to bail Batista out, as it had for several other Cuban heads of state, and in March it imposed an arms embargo on the Batista regime. This did not, however, stop the flow of American arms to Batista through the dictatorial governments of Nicaragua and the Dominican Republic.

The United States did not send in the marines for one basic reason: it did not fear the Revolution. Though the nation was emerging from the height of the Cold War and from Senator Joseph McCarthy's anti-Communist frenzy, it was inconceivable to the U.S. policy makers that a revolution in Cuba could turn out badly for them. After all, U.S. companies owned the country.

The last unraveled strands of the Batista government's forces were backing down under fire from the Sierra Maestra, into the sanctuary of the plains. They left behind them by the ton tanks, mortars, bazookas, rifles, machine guns, carbines, crates of ammunition, radio transmitters, secret codes, and cannons.

And they took away with them something more important and deadly to the regime. They had met the enemy and come to know him. They had been lied to and betrayed by their officers. They had fought and been defeated in several battles by the Mariana Grajales women's platoon.

They had been treated, many for the first time in their lives, like human beings—by the enemy. Carried back to the military barracks, homes, and neighborhood bars, this experience became a dangerous thing for Batista.

This was the moment for which Fidel had been preparing since his days in jail when he poured over the memoirs and accounts of the invasion of the western part of the island by Antonio Maceo in 1895–96.

As in 1868 and 1895, the Revolution was strongest in Oriente, weakest in Havana where the Spanish and later the Americans had concentrated their forces and influence. It was necessary to carry the Revolution into the plains and cities of the west, proving to the enemy and the people that the dictatorship was vulnerable in every town and province. This is what Maceo had accomplished in the war of independence.

Fidel planned to duplicate this epic by launching two invasion columns led by Camilo Cienfuegos and Che Guevara. It was an audacious plan and may be the only example in military history of a tactic used twice in the same country, sixty years apart, both times successfully.

"I'd like to carry out our mission to the end," Camilo Cienfuegos told his men before their column left the mountains, "but at the same time I sort of hope the war will end first, so Maceo will be the only one to have this feat to his credit."

The two columns—Che's with one hundred and fifty men,

Camilo's with sixty-five—left their mountain base camp on August 21, 1958, under a torrential rain.

Their advance was slow, the path tortuous. The rebels walked at night and rested by day. They ate *jutias,* an edible rat. One day Camilo's entire column shared two *jutias* as their only food.

To make matters worse, many of the peasants who lived in this sparse, forlorn region were afraid to help the rebels. Bandit gangs operated in the area, taking advantage of the chaos the war created, sometimes passing themselves off as revolutionaries.

Orestes Guerra, leader of Camilo's advance platoon, remembered a dramatic confrontation in a peasant cottage:

> It was night. We knocked on the door [of a *campesino*] and one of them opened it. When they realized we were rebels, one of them inside the house started to scream hysterically. . . . We had to stuff his mouth with a handkerchief to shut him up, for the Army was close by and could have heard. . . .
>
> But in that moment, to the surprise and emotion of all of us, a little boy of 6 years said to him, with words that seemed to be coming from a grown man, "You are a coward. If I wasn't so little, I'd guide them, because they're lost."

Their path intertwined with the route taken by Maceo sixty-three years before. Like the ghosts of a past invasion, Camilo's troops skirted the villages and towns, passed through a drainage culvert under the Central Highway and emerged into the northern part of Camagüey province, above the city of Ciego de Avila. Crouched in a sugarcane field, they could hear the cars passing on the highway.

Only a few miles away were the foothills of the Escambray Mountains and the border of Las Villas province, where a guerrilla group organized by the Popular Socialist Party (PSP—the Communist Party) was operating. When they crossed the river into Las Villas, Camilo kissed the earth. They had eaten only eleven times during the thirty-one days of march, including the time that, as Camilo said, "we ate a horse raw and without salt."

Having endured a similar ordeal, Che's column was entering the Escambray Mountains in the southern part of the same province.

A tradition of militancy among the sugar workers of northern Las Villas province extended back to the 1930's. During the revolutionary upheavals that overthrew the Machado dictatorship, the workers of the Narcisa sugar mill had formed a cell of the Communist Party.

A guerrilla detachment of the PSP was active there when Camilo's column arrived. The column, the PSP detachment, and the local M-26-7 guerrillas joined forces. By the end of October, they had liberated a large area north of the Central Highway.

In Oriente province, the Sierra Cristal mountains, controlled since April by the "Frank País Second Front" of Raúl Castro, had also been the scene of generations of struggle between the peasants and the plantation owners. In September, Raúl convened a "Congress of *Campesinos* in Arms" at his headquarters.

This alliance between the rebels and the peasants allowed Raúl Castro's forces to liberate within a few months and with minimal losses some twelve thousand square kilometers of land with half a million inhabitants. The revolutionary forces organized schools and hospitals, built roads and telephone lines, and organized the administration of the liberated towns.

On October 10, 1958, the ninetieth anniversary of the 1868 war of independence, the Rebel Army issued its first agrarian reform law. This law proclaimed the right of the peasant to his land and became the basis for the distribution of land in all the liberated zones.

The Rebel Army was no longer a tiny band of men. It had been welded into a disciplined army of workers and peasants. Long before victory arrived, they had ceased to be guerrillas and had become, as they would often say later, "the people in arms."

In a last-ditch effort to don the clean clothes of legitimacy, Batista scheduled a general election for November 3, 1958. Three nights before the election, United States Secretary of State John Foster Dulles and his wife dined with the Cuban ambassador in the Cuban Embassy in Washington. Havana papers headlined it on page one: "DULLES TOASTS BATISTA."

To top it all off, the dinner was to commemorate Teddy Roosevelt, who had refused to allow the *mambisi* liberating army to enter the city of Santiago in 1898.

However, on November 3, at least 75 percent of the voters in Havana boycotted the polls. Abstentions ran higher in the provinces, reaching 98 percent in Santiago.

Four days later, Fidel closed his headquarters in the Sierra and marched at the head of a column of three hundred men to the plains, setting in motion the final campaign of the war: Operation Santiago.

On November 20, in the northern foothills of the Sierra, the Rebel Army waged the first pitched battle of the war on the plains, involving stationary positions under tank, artillery, rocket, and air attacks. At stake was control of the Central Highway, the major access route to Santiago. The army of Batista put up a desperate fight that raged for ten days up and down the highway.

At the end, the rebels had lost fifteen dead and wounded; the Batista forces, two hundred. Among those who distinguished themselves were a squad from the Mariana Grajales women's platoon, which had held one of the most dangerous positions by the side of the highway.

Ten days later Fidel's "José Martí Column" took the town of Baire. The forces of Raúl Castro's column pushed outward in an expanding circle from the Sierra Cristal, taking coastal towns and garrisons to the north and west, and moving steadily southward toward Santiago. At Palma Soriano, the last large town on the highway west of Santiago, the three forces of three *commandantes* —Fidel, Raúl, and Juan Almeida—met.

Radio Rebelde could be heard all over the dial, broadcasting in both shortwave and long-wave transmission from the captured cities.

On the twenty-eighth of December, General Eulogio Cantillo, chief of operations of Batista's army in Oriente, paid a "friendly visit" to Fidel at a sugar mill near Santiago.

The general flew in by helicopter. Fidel explained to Cantillo that if he was to cooperate, three conditions must be met: (1) Batista was to be arrested; (2) no talks were to be held by Cantillo with the army generals nor with the United States ambassador to Cuba about anything; (3) no military coup was to be carried out behind the back of the Rebel Army.

Cantillo "agreed" that on December 31 at 3 P.M. he and his troops would rise against the government, join the Revolution, and surrender the Moncada garrison to the Rebel Army.

After he left the sugar mill, Cantillo went to Havana, not Santiago. There he consulted with Batista and the United States ambassador to Cuba and agreed to let Batista flee the country and to set up a military government without notifying the Rebel Army.

The day of the meeting at the sugar mill, Che Guevara's troops were advancing toward the city of Santa Clara in central Cuba.

The general staff of Batista's army dispatched a seventeen-car armored train carrying four hundred soldiers and loaded with $1,000,000 in arms, ammunition, and armored cars, just purchased from England. The officer assigned to command the train saw it off at the railroad terminal in Havana, and then discreetly boarded his yacht at the Biltmore Yacht Club and sailed for Miami.

The moment the rebels entered Santa Clara, they were joined by a popular uprising. The local chapter of the July 26 Movement was distributing guns to the people. Cars were overturned in the streets to block government tanks; Molotov cocktails were dropped from the roofs. The fighting was so close that government bombers were unable to distinguish the rebels from the army troops.

When the armored train arrived, it was blocked by the trailers and gasoline trucks that Che's troops had pulled across the tracks. The rebels hurled hundreds of Molotov cocktails against the armor. The soldiers trapped inside could only fire wildly through the slits in the armor plate. Too late, the engineer put the train in reverse: the rebels had torn up the tracks behind them; the last car tilted and turned over on its side. A white handkerchief on a gun barrel was poked out a window.

January 1, 1959: The plane stood on the runway, its propellers howling. General Batista, now ex-President Batista, stood on the gangway, wearing his customary white suit despite the cold air. He was trying to smile as he said a few last words to General Cantillo. In his suitcase aboard the plane were several million dollars.

As Cantillo saluted, Batista tried to put some energy into his traditional *"Salud, salud."*

Moments later, the aluminum nose of the plane lifted off the runway to the east on a voyage without return.

Manuel Fajardo of the Frank País Second Front was driving along country roads to a village near Santiago to meet other rebel officers that morning.

When we passed by a sugar mill, all the people were in the streets yelling, "The Man is gone; The Man is gone!" When we arrived, I heard the news that Batista had fled.

I stood for a moment with my head bent, thinking, and a woman asked me if the news didn't make me happy. I told her that for us the struggle was going to be much more difficult, because up till then we'd been fighting an enemy who was out front, but beginning now it would be against hidden enemies.

And more, I was thinking that the blood of our fallen comrades had not even dried—those who dreamed of this day and had thousands of plans, and who, nevertheless, had not lived to see the victory.

Fidel heard the news at 8 A.M. that the Batista generals remaining in Havana were establishing a military government:

The chief [Fidel] leaped to his feet, more fury than surprise in his face. He strode to the door of the dining room, tugging at his beard. Finally he said aloud, "This is cowardly betrayal! They're trying to prevent the triumph of the Revolution. We have to take Santiago right away!"

ANNOUNCER: This is *Radio Rebelde,* at the doors of Santiago de Cuba. Attention: This is very important. Dr. Fidel Castro, the leader of the Cuban Revolution, is now coming to the microphones of *Radio Rebelde* to make a very important announcement.

MAJOR FIDEL CASTRO: Instructions to all Commanders of the Rebel Army and to the people:

Regardless of the news coming from the capital, our troops are not to cease fire, no matter what. Our forces continue their operations against the enemy on every battlefront.

The dictatorship has crumbled as a result of the crushing defeats dealt it in the last few weeks, but this doesn't mean that the Revolution has triumphed.

Revolution, yes! Military coup, no!

Then to the people of Santiago:

Santiago de Cuba, you are not free yet. Those who oppressed you for seven years, the murderers of hundreds of your best children, are still walking free in your streets. The war is not yet over, because the murderers are still armed.

The military men are trying to keep the rebels from entering Santiago de Cuba. . . . The story of 1895 will not be repeated! This time, the *mambises* will enter Santiago de Cuba!

Fidel then called for a general strike in all the territories not yet liberated.

This time the general strike was complete, demonstrating beyond doubt the support of the Cuban working class for the Revolution. The patient organizing work done by the Communists and the labor wing of the M-26-7 had paid off.

A letter arrived at Fidel's camp from the commander of the Moncada garrison, surrendering unconditionally.

Shortly before one o'clock on the morning of January 2, 1959, Fidel rode at the head of a column of men and women of the Rebel Army into a delirious Santiago, walked up the short flight of stairs through the doors of the military barracks he had tried to storm five years, five months, and five days earlier, and received the surrender of the army of the Batista dictatorship in Oriente.

Havana, New Year's Day: A car crossed the street. Overflowing from its windows flew a red and black flag that snapped in the wind. Cuban flags clustered in the balconies of buildings. Before the stone steps of the University, a crowd had gathered. An auto passed at high speed, shooting wildly. No one was wounded, but the crowd was infuriated. The torturers still ran free.

An old man had a sledge hammer and began to destroy a parking meter. On the third blow it shattered on the pavement spewing out its nickels and dimes. All over the city the first outlet was the parking meters.

The crowd entered the Deauville Hotel timidly at first. Seeing that nothing happened to them, they took the slot machines, the roulette wheels and the dice tables into the streets and kicked them apart. Someone brought gasoline and they built a huge pyre. Some walked around the fire catching the money that fell from the machines.

The road to the airport was jammed with abandoned Cadillacs and Chryslers. The officials ran for the airplanes. They demanded seats at the point of the guns they carried even in their tuxedos. Others ran for the embassies and at the door stumbled into the exiled revolutionaries returning to the streets.

In the Parque Central the crowd was running to take shelter in the portals. The Tigers of Masferrer were entrenched in the Manzana de Gómez, shooting sporadically. . . . Toward the old city a column of smoke rose: it was Masferrer's newspaper *Tiempo* burning.

At noon the gates of Principe Prison were opened. The political prisoners rushed down the stone steps, crying "Freedom, freedom!"

HAYDÉE SANTAMARÍA: On the first of January in the midst of the joy of triumph, there came to my mind so many memories of so many dead. . . . The first of January was when I truly realized that Abel was dead, that Enrique was dead, that they all were dead. When I saw the parade and I looked and they were not there.

The bodies of slain revolutionaries lie outside the Moncada garrison after the attack
Prensa Latina

The Moncada garrison after the attack on July 26, 1953   *Prensa Latina*

Slaves cutting sugarcane   *Bohemia*

Carlos Manuel de Céspedes
Bohemia

Antonio Maceo
Bohemia

José Martí
Prensa Latina

United States President Calvin Coolidge and Cuban President Gerardo Machado *Bohemia*

Julio Antonio Mella

Prensa Latina

Antonio Guiteras,
leader of the revolutionary
government of 1933

Bohemia

Blas Roca

Prensa Latina

Fulgencio Batista during
the 1952 coup d'etat
Bohemia

Young Fidel Castro
protesting the military coup
Bohemia

Haydée Santamaría *(left)*
and Melba Hernandez
(right) in prison
after the 1953 attack on the
Moncada garrison *Bohemia*   Abel Santamaría   *Prensa Latina*

Anti-Batista demonstrators attacked by police   *Bohemia*

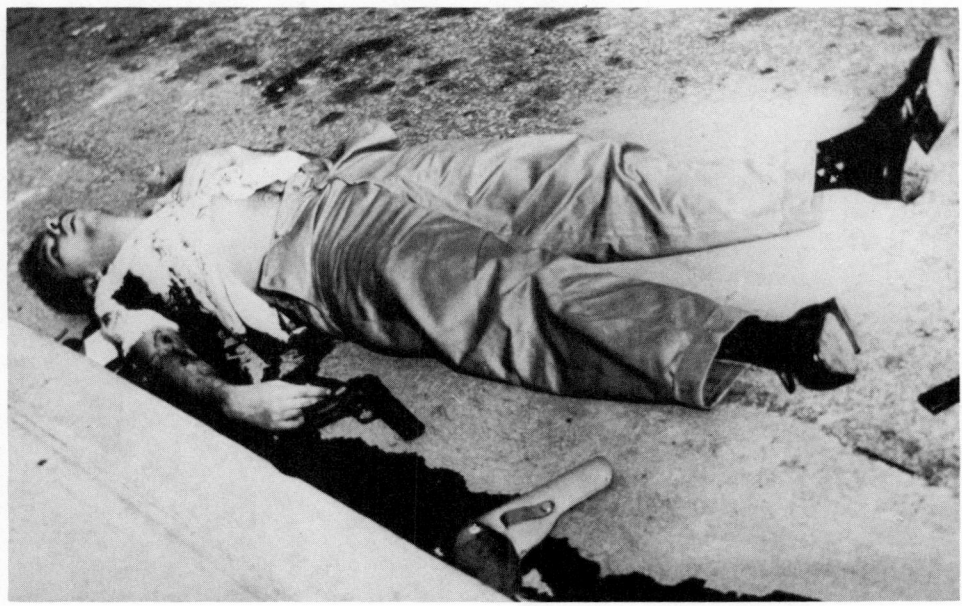

Leaders of the Rebel Army in the Sierra mountains *Bohemia*

The body of urban revolutionary leader Frank País *Bohemia*

The troop train derailed by rebels during the battle for Santa Clara   *Bohemia*

Fidel and his supporters enter the Moncada garrison, January 1959.   *Bohemia*

José Antonio Echeverría,
revolutionary student leader
Prensa Latina

Juan Almeida
Bohemia

Camilo Cienfuegos in Las Villas
province in the last days of the war
Bohemia

Camilo Cienfuegos and
Fidel Castro entering
Havana in January 1959
Bohemia

A peasant woman receives
the title to her land
from the agrarian reform
program in 1959.
Prensa Latina

A peasant *bohio*   *Prensa Latina*

PART II

THE FIRST YEAR

Winning the Right to Make the Revolution

Winning the war was not the Revolution. It gave us the right to make the Revolution.

— *FIDEL CASTRO, 1959*

The war correspondent for the Chicago *Tribune,* who had witnessed the liberation of Paris in World War II, said there was nothing else to which he could compare the entrance of Fidel Castro into Havana, January 9, 1959, at the head of the columns of the Rebel Army.

That night, before a million people on the grounds of conquered Camp Columbia, and during the days and nights afterward, Fidel and the other leaders of the Revolution drove home to their people in their ecstatic hour a single idea: this is a *real* Revolution, not an exchange of one ruling group for another.

"This Revolution is not about to repeat the mistakes of the thirties," Che Guevara told a television audience, "by simply throwing one man out without taking into account that that man is the representative of a class and a state of things, and if the whole state of things is not destroyed, the enemies of the people will invent another man.

"Therefore," Che said, "the Revolution must destroy at its roots the evil that afflicted Cuba. I would have to quote Martí— that 'radical' means to go to the root; one can't be called a radical who doesn't see the basis of things. This Revolution proposes to pull up the roots of injustice. . . ."

Only a handful of Batista's henchmen had found seats on his plane to Santo Domingo. Some left in private yachts; some sought asylum in foreign embassies. But most of them were still in the streets. They shed their uniforms and some their names; they moved, hid, pretended to be revolutionaries; but for most of them there was no hiding place.

Mass graves of victims of Batista's army were being uncovered the length of the island. Centers of torture were found, full of instruments. Whole families had been beaten to death, homes burned, towns destroyed. It is estimated that during his seven-year reign, Batista's armed forces, police, military intelligence, Bureau to Repress Communist Activities, and hired thugs had killed some twenty thousand Cubans.

The people began to demand justice. Immediately the Rebel Army established public tribunals to try the most notorious killers of the old regime. Once the tribunals were created, people who had been forced to live for years in the same town with the torturers of their children, parents, or friends, instead of lying in wait and shooting them, turned them over to the Rebel Army.

There was no lack of evidence. Like the Nazis, who thought their regime would last a thousand years, Batista's torturers had not tried to hide their crimes. One had given his twelve-year-old son the skulls of revolutionaries to play with. Many of the grisly photos used in the trials had been taken by the torturers themselves to decorate the walls at parties.

The furious protests in the U.S. press, portraying the trials and executions as "kangaroo courts," baffled and angered the Cubans. "Public opinion in this country," Jules Du Bois, correspondent in Cuba for the Chicago *Tribune,* wrote in February 1959, "from the poorest worker to the richest sugar magnate, from the atheist to the hierarchy of the Roman Catholic Church, supports Castro's firmness on this subject."

A survey taken in that same month by *Bohemia* magazine asked, "What are the best things the Revolution has done?" At the top of the list was "revolutionary justice." As Juan Almeida said, "We have to establish forever in this country—forever!—that there is no pardon for those who torture and kill."

As the trials continued, the United States government offered asylum to the worst criminals of the Batista regime, while the U.S. press campaigned, not against the torturers, but against those who brought them to justice. For many Cubans this was their first break with their northern neighbor—over the fundamental issues of justice and morality. It was the first hostile act by the United States against the new Cuban government. More were to come.

There is no mystery about what happened between the United States and the Cuban Revolution. The morning Batista fled, two forces came into head-on conflict: the needs of the Cuban people versus the economic policies of the United States corporations that owned the factories and fields of Cuba. As economist Edward Boorstein, who served as an adviser to the revolutionary government, wrote, "The victory over Batista meant that the Cuban people had done away with the local overseer; now they confronted the owner of the plantation—American imperialism."

The word imperialism will recur often from now on. What do the Cubans mean when they use it?

The natural development of capitalism in the nineteenth and twentieth centuries concentrated economic power in a few monopoly corporations and banks. Nowhere is this fusion of industrial and financial power so advanced as in the United States. This is imperialism: the most advanced, monopolized stage of capitalism.

There came a point late in the nineteenth century, when the monopolies began to search outside the boundaries of the United States for profitable ways to invest their wealth and sell their products. That was when the sugar trust and the Rockefeller and Mellon financial empires discovered Cuba. The effect on the Cuban economy, as described by Boorstein, was disastrous:

> The monopolies did not deliberately plot to strangle Cuba. They simply acted naturally. They made sure of the land and labor they needed, took control of mineral resources the way monopolies do everywhere, secured easy access into Cuba for their exports. They took control of resources and markets not only for their own use but to deny them to others. And just by being themselves, by taking normal advantage of their size and strength to promote their interests, the monopolies could not help but strangle the Cuban economy.

From January 1, 1959, therefore, the question became, Who is going to determine what happens in Cuba—the people of Cuba or the government and business interests of the United States? If the Revolution was going to carry out the radical reforms it had been promising since 1953, a clash was inevitable.

The July 26 Movement chose as provisional president of the Republic of Cuba Dr. Manuel Urrutia, a respectable and nonpartisan figure. As judge in the Court of Appeals in Oriente, Urrutia had declared at the trial of the captured survivors of the *Granma* landing that it was no crime to organize an insurrection against the dictatorship. The new Prime Minister was Dr. José Miró Cardona, president of the Havana Bar Association.

By the end of the first month it became obvious that there were actually *two* revolutionary governments: one in the presidential palace; the other in the Havana Hilton Hotel where Fidel and several hundred rebel soldiers were quartered. It was to Fidel, the spiritual and political hero of the country, and not to the "respectable" politicians, that the people turned for solutions to their desperate problems. The Hilton was the center of revolutionary ferment and creativity. The palace operated like a clean version of the governments of the past.

In an attempt to solve this contradiction, Miró Cardona resigned in mid-February and the Council of Ministers—chosen by the revolutionary leaders and given both executive and legislative powers—elected Fidel to the post of Prime Minister. Still, the new government was dominated by old-style politicians. Most of the bureaucracy remained and had to be constantly shaken to get the dead wood out.

With Fidel at the head of the government, a stream of basic reforms poured out of the Council of Ministers. During its first hundred days, the Revolution:

• Slashed rents. Rents less than 100 pesos (one peso = one U.S. dollar) a month (the majority of apartments in the country) were cut in half. Rents of 100–200 pesos were cut by 40 percent, those of more than 200 by 30 percent. "There were a few individuals who were upset," Fidel told the United Nations General Assembly a year later, "the few who owned the apartment buildings, but the people rushed into the streets rejoicing, as they would in any country, even here in New York, if rents were reduced by fifty percent."

• Cut in half the telephone rates of the ITT-owned Cuban Telephone Company. At a meeting of telephone workers in support of the reform, the head of the revolutionary trade-union confederation (CTC-R) said, "The whole world is watching the intervention in the Telephone Company, because this is the first time that a government in America has intervened in such an important company." The telephone workers painted "We Support the Intervention" on manhole covers and telephone-repair trucks.

• Set up a "Ministry for the Recovery of Illegally Acquired Properties," which began to poke at the mountain of corruption, embezzlement, theft, bribery, fraud, blackmail, and gangsterism by which those close to the Batista dictatorship had enriched themselves. By the end of the year the ministry had recovered some $400,000,000 worth of farms, buildings, plantations, jewelry, yachts, and a thousand other ill-gotten gains. Among the two thousand buildings seized was Batista's fabulous country estate, which became a residence for schoolchildren.

• Turned the old military garrisons of the dictatorship into schools.

• Began to clean up the gangster-ridden trade unions. Officials forced on the workers by violence and bribery were ousted; workers fired for political reasons were reinstated; free elections were held for new leaders.

• At first closed the gambling casinos, then reopened them (when it was realized that thousands of Cubans would be put out of work), with the profits going to the state. Later, when new sources of employment opened up, the casinos were closed permanently.

• Outlawed prostitution and opened special schools to retrain the thousands of young women who had been forced into the trade.

As each measure passed, a few more of the little signs that said *"Gracias, Fidel,"* which had appeared in the windows of homes and cars in early January, vanished from some of the richer houses and Cadillacs. Certain people began leaving the country: old corrupt trade-union leaders, owners of tenements and apartment houses, and people with dubious sources of income.

Racism and racial discrimination were never as deep or widespread in Cuba as they were in the United States. For centuries, black Cubans had played a recognized role in the struggle for independence. As one Cuban scholar put it, "The term *Cubano* in its very inception was a multiracial term."

Segregation came to Cuba in 1898 with the occupying (and segregated) armed forces of the United States. "With the U.S. domination of Cuba," Fidel said in 1975, "race discrimination, which should have been wiped out forever by the blood shed in common on the field of battle . . . became especially acute. In the parks of many cities one could observe the disgraceful sight of blacks and whites segregated in separate areas. Many educational, economic, cultural and recreational establishments were barred to black citizens, who were denied the right to study, work, and enjoy culture, and what is more important, human dignity."

Despite this, the ideology of racism failed to embed itself deeply among the peasants and workers, and it was fought strenuously by all progressive and left-wing movements and organizations. Practically no trade union in Cuba after 1902 barred black members. Cuban historian Pedro Serviát, a specialist in studies of Cuban race relations, stated in 1976 that in the entire history of Cuba he could find only two cases of the lynching of black Cubans by whites.

This is not to say that racism had not been fostered by those in power. In 1912, black Cubans in Oriente province were forced to rise up against the racist practices of the Cuban government and the degrading treatment of black veterans who had fought in the war of independence. The United States landed troops to defend the government, and the rebellion was suppressed.

The antiracist tradition of Maceo, Céspedes, and Martí was

continued by the revolutionaries who overthrew Batista. The M-26-7, the Cuban Communist Party, and the Revolutionary Directorate gathered in their ranks men and women of all colors. When the Rebel Army entered Havana, it swept before it not only the government and army of the dictatorship, but the social conventions, hierarchical structures, and racial practices that had supported dictatorial rule.

Two months after the victory, Fidel told a rally of workers in Havana:

> It should not be necessary to dictate a law against an absurd prejudice. That which should be dictated is the public condemnation against any people so filled with old vices and prejudices that they would discriminate against Cubans over questions of lighter or darker skin.
>
> We are a mixed race from Africa and Spain. No one should consider themselves a pure race, much less a superior race.
>
> We are going to put an end to this odious and repugnant system. . . .

His speech was interrupted by cheers. Fidel was speaking to a deeply felt desire.

"The Revolution showed it meant business right away," recalls economist Edward Boorstein:

> They opened up the beaches, they opened up the hotels, they opened up everything. Once they put the weight of the society, once they put the weight of a *revolution* in a society against racism—that was it!
>
> The whole thing took place with surprising speed, with surprisingly little opposition. The Cuban people sort of sighed with relief . . . as though they had been relieved of a burden.

All hopes and dreams were stirred in the "rich pandemonium" of that year. Nicolás Guillén, Cuba's black poet laureate, summed up in a poem, "Tengo," (I have) the feelings of black Cubans in that moment, particularly to the opening of the once-segregated beaches:

When I look at and touch myself
I, John-only-yesterday-with-Nothing,
and John-with-Everything-today,
with everything today,
I glance around, I look and see
and touch myself and wonder
how it could have happened

. . . .

I have, let's see:
that being Black
I can be stopped by no one at
the door of a dancing hall or bar
Or even at the desk of a hotel
have someone yell at me there are no rooms,
a small room and not one that's immense,
a tiny room where I might rest.

I have, let's see:
that there are no rural police
to seize me and lock me in a precinct jail,
or tear me from my land and cast me
in the middle of the highway.

I have that having the land I have the sea,
no country clubs,
no high life,
no tennis and no yachts,
but, from beach to beach and wave on wave,
gigantic blue open democratic:
in short, the sea.

. . . .

The first giant step that proved to all that this was no half-way revolution was taken on May 17, 1959, when the agrarian reform law was passed. The law liquidated the huge plantations, whether held by Cubans or foreigners. Those peasants who farmed land for their own use were given title to that land—free. In a stroke, the ancient dream of the peasants, who before, as Fidel has said, "couldn't even plant a cedar or an orange tree for they never knew when the Rural Guards would come and evict them," was made true.

One fourth of the best land in Cuba had been owned by Americans. This meant that the five-month-old Revolution had to clash directly with the most powerful country in the world over her most basic natural resource, the land.

The greater part of the land had been welded by the landlords and corporations into plantations that sometimes stretched from horizon to horizon. These were kept intact and passed to the ownership of the nation as a whole.

Such state-owned farms—known elsewhere as collective farms—are a socialist form of agriculture. A state organization, INRA (the National Institute of Agrarian Reform) was set up to administer them. No one planned it this way because it was "the socialist thing to do." It just made sense. The great landholdings already existed. The question was, in whose interest were they going to be run? Private owners or the people as a whole?

The largest piece of land one could privately own was set at a thousand acres. Considering that a relatively small North American firm, the Cuban Trading Company, owned 72,870 acres, this law eliminated the huge plantation holdings in a single stroke. Some 40 percent of all rural land was transferred from the sugar trust and the latifundists to the revolutionary government. A hundred thousand peasant families were given deeds to the land on which they lived and worked.

There is no revolution without counterrevolution. The old does not give way without a struggle. Once the agrarian reform law was passed, the former plantation owners, North American and Cuban, passed over to the side of the counterrevolution, sweeping with them many of their friends among the country's industrialists.

These once-powerful people no longer had any formal political or military power. The rebels had done away with that. But they did possess a weapon—anti-Communism—and a formidable ally —the United States of America.

The defeated *Batistianos* were the first to raise the cry of "Red menace" as soon as they reached Miami. When the large landholders arrived a few months later, they did the same. Soon the leaders of the Revolution couldn't appear for a press conference without reporters demanding to know if they were "Communists."

The purpose of this outcry was twofold: to prevent the revolutionary leaders from passing radical measures for fear of being labeled Communist, and to provoke them into making what could be interpreted as pro-Communist statements that would isolate them from some of their followers. It had nothing to do with the nature of the government: its leaders were not then Communists. They were doing what they believed to be merely just and humanitarian.

The most outrageous rumors were making the rounds inside Cuba, believed by many people: all the children were going to be taken to the Soviet Union; the antipolio vaccine given out in candy balls by the Ministry of Public Health was really a chemical that turned you into a Communist. . . .

The campaign affected some vacillating members of the revolutionary army who had imagined they would be rewarded with wealth and privilege after the Revolution and were disappointed. It also appealed to middle-class politicians to whom offending the Americans was "just not good politics." It shook those who feared the Revolution's determination to go to the root of Cuba's problems. They began to blame "the Communists" for making the Revolution radical.

In June, the first small planes started coming across the Florida Straits from the United States, dropping incendiary bombs and hand grenades on sugar fields and mills. On July 12, the head of the rebel air force, Díaz Lanz, under investigation for incompetency, resigned, charging Communist infiltration of the government. *Bohemia* magazine, no left-wing journal at that time, featured a two-page spread of three photos: Díaz Lanz, Benedict Arnold, and Judas.

There was anger against the counterrevolution, but there was also unease in the air. Things seemed to be bogging down; the Revolution was losing momentum. The contradiction between the old-time politicians and the new revolutionary leaders, between those who only wanted to rid themselves of Batista and those who wanted to make the Revolution, was coming to a head.

On the morning of July 17 the newspapers hit the streets with a banner headline: FIDEL RESIGNS! The country came to a virtual halt: students stood anxiously in the halls outside their classrooms; work in the factories stopped; the telephone lines were jammed with people calling the newspapers and radio stations.

At 8 P.M. Fidel arrived at the CMQ-TV studio and explained to the nation why he had resigned.

President Urrutia was dragging his feet, Fidel charged. Work was bureaucratically jammed up; needed reforms were not being made.

Fidel could have maneuvered to kick Urrutia out behind the scenes, but backdoor deals were not his style. Instead he went on television, having first resigned in order to speak as an individual. He was putting the problem before the people, he said; it was up to them to solve it.

When Fidel finished his speech, the cameras focused on him and the reporters and audience in the studio. Everyone waited.

Telegrams supporting Fidel began to pour in, from the university students, from the Committee of Cuban Institutions (which had demanded Batista's resignation in 1958), from the labor unions, from the Association of Cuban Mothers.

The students announced that they were marching on the presidential palace. Fidel advised them not to march because it might seem like a physical threat, but they were already in the streets.

Shortly after midnight a telegram arrived at the television studio from the presidential palace. Urrutia had resigned.

The new president, appointed by the Council of Ministers, was Osvaldo Dorticós. Born in Cienfuegos in 1919, he was sixteen when the 1935 general strike, in which he participated, was crushed. After graduating from the University of Havana Law School in 1941, he opened up a law office in Cienfuegos where he practiced civil and criminal law. When Batista seized power, Dorticós joined the Movement of Civic Resistance, a coalition of professional groups, and had been arrested after the September 1957 uprising in Cienfuegos. Later released, he joined the July 26 Movement, becoming its coordinator in Cienfuegos, supplying Che Guevara's invasion column in the nearby Escambray Mountains. In the final months of the war, he was arrested by Batista's military intelligence, but was exiled rather than jailed, due to his position as dean of the Cienfuegos Law School. Though older than most of the Rebel Army leaders, at forty he was Cuba's youngest president.

Since the days of the Moncada attack, the leaders of the revolutionary movement had promised that when they came to power, they would hold elections. After the victory over Batista, they continued to plan for elections once the conditions for holding them fairly had been established. They assumed the people felt the same.

Yet at the end of February 1959 when *Bohemia* magazine's opinion poll asked its readers, "What has the government not yet done that it should do quickly?" only 1.3 percent mentioned elections. A profound change had taken place among the people— subjected for years to farcical and corrupt elections—which even Fidel did not notice. During a mass rally in March, Fidel mentioned elections as one of the goals the Revolution would soon take up. *Bohemia* reported the reaction:

> An outcry of rejection, almost angry, drowns out his voice. Fidel, a little perplexed before the indignant reaction, crosses his arms and waits for the gale to pass. No one wants to hear talk of nominations, candidates, shouting aspirants for office. A spontaneous refrain breaks out:
> "Elections—No!"
> It is a new Cuba. . . . No one now wants to hear of parties, committees, political cartoons and the counting of votes. First is the Revolution. . . . The people, forgotten and trampled on for seven years, are conscious that they are now the protagonist in their own destiny.

What was taking place? The people had seen more happen in three months of revolution than in thirty years of pseudo democracy. Racial discrimination, gambling, prostitution, corruption, terror, and injustice had been seriously challenged—without elections.

That realization is a profound moment in a revolutionary process, when people understand that parliamentary elections are only a means to an end, not an end in themselves, and are often an inadequate way of achieving what is needed at the moment. Free secret balloting would return to Cuba—but it would be very different from the commercial hurly-burly of the elections of the past.

When the old-line politicians, who all their lives had made a career of being elected to office, saw that the people rejected elections in favor of direct revolutionary action, they, too, began leaving for Miami.

After half a year, *Bohemia*'s poll showed that 90.29 percent of the people backed the Revolution; 1.3 percent were opposed.

In the middle of October, the American Society of Travel Agents (ASTA) opened their annual convention in Havana, a gala occasion of meetings, parties, and dances. Cuba's economy, heavily dependent on tourism, needed such a boost. The counterrevolution chose the days of the convention to begin their first offensive.

The government had been concerned for some time about the activities of Major Huber Matos, rebel commander of Camagüey province. Matos had had close relations with the defector Díaz Lanz, and worse, with the local plantation owners. On October 20, in the midst of the ASTA convention, Matos sent a letter of resignation to Fidel, calling on him to "rectify his errors—if there is still time." He charged "Communist infiltration" of the government. . . .

On the morning of the next day the Rebel Army moved troops to cover strategic points outside the city of Camagüey. At half past eight Camilo Cienfuegos arrived. The city was in a state of severe tension. The local leaders of INRA publically accused Matos of treason for having conspired with the latifundists to stop agrarian reform. Crowds gathered in the streets.

At ten o'clock Fidel entered the city and went to the radio station where ten thousand people had gathered. Unarmed, he mounted a pickup truck and asked the people to come with him to the garrison. A river of people moved through the streets to the military headquarters where Matos and his officers waited. When they arrived, the soldiers guarding the headquarters let them pass.

At the gates of the garrison, Fidel spoke to the crowd.

He reminded them of what had happened under Batista when there was a conspiracy in the army: Batista had brought in tanks and troops and slaughtered them. Now Fidel had only to bring the people. They waited. The city shimmered under a roasting sun.

At noon Matos surrendered.

"The seriousness of Matos's treason," Fidel stated later, "was his primary intent to use the soldiers against the Revolution, against the rights of the Cuban people. The forces of reaction want a disarmed people, a corrupted army which one day would harm the Revolution and send our country hurtling backward."

Returning from the confrontation in Camagüey, Fidel's car was entering Havana, when he heard explosions in the city. People on the streets were saying they'd been attacked by a plane, that there were many killed. "Fidel, look what they've done!" they were yelling.

Díaz Lanz, taking off from Florida, had arrived over Havana in a Mitchell B-25 bomber at six, the hour when most people were in the streets. His copilot was Frank A. Sturgis, who thirteen years later was one of those who broke into the Democratic Party headquarters at Watergate.

Lanz first dropped a wave of leaflets signed by himself, containing the charges of Communism. On his second turn he machine-gunned along the streets. On the third he dropped hand grenades into the evening crowds. Two people coming home from work were killed, forty wounded. Lanz's purpose was to show the ASTA agents that Havana was unsafe for tourism.

A week later, another tragedy occurred. On October 28, Camilo Cienfuegos, a pilot, and an escort took off from Camagüey for Havana in a two-engine Cessna-310. The flight should have taken three hours. It never arrived.

The army and the people searched for the plane from that day to the twelfth of November with no results. They searched in planes, helicopters, and boats. On the ground, they searched with jeeps and on foot and on muleback. No wreckage, no trace, was ever found.

Every year on the twenty-eighth of October, the childen of Cuba throw flowers into the sea for their lost *commandante,* "A flower for Camilo."

At the end of the first year of the Revolution, much was uncertain; even the survival of the Revolution itself was not certain. But the determination and vision of the guerrillas—which had carried them from a handful of men and women to a victorious national movement—were becoming fixed in the people of Cuba as a whole. During the next dangerous year, the question of where Cuba was going would be resolved.

THE MONCADA GARRISON IS TURNED INTO THE "26TH OF JULY SCHOOL CITY," JANUARY 28, 1960

On the one hundred and seventh anniversary of José Martí's birth, the Moncada garrison in Santiago became a school. Several thousand children attended the opening ceremony; they stood acres deep in the open area before the school. The bullet holes from the 1953 attack were, and still are, visible. The children stood on the grass, which had been matted in blood and strewn with the tortured bodies of Luís Tasende, Abel Santamaría, and others seven years before.

FIDEL: Why have we converted this fortress into a school? Who defended the government before? The army—that army. Who defends the Revolution today?
CHILDREN: The people!

FIDEL: Where are the fortresses of the Revolution today?

CHILDREN: In the people!

FIDEL: Now we have much work to do, we have many roads to construct, many dams, many towns, many factories; we have to plow the fields, construct beaches and tourist centers. We have a great job to do and there are not enough people who know how to do these things and therefore our greatest hope is not in what we are doing today, but in what you are going to do tomorrow.

You will finish the work that we are doing today; because we are going to do no more than a part, and you will have to do the rest. Do you understand this well?

CHILDREN: Yes.

FIDEL: Or do you not understand?

CHILDREN: Yes!

FIDEL: You *do* understand?

CHILDREN: Yes.

FIDEL: You understand that you will have to finish the work that we are doing now?

CHILDREN: Yes.

Raúl Castro was standing in front of the school, holding the young daughter of slain Luís Tasende in his arms. He pointed to the building. "This is the work of your father," he told her. They were both crying.

1960

Cuba Becomes an Ex-Colony

We understood perfectly that the life of a single human being is worth a million times more than all the property of the richest man on earth.

— *CHE GUEVARA, August 19, 1960*

The year 1960 marked the beginning of Cuba's "war of economic independence" from the United States, a war fought on two intermingling fronts. One was a war of ideas—against fear, anti-Communist prejudices, and lingering feelings of dependency on the great northern neighbor.

The second was economic. The United States government, aware of Cuba's dependency on U.S. experts, technology, machinery, and spare parts attempted to pressure the revolutionary government by withdrawing these resources from the island.

The two fronts were closely related. As the revolutionary enthusiasm of the Cuban people increased, the United States escalated its economic pressure and its propaganda. As the pressure rose, the Cuban people rallied closer around their new government.

Economic independence from the United States was a goal that no Latin American country had ever achieved. Cuba's leaders were acutely aware of two previous radical movements that had reached this very point only to be defeated: the Cuban revolution of 1933, and that of the Arbenz government of Guatemala, overthrown by the CIA in 1954.

In the spring of 1960, the political ferment could be felt everywhere in Cuba. An intense national debate was going on in every factory, school, neighborhood, social club, association, and farm. People were discussing the political and economic issues that would determine the future of their country: Is socialism better than capitalism? Should workers strike? Could they survive without the United States? What should they do about the counterrevolution and sabotage? Were the rumors about the Communists true? As never before, the country debated, listened, learned.

The men and women trade unionists listening to Fidel at the Blanquita Theater in Havana on the night of February 24, 1960, did not care that his speech was long. They were hearing what few prime ministers ever dare tell their people: the real problems of the economy.

Several months earlier, their organization—the CTC (Confederation of Cuban Workers)—had agreed after much debate to donate 4 percent of their wages to the government to invest in economic development.

The only way they could solve the problems of unemployment, low wages, poor housing, bad health care, Fidel was explaining, was to increase production. If Cuba was to be economically independent, she had to expand her industries and build new ones.

"For a country to industrialize it needs what is called 'capital,' " Fidel said. "Capital is simply the investments one has to make in machinery or in work to improve the resources of a nation. If a country doesn't have that capital, it must obtain it by saving a part of what it produces."

What would the government do with the industries built with the CTC donation?

"We will return the profits to the people, not to some absentee company. These factories will belong to 'People Company, Inc.' They are industries of the people and the people will receive the benefits, because the state—why does it need money? The state is not a company; the state is not a boss. . . ."

The Blanquita Theater shook with the ovation. The workers' donation was not only a victory for Cuban economic independence; it showed the unity of the Cuban workers with the Revolution. They were not afraid of independence, even if it meant a sacrifice.

Had the State Department and CIA experts understood how firmly Cuban workers supported the Revolution, they might have known that the United States was dealing with something it could scarcely hope to defeat. A year later, after the invasion of Cuba at the Bay of Pigs had been crushed, they understood; but it was too late. The United States was basing its policy on too many incorrect premises, the most fatal being that Fidel lacked real popular support.

Inside Cuba, old fears and prejudices were withering. People were judged by the way they acted. When anti-Communists like Díaz Lanz turned traitor, their arguments were weakened in the public mind. When Communists, on the other hand, proved themselves to be among the firmest defenders of the Revolution, and when their predictions about the course of events more often than not came true, public respect for them grew.

On March 4, the French ship *Le Coubre,* carrying Belgian arms purchased by the revolutionary government, blew up while being unloaded in the harbor of Havana. Half the ship disappeared in a volcanic blast that darkened the afternoon with a mushroom cloud from some thirty tons of exploding rifle grenades and ammunition. Cuban longshoremen, members of the French crew, and Rebel Army guards were torn apart and hurled through blocks of destruction. Almost one hundred people were killed, two hundred wounded.

All the evidence pointed to sabotage. We now know that on March 17, two weeks after the explosion, President Eisenhower officially ordered the CIA to prepare an invasion of the island. In the light of later revelations about CIA activities, it is fair to say that though Fidel had no concrete evidence at the time, he at least had reason on his side when two days after the blast he accused the United States of being responsible for the slaughter.

As Eisenhower's CIA was planning the Bay of Pigs invasion, those who would defeat it were solemnly parading through the streets of Havana to the cemetery where the *Le Coubre* dead were to be buried.

Above the graves that contained only mangled bits of flesh, Fidel first used the words that became the fighting slogan at the Bay of Pigs: *Patria o muerte!* "Our country or death!"

The hostility expressed toward Cuba by the United States told the leaders of the Revolution that more serious economic warfare was coming. They began to prepare by diversifying the markets to which they sold their major products and from which they received their essential supplies.

Anastas Mikoyan arrived in Havana at the head of a trade delegation from the Soviet Union on May 4, 1960. Ten days later the two countries signed a major trade agreement. The Soviet Union would buy one million tons of Cuban sugar a year for the next five years, paying for most of it in goods: oil, newsprint, machinery, wheat, and chemical products.

"This agreement constituted a virtual declaration of political and economic independence by Cuba," writes economist Edward Boorstein. Trade agreements with other socialist countries—China, the German Democratic Republic, Poland, and Czechoslovakia—followed.

Cuba has no oil of her own. Every drop that fuels and greases her trucks, cars, tractors, and industry comes from abroad. In

1960 Cuba was spending $70,000,000 a year (10 percent of all her imports) on oil. She welcomed the opportunity to buy petroleum from the Soviet Union in exchange for goods rather than dollars, which were in short supply. The price of Soviet oil was one third less than oil bought from United States corporations—a saving to Cuba of some $20,000,000 a year.

When the Cuban government asked the three foreign oil companies operating refineries in Cuba—Texaco, Standard Oil, and Shell —to refine the Soviet oil, they refused. The revolutionary government then seized the refineries under a 1938 mining law that gave Cuba the right to have oil from any source refined by foreign-owned companies.

Early in July 1960, the first Soviet tanker sailed past the light-house of Morro Castle into the Havana harbor. Since then, more than three thousand Soviet oil tankers have docked in Cuba, one every fifty-six hours, a fleet of ships strung in a continuous line from the harbors of the Black Sea to the Caribbean. It has been the most massive "oil lift" in history, providing more than eighty million tons of petroleum for Cuba's industry. Through blockades and oil "crises," Cuba has never suffered a shortage of petroleum.

For half a century, the sugar quota had been an object of fear and veneration to Cubans. It dominated Cuban agriculture and tied her economy to the United States.

The quota guaranteed that a certain part of sugar consumed by the U.S. each year would be purchased from Cuba. The quota subordinated all Cuban agriculture to the great U.S. sugar-refining companies; its terms required that Cuba purchase goods almost entirely from the United States, and it prevented her from competing with U.S. sugar growers in the Philippines, Puerto Rico, and Hawaii.

Without warning, on July 6 the news came over the wires that President Eisenhower had cut the 1960 Cuban sugar quota by seven hundred thousand tons, eliminating in a single stroke 95 percent of what the United States was supposed to purchase during the rest of the year. Eisenhower hoped to force the Cuban government to cease its radical measures and to replace Fidel with a "moderate" who could get along with the United States.

Instead, it galvanized the Cuban people in anger. "Is that what you want, to crush us with hunger?" Fidel said at a stormy rally the following night. "No, you will not succeed!" A popular slogan appeared on walls, on signs, in speeches, beginning that day: *Sin cuota, pero sin amo* ("Without a quota, but without a boss").

CIA-organized counterrevolutionary rings were being uncovered inside Cuba almost daily. After the sabotage of *Le Coubre,* no one doubted that a military attack was inevitable. It was public knowledge that an invasion force was being trained in Florida and Guatemala.

Two days after the sugar quota was cut, Soviet Premier Nikita Khrushchev surprised both the United States and the Cuban governments by announcing that the Soviet Union would defend Cuba against any attack—with its own missiles, if need be. This was followed by a Soviet offer to purchase the seven hundred thousand tons of sugar that the United States refused to buy. Posters appeared around Havana: *Cuba no está sola* ("Cuba is not alone").

Cuba had reestablished diplomatic relations with the Soviet Union only two months earlier. Though relations were good, nothing had indicated the extent of Soviet willingness to defend the Revolution.

In Washington, politicians invoked the Monroe Doctrine and accused the Soviet Union of "foreign interference," to which Cuba's ambassador to the United Nations, Raúl Roa, replied:

Who is intervening in the internal affairs of the hemisphere—the great power which with all its military might is threatening a small and unarmed country, or the other great power which takes a step to stop this? Is it the one who robs a small country of its sugar quota, or the one who is offering to take it up?

"If they take away our quota pound by pound," Fidel announced, "we'll take away their sugar mills one by one."

On the evening of August 6, Fidel stood before a crowd massed in the Havana sports stadium and dramatically announced that Cuba was nationalizing most of the U.S.-owned properties in the country. Cuba was no longer an appendage of the United States economy.

The five top United States companies nationalized, with the amounts of their worth (rounded off to the nearest million), were Cuban Electric Company, $267,000,000; International Telephone and Telegraph, $130,000,000; North American Sugar Industries Inc., Cuban-American Mercantile Corporation, West India Corporation (joint claim), $109,000,000; Moa Bay Mining Company, $88,000,000; United Fruit Sugar Company, $85,000,000.

The total claimed value of the nationalized industries came to $1,800,000,000. The Cuban Electric Company alone provided more than 90 percent of Cuba's electrical energy.

On October 13, the revolutionary government nationalized 382 large Cuban-owned companies, including all the banks. The following day it passed a law of urban reform, which over a period of time turned ownership of homes and apartments over to those who rented them, putting an end to the landlord class in Cuba.

No one used the word *socialism* yet, but by November of that year, Cuba was basically a socialist nation, a country without capitalists, factory bosses, landlords, plantation owners, bankers, or aristocrats.

It had been a rapid and sometimes harsh process. With the candor that marked the leaders of the Revolution, Raúl Castro acknowledged during a 1960 television address the errors and injustices that had occurred:

No one knew anything; everyone had to start learning, and we went here and we blundered, we went there and committed an error, and we still continue making errors and we will go on making them, but with the best intentions in the world.

Fortunately, every time the people see some nonsense, they at least say, "Fidel isn't aware of that." It's a reality, we have to be constantly vigilant and critical. Today as the farmers say, *Halar parejo.* Everyone has to pull together.

Ironically, it was not the blunders of the Revolution but the successes that put it in greater peril. Those who opposed the Revolution for one reason or another, those who had abandoned their country in the hopes that the United States would restore them to power, were being leashed together by the Central Intelligence Agency—not to influence, reform, or pressure the Revolution, but to destroy it.

FIDEL: HOW I BECAME A COMMUNIST

I was the son of a landowner—that was one reason for me to be a reactionary. I was educated in religious schools that were attended by the sons of the rich—another reason for being a reactionary. I lived in Cuba, where all the films, publications, and mass media were "Made in USA"—a third reason for being a reactionary. I studied in a university where out of fifteen thousand students, only thirty were anti-imperialists, and I was one of those thirty at the end. When I entered the university, it was as the son of a landowner—and to make matters worse, as a political illiterate!

 . . . . And mind you, no party member, no Communist, no socialist or extremist got hold of me and indoctrinated me. No. I was given a big, heavy, infernal, unreadable, unbearable textbook that tried to explain political economy from a bourgeois viewpoint —they called that political economy!

And that unbearable book presented the crises of overproduction and other such problems as the most natural things in the world. It explained how in Britain, when there was an abundance of coal, there were workers who didn't have any, because by the inexorable natural and unchangeable laws of history, of society and nature, crises of overproduction inevitably occur, and when they do, they bring unemployment and starvation. When there's too much coal, workers will freeze and starve!

So that landowner's son, who had been educated by bourgeois schools and Yankee propaganda, began to think that something was wrong with that system, that it didn't make sense. . . .

As the son of a poor man who later became a big landowner, I had the advantage of at least living in the countryside, with the peasants, with the poor, who were all my friends. Had I been the grandson of a landowner, it's quite possible that my father would have taken me to live in the capital, in a superaristocratic neighborhood and those positive factors at work on me wouldn't have been able to survive the influence of the milieu. Egoism and other negative traits we human beings have would have prevailed.

Luckily, the schools I studied in developed some of the positive factors. A certain idealistic rationality; a certain concept of good and evil, just and unjust; and a certain spirit of rebelliousness against impositions and oppression led me to an analysis of human society, and turned me into what I later realized was a utopian Communist. At the time, I still hadn't been fortunate enough to meet a Communist or read a Communist document.

Then one day a copy of the *Communist Manifesto*— the famous *Communist Manifesto!*—fell into my hands and I read some things I'll never forget. . . . What phrases, what truths! And we saw those truths every day!

I felt like some little animal that had been born in a forest which he didn't understand. Then, all of a sudden, he finds a map of that forest—a description, a geography of that forest and everything in it. It was then that I got my bearings. Take a look now and see if Marx's ideas weren't just, correct, and inspiring. If we hadn't based our struggle on them, we wouldn't be here now! We wouldn't be here!

Now then, was I a Communist? No. I was a man who was lucky enough to have discovered a political theory, a man who was caught up in the whirlpool of Cuba's political crisis long before becoming a full-fledged Communist. . . .

I went on developing. Afterwards, I had the opportunity to know imperialism more concretely than I had through Lenin's book. I got to know it in Cuba, at a distance of only ninety miles. I had the opportunity to know imperialism—the worst and most aggressive of all. . . . And I believe life has given me a better understanding of reality. It has made me more revolutionary, more socialist, more Communist. . . .*

---

*At a question-and-answer period with Chilean students, University of Concepción, Chile, November 18, 1971.

THE
COUNTERREVOLUTION
AND THE BAY OF PIGS

"The First Defeat of Imperialism in America"

Who practices subversion and who is the victim of subversion? Who constitutes a danger to the security of another country and who is the victim of this danger? The United States, who organized the invasion of April, 1961? Guatemala, where the mercenaries were trained? Nicaragua, from which they were launched? Or Cuba, where they landed?

— *CUBAN COUNCIL OF MINISTERS*

To every action there is a reaction. To every revolution there is a counterrevolution. That there was an organized Cuban counterrevolution of any strength was due to the consistent support it received from the United States government and particularly the Central Intelligence Agency.

DWIGHT D. EISENHOWER: Within a matter of weeks after Castro entered Havana, we in the administration informally began to examine measures that might be effective in restraining Castro if he should develop into a menace. . . .

One suggestion was that we begin to build up an anti-Castro force within Cuba itself. Some thought we should quarantine the island,

arguing that if the Cuban economy declined sharply, Cubans themselves might overthrow Castro. . . .

On March 17, 1960 . . . I ordered the Central Intelligence Agency
to begin to organize the training of Cuban exiles, mainly in
Guatemala. . . .

No American properties in Cuba had been nationalized when
Eisenhower gave his order to overthrow the Cuban government.
No Soviet oil had been imported. The Soviet Union and Cuba had
not even established diplomatic relations. Yet the United States
government was embarking on a two-pronged offensive: to de-
stabilize the Cuban economy and to prepare a military force that
would break the Revolution if it could not be bent.

The CIA's first plan was to infiltrate counterrevolutionary guerrillas into Cuba over a long period, supplying them with arms and
material dropped by plane. But where inside Cuba would be the
best place to organize these guerrilla bands? The Sierra Maestra
was out—the peasants there completely supported the Revolution.

More fruitful soil for the CIA were the Escambray Mountains
of central Cuba. To understand why, we have to return to the days
of the revolutionary war, at the moment the invasion column of
Che Guevara was entering those mountains in October 1958.

Che discovered that there were three guerrilla movements in the
Escambray. Two of them—the July 26 Movement and the Revolutionary Directorate—quickly united with him. The third group
at first refused. The "Second Front of the Escambray," as it was
called, turned out to be little more than a bandit gang. Some
peasants called them the "cow-eaters," from their habit of seizing
peasants' cattle without paying. These were the only "revolutionaries" many peasants in the Escambray had ever met, and they
gave the Revolution a bad name.

Fidel and Che later criticized themselves for having cooperated
with the "cow-eaters" in the name of unity against Batista. The
Revolution paid for its mistake when the Escambray, where the

Revolution was weakest, became the CIA's base of operations.

Early in 1960 a wealthy Havana apartment owner traveled to the United States for CIA training. When he returned, under the *nom de guerre* of Major Agosto, he established a unified command of counterrevolutionary bands operating in the Escambray. Then he went looking for a man to command them.

Soon he came up with a real find: Tony Santiago, a man in his late thirties, who had fought with the United States Army during World War II, had joined Fidel's rebels in the mountains, and was now discontent with the Revolution for its "creeping Communism."

Santiago agreed to take on the job, and Agosto arranged for a series of meetings at the United States embassy in Havana between himself, Santiago, the United States ambassador, and the head of United States Caribbean military intelligence (headquartered in the embassy). There they briefed Santiago on plans for infiltration, arms drops, and an eventual invasion, and appointed him head of the entire Escambray operation.

But Tony Santiago was *not* discontent with the Revolution. He was a member of its Department of State Security. Before he left for training in the United States, he recruited ten "counterrevolutionary" soldiers—all members of State Security—and sent them to the Escambray. Then he left for Miami one moonless night in a fishing boat with three fishermen and a CIA agent. Those in State Security waited for his first reports from Miami. None came. Months later the nameplate of the boat in which he had left washed up on the northern shore.

Santiago's disappearance remained a mystery for years, until a Cuban agent who had infiltrated the counterrevolutionary movement in the United States got into a conversation with a drunken Cuban exile who was bragging about his exploits as a free-lance pirate. He used a high-speed launch with a cannon mounted on the deck to prey on fishermen off Cuba's northern coast. In all the time he plied his trade, he said, only one boat had ever put up any resistance, and he named the boat Tony Santiago had been in.

He had come upon it in the night and fired once with his cannon but missed. Santiago had returned the fire. The next shells ripped the boat in half. The pirate then shot the swimming men to death.

Tony Santiago was one of hundreds of Cuban men and women who labored for years in obscurity and danger, infiltrating the ranks of the counterrevolution, working closely with loyal Cubans —many of whom had members of their families in the counterrevolution.

They, together with thousands of peasants, were the backbone of the fight against the counterrevolution, and the reason why the CIA's plans for organizing guerrillas inside Cuba were notoriously unsuccessful.

The Revolution kept military confrontations at a minimum. It did not want to risk lives unnecessarily, nor to disrupt the thousands of projects—the building of schools, agrarian reform, the campaign against illiteracy—which were going on as the battle against the counterrevolution unfolded.

In the final phase of the Escambray operation, the revolutionary army trained a thousand peasants from the area who volunteered to fight the armed gangs in the mountains. They were joined by five hundred militiamen from the Sierra Maestra. By the time of the Bay of Pigs invasion, they had crippled the counterrevolutionary bands in the Escambray, but not until 1965 were the bands totally eliminated.

In September 1960, Fidel came to New York City, where he addressed the General Assembly of the United Nations. His visit was dramatic, with the press reporting spurious stories of the Cuban delegation keeping live chickens in their hotel rooms.

Back in Cuba on the twenty-eighth of September, Fidel was telling a welcome-home rally outside the presidential palace the story of his adventures in New York, when two bombs went off at the edge of the massive crowd.

Fidel interrupted his speech to say to the angry audience:

We're going to establish a system of revolutionary collective vigilance. If they think they can come up against the people, they're in for a disappointment. We're going to have a committee of revolutionary vigilance on every block, so the people can watch, so that there's no imperialist, no sellout to the imperialists who can move an inch.

With this, the spontaneous struggle and protest against the counterrevolution took on a form and a name—*Los Comités de Defensa de la Revolución* (the Committees for the Defense of the Revolution) or CDR.

CDR filled a need that many Cubans people felt strongly—the need for a *community-based* organization, separate from the army or the militia, controlled by the people, that would fight the counterrevolution. Six months later, when the Bay of Pigs invaders landed, there were eight thousand CDR chapters in the country. Two years after Fidel made his suggestion there were a hundred thousand—one on almost every block and neighborhood in the island.

All were aware that a battle was coming. On January 2, 1961, the second anniversary of the triumph of the Revolution, the people paraded for nine hours through the Plaza de la Revolución, past the towering statue of José Martí.

Fidel told the assembled crowd:

A revolution is not a bed of roses. A revolution is a struggle to the death between the future and the past. The old order always resists to the death, and the new society fights with all its energy to survive. Either the counterrevolution destroys the Revolution or the Revolution destroys the counterrevolution.

The next day President Eisenhower ordered diplomatic relations broken with the government of Cuba.

Three weeks later, John F. Kennedy was inaugurated President of the United States. The CIA's guerrilla movement in the Escambray had collapsed. The CIA turned toward a full-scale invasion.

The main training base for the nine-month-old invasion force was in Guatemala. The CIA also trained ground troops in Louisiana, Florida, and the Panama Canal Zone. The men in charge of training were CIA personnel, United States military officers, and Green Berets.

To give it the public image of a Cuban exile project, the CIA united five small exile organizations into an umbrella group: the *Frente Revolucionario Democrático.* Its leaders were Tony Varona, Aureliano Sánchez Arango, Justo Carrillo, José Ignacio Rasco, and Manuel Artime.

Howard Hunt, the CIA agent who paid these men, described them this way:

> With the exception of Rasco, they were all professional politicians whose trade was public demagoguery and private intrigue. . . . I considered them shallow thinkers and opportunists who owed a large debt (their lives) to the United States Government and specifically to the CIA.

Hunt was paying them $115,000 a month, mostly for salaries and rentals, which he delivered in cash in a briefcase. The military expenditures were a separate account that came from the $13,000,000 budget for the operation approved by President Eisenhower.

So subservient were these Cuban "leaders" to the CIA that they were not even allowed to see the plans the CIA was drawing up for the invasion of their own native land.

Though the invasion plans had been kept secret from the American public, the government in Havana knew what the CIA strategy would be: to seize a beachhead of Cuban territory and hold it against counterattack long enough to fly in a provisional government of exiled leaders. The United States would recognize this body as the government of Cuba and send in all necessary military support. They would then blockade the island, crippling its economy.

The Revolution marshaled its forces for a multiple invasion. Pamphlets were distributed to every family in the country, explaining how to defend themselves, what to do in case of paratroop landings, where and how to report.

In Washington, CIA agents pored over maps of Cuba looking for the right location, finally settling on an area of Cuba's southwest coast, bordering the *Bahia de Cochinos* (Bay of Pigs).

The bay is a long, narrow finger of water cutting into the enormous Zapata Swamps which stretch for miles to east and west. The soil is rocky at the beach and hard for up to six miles inland, where it becomes impassable.

In choosing this area, the CIA was thinking defensively; there were only two highways leading through the swamps to the landing area. The beach would therefore be easy to hold but hard to leave. In the CIA's paramilitary section, the joke went around that Castro would be completely fooled, because "no one in his right mind would believe the Bay of Pigs had been chosen for the main assault."

What the CIA did not know was that the poverty-stricken Zapata Swamps were a region where the Revolution had worked hardest in the previous two years. It had built 120 miles of highways and roads for the farmers to bring their charcoal to market. The average income had increased markedly. At the time of the invasion, there were two hundred young teachers in the swamp, part of the year-long campaign to eradicate illiteracy in Cuba. Three hundred children of local farmers were studying in Havana, learning skills they could use back home. The population surrounding the Bay of Pigs was entirely with the Revolution.

Meanwhile, in the United States and Guatemala, the counterrevolutionary coalition was coming apart at the seams. Its president, Miró Cardona, wrote a political manifesto that Kennedy's special aide Arthur Schlesinger, Jr., called "so long-winded and so devoid of ideas that it aroused doubts as to the kind of people we intended to send to Cuba. . . . The Council's* program was most alluring to foreign investors, private bankers and dispossessed owners, but it had very little to say to the workers, peasants and Negroes."

A deeper question was, What kind of government could have been established by a group of exiles who could not agree among themselves, but who had to be welded together by one of the least democratic organizations in the world—the CIA? They couldn't provide their own arms or their own plan. Until a few hours before they landed they were not told where their invasion would be. Could they have formed an independent government?

On April 4, 1961, President Kennedy met with his top advisers to review the project and give it the final seal of approval.

The next day the invasion forces left Nicaragua's port city of Puerto Cabezas for Cuba. The Nicaraguan dictator, Somoza, his face all powdered, "dressed like a musical comedy potentate," and surrounded by gunmen, came to see them off. "Bring me a couple of hairs from Castro's beard," he told them.

The fleet was made up of five merchant ships, the *Houston,* the *Atlantic,* the *Rio Escondido,* the *Caribe,* and the *Lake Charles.* The fifteen hundred men were armed with landing craft, tanks, cannons, antitank guns, and thousands of automatic rifles.

Fidel had taken to sleeping in the afternoons and staying awake at nights in the General Staff headquarters in Havana. He was there at 6 A.M. on Saturday, April 15, "when a B-26 flew near and

---

*Shortly before the invasion, the CIA replaced the *Frente Revolucionario Democrático,* which had become hopelessly divided, with the "Cuban Revolutionary Council," the provisional government that was to be flown to the Bay of Pigs.

almost immediately, a few moments later, we felt the blast of the bombs and the antiaircraft fire."

"This is it," Fidel said to those in the room. "This is the aggression."

Nine CIA planes had taken off that morning from Puerto Cabezas: eight for Cuba and one directly to Miami. The mission of the eight was to smash the Cuban air force before it could get off the ground. Each plane bore an imitation of the Cuban Air Force insignia.

The single pilot bound for Miami was to arrive there just after the others had bombed Cuba. He was to spread the story that the bombs had been dropped by defecting members of the Cuban air force. The trick was supposed to convince the world that Fidel faced serious unrest inside his own armed forces, while distracting attention from United States involvement.

The eight bombers attacked three Cuban bases. The pilots reported to the CIA that they had destroyed between twenty-six and thirty planes. If the report had been true, it would indeed have been the finish of the Cuban air force—which the CIA estimated at twenty-nine planes. But their report turned out to be fantasy. The Cuban air force actually lost only *two* combat planes.

It did not take long for the cover to come off the story the CIA pilot who flew directly to Miami told the press. An enterprising reporter got close enough to his plane to notice that dust and grease covered the bomb-bay doors and that the muzzles of the guns were taped shut. The plane had obviously not participated in any attack.

Whether he believed the pilot's story or not, the United States representative to the United Nations, Adlai Stevenson, tried desperately to convince the world that it was true.

"The United States has committed no aggression against Cuba," Stevenson told the United Nations. "Nor has it launched any attack either from Florida or any other part of the country. . . ."

The day after the attack was a Sunday. The bodies of the slain Cubans were carried in a sad procession thirty blocks long through the streets of Havana. Ten thousand men and women, most of them armed, massed at the cemetery.

Fidel recalled to them the attack on Pearl Harbor by the Japanese, "an event which became a symbol of treason." And yet, he said, the Japanese government admitted its participation, unlike the United States, which was trying to deceive the entire world.

FIDEL: The imperialists plan the crime, organize the crime, furnish the criminals with weapons for the crime, pay the criminals, and then those criminals come here and murder the sons of seven honest workers, after which they land in the U.S. and though the whole world knows of their deeds, just state that they were Cuban pilots, make up a ridiculous tale and broadcast it to the whole world!

A few minutes later, the Cuban Revolution took a conceptual leap forward:

Why are they doing this? They can't forgive our being right here under their very noses, seeing how we have made a revolution, a socialist revolution right here under the very noses of the United States!

As far as the eye could see, there were guns being raised, the rifles of the militia, a metal sea rippling across the cemetery and down the streets.

The people were shouting, *"Venceremos! Venceremos!"* ("We shall win!")

Whose hands are those that are raising these weapons? Are they the hands of the rich?

"No!"

Comrades, workers and peasants, this is a *socialist and democratic* revolution of the poor and destitute. And for this Revolution of the poor, by the poor and for the poor, we are ready to give our lives!

The shouts died down. They began to sing the Cuban national anthem. The last announcement told the militia to go to their battalion headquarters. "Make ready to face the enemy. . . ."

Fidel's speech was the first announcement that the Cuban Revolution was socialist. "There were some," Fidel said later, "who wondered why the socialist character of the Revolution was announced at that time. But when aggression comes, it is then that the banners must be flown higher than ever before."

Every Cuban who fought the invasion thus knew exactly for what he or she was fighting.

Monday, April 17: Fidel had lain down the night after the funeral to get some sleep but was awakened at 3:15 on Monday morning and told that there was fighting at Playa Girón and Playa Larga on the edge of the Zapata Swamps.

The area around the Bay of Pigs is essentially an island. On one side, the bay and the sea, on the other an impassable swamp, cut by two major access roads. Defensively it was perfect for the invaders. Once taken, it could be supplied by ship and air. The revolutionary forces would have to attack along the two highways through the Swamp, completely exposed; only the highways were passable.

At the moment of attack, the nearest revolutionary force was Battalion 339 from Cienfuegos, stationed at the Australia sugar mill to the north, and various platoons of armed charcoal workers inside the area. Fidel ordered Battalion 339 to advance immediately down the road to Playa Larga. At dawn they were fighting the advance units of the invasion force.

Shortly after dawn, the invaders dropped paratroops behind Battalion 339 fighting at the beach, cutting them and several smaller militia units off from the rear. Another paratroop drop seized the road to Covadonga.

At all costs, the revolutionary forces had to get through the swamp to the beach, to keep the invaders from sealing off that easily defended area.

When the paratroops landed, Fidel ordered a battalion of men attending a militia leaders' school in Matanzas to move to the Australia mill and from there down the road through the swamp to link up with the trapped Battalion 339 at Palpite.

The battalion of militia leaders, commanded by Major José Fernandez Alvarez (today a member of the Central Committee of the Cuban Communist Party) arrived at the mill about 7 A.M. About seven hundred farmers from the Zapata had gathered there, demanding weapons to fight the invasion. Major Fernandez had no extra weapons to give them.

The sugar-mill administrator told him that enemy planes, bearing the insignia of the Cuban air force, were bombing in the area. During the next day, many Cubans died, standing and waving their arms to welcome what they thought were their own planes, only to be machine-gunned on the powdery roads of the swamp.

Fidel arrived at the Australia sugar mill at noon. By then the road from the mill to Playa Larga was an inferno. The attacking B-26s passed over again and again, machine-gunning everything that moved. The advancing Cuban forces were unable to maneuver on the narrow road. Contrary to all rules of warfare, their tanks had to approach the enemy in single file along a treeless road.

At Palpite, the battalion under Alvarez split in two, half taking the road to Sopillar, where they joined sixty militiamen from Battalion 339 and ten peasants with old shotguns who had stayed to defend the land given them by the agrarian reform. The rest of the battalion continued toward Playa Larga and the coast.

Not far away, the six operable planes of the Cuban air force were carrying the war to the invaders' ships. The first to discover that the Cuban planes had not been wiped out as reported to the CIA were those in the landing craft. Aboard the *Houston,* "Rip," an American ex-marine and personal friend of the Nicaraguan dictator, Somoza, was screaming at the members of the invading Fifth Battalion who were reluctant to get off the ship.

"It's your war, you bastards! Get off!" he was yelling, when a Cuban B-26 attacked. At 9 A.M., a rocket sank the *Houston.* Those in the Fifth Battalion who made it ashore huddled under the trees, awaiting orders. They never fought.

Almost simultaneously, a Cuban Sea Fury, diving out of the sun, made a direct hit on the *Rio Escondido,* which was carrying all the supplies for the first ten days of the campaign. Less than 10 percent of the invasion's ammunition had been landed.

The other ships scattered to sea. Pursued for miles by the Cuban air force planes, they never returned.

On the eastern front the situation was not good for the revolutionary forces. The invaders were less than a mile from the Covadonga sugar mill, defended by eleven militiamen who had been ordered to resist at all costs.

But as darkness fell Monday evening, the Cuban militia had seized Sopillar, securing a firm foothold inside the swamp. The tiny Cuban air force had sunk two of the invaders' five ships and shot down five of their planes.

Tuesday, April 18: At six in the morning the report came that the enemy was retreating toward Girón. This was the turning point of the invasion.

In Opa Locka, Florida, the Cuban "leadership" of the invasion was in what CIA agent Howard Hunt called "voluntary sequestration" in a barracks. Only the CIA officer who was with them was allowed to contact the outside.

On Monday night the CIA-written press releases had been altered to read that there was actually no invasion at all, just a "tactical supply landing." The reported fighting was "internal." Invasion? What invasion?

"In the War Room," recalled Howard Hunt, "there was an air of bitter hopelessness."

At the Bay of Pigs the battle was tumbling fiercely to a conclusion. On the northern front the revolutionary troops consolidated their position at Playa Larga, then at two o'clock in the afternoon began moving down the highway to Playa Girón in pursuit of the retreating invaders. They advanced slowly, under attack from U.S. Sabre jets, which caused many casualties.

At three, Major Pedro Miret, veteran of the revolutionary war, arrived with tanks and heavy artillery at the Covadonga sugar mill. "All along the way," he said, "we were amazed to observe the calmness with which the people of Cuba had accepted the news, how preparations were being made to repel the aggression everywhere and by every means, how all the workers remained at work with their rifles at their sides, how the Covadonga sugar mill in spite of being so near the enemy was operating normally."

The rest of the day was spent feeling out the enemy, moving cautiously toward Playa Girón from the north and San Blas from the east.

Wednesday, April 19: The invaders abandoned San Blas at eight in the morning, under an artillery barrage from the revolutionary forces. Fidel, who was moving south with the troops of Major Fernandez, met Pedro Miret's men at the junction of the Cayo Ramona Road. The united forces proceeded toward Playa Girón.

At five thirty in the afternoon they entered Playa Girón practically without firing a shot, and found it almost deserted. Tanks, artillery, rocket launchers, and ammunition boxes were still in position where they had been abandoned by the retreating enemy.

Earlier in the afternoon two United States Navy destroyers had been seen moving in rapidly toward the Girón beach. Thinking it was a naval attack, Fidel halted his troops. It was not; the destroyers were answering a call to rescue the survivors. Some of the invaders had seized fishing boats and rubber rafts and were paddling out to meet the ships. Others, on the shore, furious and feeling betrayed, fired at their own men in the boats.

Defeated men ran for the swamps and the inland woods, each for himself. The invasion had lasted seventy-two hours.

An exhaustive investigation was carried out to determine just who the captured invaders were. The Cubans discovered that the bulk of the 1,197 captured troops were composed of:

100 plantation owners
67 landlords of apartment houses
24 large property owners
112 big businessmen
194 ex-soldiers of Batista (including 14 wanted for murder and torture during the revolutionary war)
179 "idle rich"
35 industrial magnates

Together they had owned:

923,000 acres of land
9,666 houses and apartment buildings
70 factories
10 sugar mills
3 banks
5 mines
12 nightclubs and bars

Accusations, debate, and recriminations battered Washington. All the hindsight explanations of what went wrong were limited by the same mentality that had created the problem in the first place: a mentality that saw the world in terms of "capabilities," calculations, bribes, merchandise, anti-Communism, and brute force. The fantasy-like quality of the plan to conquer Cuba was the product of a large nation attempting to wield an imperial power it no longer had.

The Cubans call it, "The First Defeat of U.S. Imperialism in the Americas."

It was also a decisive turning point in the history of our hemisphere. As Raúl Castro later said, "The battle of Girón consolidated the presence of socialism in Latin America." To know why one dies is not given to everyone. But every man and woman who died defending Cuba at the Bay of Pigs knew exactly why. The Revolution had given them that.

THE MISSILES
OF OCTOBER

It seems to me that there is a question to be defined: Where does the danger of war lie—in the weapons that Cuba has, or in the aggressive plans of the United States against Cuba?

—PRESIDENT DORTICÓS, DURING THE MISSILE CRISIS

The Cuban militia was still picking up half-naked and starving survivors of the Bay of Pigs invasion force in the Zapata Swamps when powerful voices began to be raised in the United States in favor of a direct invasion of Cuba, either by an "allied" force of United States and Latin American nations or by the United States alone.

Cuba realized that she was in greater danger than before. The United States remained committed to overthrowing the revolutionary government. The attempt at the Bay of Pigs had ended in humiliation, and there is nothing quite so dangerous, the Cubans knew, as having a hostile, well-armed, and humiliated neighbor.

A week after Playa Girón, the United States government placed an economic embargo on all United States goods shipped to Cuba.

In October a Cuban workman was tortured to death at the

REVOLUTIONARY CUBA   152

Guantánamo naval base. United States military overflights, in violation of Cuba's airspace, continued throughout the year. CIA plots to assassinate Fidel sprouted like mushrooms. The U.S. Senate Select Committee to Study Governmental Operations concluded in 1975, "We have found concrete evidence of at least eight plots involving the CIA to assassinate Fidel Castro from 1960 to 1965." The Cuban Department of State Security identified twenty-four such attempts.

On August 20, Secretary of State Dean Rusk slammed the door to any negotiations between the United States and Cuba. "The essential problem in our relations with Cuba is the alignment of Cuba with the Sino-Soviet bloc," he said. "We have no indication that they are ready to break their alliance and join the community of American states on a normal basis."

The six largest Latin American states refused to go along with Rusk's demand that they expel Cuba from the Organization of American States (OAS).

In January 1962, Secretary of Defense Robert McNamara told a meeting of top United States military men, "The security of the countries of this hemisphere is threatened by Communist subversion, particularly from Cuba."

Cuba's response to these threats was a passionate document ratified by an assembly of a million Cubans in Havana on February 4, 1962.

The Second Declaration of Havana traces the history of colonialism and records Cuba's political view of Latin America, the United States, and the world, a view it has maintained ever since. It is the "History Will Absolve Me" of the Cuban Revolution as a whole:

What is hidden behind the Yankee's hatred of the Cuban Revolution . . . a small country of only seven million people, economically underdeveloped, without financial or military means to threaten the security or economy of any other country?

What explains it is fear. Not fear of the Cuban Revolution but fear of the Latin American Revolution . . . fear that a plundered people will seize the arms from the oppressors, and, like Cuba, declare themselves free people of America.

They imagine in their delirium that Cuba is an exporter of revolutions. In their sleepless merchants' and usurers' minds there is the idea that revolutions can be bought, sold, rented, loaned, exported and imported like some piece of merchandise. . . .

On April 9, 1962, the United States massed the largest naval force ever seen in the Atlantic and Caribbean for naval maneuvers involving forty thousand marines and the carrier *Forrestal,* culminating in a simulated amphibious landing on the island of Vieques, off Puerto Rico.

Convinced that Cuba faced an imminent attack by an overwhelmingly superior force, the revolutionary government sent Che Guevara to Moscow to request nuclear missiles with which to defend their country. The Soviet Union agreed. The missiles began to arrive in mid-1962.

To leap ahead for a moment, during the entire Missile Crisis, United States government officials, military men, and politicians justified every move by the United States with the charge that the missiles Cuba received were offensive weapons. Imagined scenes of American and Latin American cities in flames from Cuban missile attacks created near hysteria in many countries.

Were the missiles offensive? Or were they defensive, as the Cubans claimed?

"A knife in the hands of one of the Playa Girón invaders is an offensive weapon," Fidel said over television at the height of the crisis, making the point that it is the use to which a weapon is put that makes it offensive. In real life one must consider to what actual purpose the Cuban missiles were installed, not merely what was possible.

In fact, no one, not even President Kennedy, seriously believed that the Cubans would use their missiles to attack the United States.

It was dreaming to think that Fidel would launch an attack against a country protected at that time by 144 Polaris missiles under the ocean in submarines, 200 land-based intercontinental missiles, 16 attack carriers with more than 400 attack bombers, 700 SAC B-52s and B-58 long-range bombers, and 700 B-47s.

When the crisis was over, Kennedy was asked if he thought the Soviet Union meant to attack the United States with the missiles in Cuba. He replied:

> Not that they were intending to fire them, because if they were going to get into a nuclear struggle, they have their own missiles in the Soviet Union. But it would have politically changed the balance of power. It would have appeared to, and appearances contribute to reality.

If there was no new or alarming military threat caused by the installation of missiles in defense of Cuba, then why were we brought to the edge of atomic catastrophe?

Why was there a missile crisis?

Kennedy's answer above is the key. The presence of missiles in Cuba would have appeared to change the balance of power between the United States and the Soviet Union. It would have been a blow to the prestige of the United States, to its image.

"The real stake was prestige," Washington analyst I. F. Stone commented later. "The question was whether, with the whole world looking on, Kennedy would let Khruschev get away with it."

After a string of what Kennedy himself called "disasters" in his first two years of office, this opportunity to "prove himself," to exert leadership, may explain why Kennedy chose to challenge Cuba's right to defend itself with missiles. But, still, why a *crisis,* why not a process of negotiations, using the machinery of the United Nations, which might have obtained the same results?

The 1962 Congressional elections were three weeks away when the presence of nuclear missiles was confirmed. Since August, the Republicans had been building the rumor of missiles into an election issue. Senator Kenneth Keating of New York was using information leaked to him by the intelligence services to hammer away at this "threat to American security." His colleague, from Indiana, Homer E. Capehart, was calling for an invasion. . . .

Had the Soviet Union installed an equal number of nuclear missiles capable of reaching the same areas of the United States as the missiles in Cuba, but placed them instead in Siberian territory forty-five miles from Alaska, there would have been no "Bering Strait Missile Crisis." But this was Cuba, a Third World country flaunting its sovereignty before the world; Cuba, which had humiliated the United States at the Bay of Pigs the year before; Cuba, which was now making an invasion too costly for the United States, blocking the only means left to squash the Revolution. The Republicans had hit on the sorest of nerves and the softest of spots in the Kennedy administration.

President Kennedy made up his mind on Saturday afternoon, October 20, as described by television journalist Elie Abel:

> He said that he preferred to start with limited action. An air attack, he felt, was the wrong way to start. The modern bomber seemed to him hardly a surgical tool, but rather a blunt instrument. Before making his final decision he wanted to talk with the tactical bombing specialists. But the blockade, he felt, was the way to begin. He asked the air-strike advocates to understand that their alternative was by no means ruled out for the future.

Generally speaking, the Kennedy administration was assuming that the missiles were not what the Cubans and Soviets said they were, that they were instead part of some grand Soviet scheme. They speculated that the Soviet Union was trying to pressure

United States missiles out of Turkey or weaken the United States position in Berlin. But no evidence has been produced to prove that the missiles were other than Cuba's hope of defending herself against a mighty military attack.

President Kennedy's televised speech to the American people on Monday, October 22, was probably the most important in his life. That night he announced, ". . . a strict quarantine on all offensive military equipment under shipment to Cuba is being initiated. All ships of any kind bound for Cuba from whatever nation or port will, if found to contain cargoes of offensive weapons, be turned back."

He called upon Premier Khruschev to withdraw the missiles from Cuba, insisting that the United States would "regard any nuclear missile launched from Cuba against any nation in the Western Hemisphere as an attack by the Soviet Union on the United States, requiring a full retaliatory response upon the Soviet Union."

At the end of the speech he called on the "captive people" of Cuba to overthrow their own government. Cuba's response was a combat alert. Fidel went on national television:

> We are a sovereign nation in our own right—not in the Yankee concept of sovereignty. And we are not sovereign in name only. We are sovereign in fact! To take away that sovereignty they will have to sweep us from the face of the earth!

The following day, Premier Khruschev transmitted to the White House the first of a series of letters that would eventually play a major part in resolving the crisis. Calling the United States quarantine a "pirate act," Khruschev refused to withdraw the missiles or to order Soviet ships—twenty-five of which were steaming toward the naval blockade line—to withdraw.

Both Cuba and the United States, meanwhile, had requested an emergency meeting of the United Nations Security Council. The

Cuban ambassador, Dr. Mario García Incháustegui, reviewed the history of the economic and military attacks sponsored by the United States against Cuba, which had obliged them to arm themselves, and read to the Security Council the position of his government:

> If the United States would give Cuba effective and satisfactory guarantees with respect to the integrity of its territory and will cease its subversive and counterrevolutionary activities against our people, Cuba would not even need an army, and would invest all its resources happily into the economic and cultural development of our nation.

Inside Cuba, Fidel's reply was firm and final.

> If they attack us, we will resist. If they totally blockade us, we know how to resist it. Anyone who wants to inspect Cuba, had better come prepared to fight their way in.

The next morning, Wednesday, October 24, Kennedy was meeting with his advisers when a note was brought in. "Mr. President, we have a preliminary report which seems to indicate that some of the Russian ships have stopped dead in the water."

They had. In Moscow, the Soviet leaders were grappling with what they perceived as a "panic" response by the United States. None of the Soviet ships were carrying missiles anyway, since all the missiles were already in Cuba.

The next move was made by UN Secretary General U Thant, who appealed to Cuba, the United States, and the Soviet Union to "enter into negotiations immediately, even this night, if possible." Kennedy was dismayed. This meant that a large block of influential countries did not support his measures. But to begin negotiations meant postponing the "crisis" until after the elections. He rejected the proposal.

Kennedy's refusal to engage in diplomacy through the UN or

directly with Khruschev meant that some initiative would have to come from the Soviets themselves.

At 6 P.M. on Friday night, October 26, a private message from Khruschev to Kennedy came over the State Department teletype. Khruschev said that he had been in two wars and knew well the death and destruction they cause. "Only lunatics or suicides, who themselves want to perish and to destroy the whole world before they die," would start a nuclear war, he said. He proposed that the weapons inside Cuba be withdrawn and that the United States in return agree never to invade Cuba.

The United States joint chiefs of staff met with Kennedy and his advisers on Saturday and presented their solution—an air strike on Monday, followed by an invasion. (After the crisis was over, the President told his brother Robert that he was distressed that most of the military leaders with whom he had dealt "seemed always to assume . . . that a war was in our national interest.")

But now Kennedy was moving toward the opening that Khruschev had provided. He decided to accept the proposal, and that night wired Moscow. If the Soviet Union would remove the nuclear weapons from Cuba "under appropriate United Nations observation and supervision," the United States would remove the quarantine and "give assurances against an invasion of Cuba."

Khruschev accepted. The crisis was over.

The Cubans were frankly skeptical and displeased. They recalled Kennedy's earlier assurances that no invasion was being planned even as exiles were being trained for that very purpose. The end dragged on for several weeks, the Cubans refusing to allow inspections by the United Nations inside their country, Kennedy insisting that he would not lift the naval blockade until United Nations observers inspected the missile sites. Finally, the United States was forced to accept overflight inspection of Soviet ships taking the missiles away. Soviet crewmen pulled off the tarpaulins covering the missiles so that United States pilots could verify and photograph them.

As years passed and the United States did not invade, Cuba's leaders realized that they had underestimated the wisdom of the Soviet decision to remove the missiles. In 1974 Fidel was asked what he thought of the way the crisis had been resolved:

> Well, we were not totally satisfied with the results of the Missile Crisis. But if we are realistic, and go back in history, we realize that ours was *not* the correct posture. The Russians believed that out of those negotiations two objectives would be gained—the promise not to invade Cuba on the one hand and, on the other, elimination of the danger of nuclear war. War did not take place and there was a period of relaxed international tensions, thus proving that the Soviet position was the correct one.

"Enemy harassment has turned us into a disciplined organized people, a nation of veterans," Fidel told his countrymen after the crisis was resolved.

FIGHTING
THE BLOCKADE

1961–65

No heaven is ever won by storm, because heaven doesn't exist. You have to build heaven before you can have it. Imperialism didn't leave us heaven, it left us hell—a hell of poverty, ignorance, need and misery. The hell of underdevelopment.

—*FIDEL CASTRO November 24, 1971*

For sixty years, the sugar trust, the latifundists, the landlords, and the businessmen of tourism, drugs, and industry had controlled Cuba's economy. When President Kennedy decreed the total economic blockade of Cuba on February 3, 1962, Cuba, for better or worse, was cut free from the economic umbilical cord that had held her in almost total dependency.

On Capitol Hill they called it a "quarantine," as if the Cuban Revolution was a contagious fever to be starved out before it reached the mainland. The Cubans refer to it as "the blockade" —though there were no U.S. warships surrounding the island— because its intent, as in a war, was to strangle the economy of their country.

The scope of the blockade went far beyond U.S.-Cuban economic relations. The U.S. Department of Commerce made every effort to convince and pressure other countries into cutting off trade with Cuba.

> FIDEL: We need steel, but we have no steel. We need tin, but we have no tin. We need ships, but we have neither the steel with which to build the ships nor the technicians, engineers, and specialists. We need chemical products for food preservation, to protect the tin, to avoid food contamination, and we have to import them from this place, from that place, from everywhere. We need paint to print the tin and we have neither the paint nor the technique, nor the machines with which to do it. Practically everything has to be imported. Now, do you realize what a situation that is?
>
> Almost 100 percent of the raw materials used in our factories came from the United States, and our equipment was adapted to operate with those raw materials. And, overnight, they prohibited the sale of those raw materials to us.

Inside Cuba, the blockade required a kind of daily heroism which was the more remarkable for the spirit in which it was carried out.

"Those were hard years, very hard," Melba Hernández recalls, "but the people worked at the maximum of their intelligence, and they triumphed. They always had a fighting attitude toward the blockade. You would go to a factory and find that the workers were accustomed to being able to get whatever spare parts they needed from the United States—a little simple screw, an instrument they needed for their work—and all of a sudden it was stopped. But their reaction was, 'We have to make it ourselves.' "

No modern country can run without technicians, engineers, and specialists. The effect of the sudden pull-out of U.S. and Cuban technicians was devastating, but Cuba's working people met it with the same determination with which they fabricated spare parts out of scrap.

Economist Edward Boorstein also remembers what it was like:

Five of us from the Ministry of Foreign Commerce, on a business visit, were being taken through the Moa nickel plant. In the electric power station . . . our guide was an enthusiastic youngster of about 22. He did an excellent job as guide, but his modesty as well as his age deceived us and only toward the end of our tour did we realize that he was not some sort of apprentice engineer or assistant—he was in charge of the plant. . . .

In another part of the complex, the head of one of the key departments was a black Cuban who had about four years of elementary school education. He had been an observant worker and when the engineer of his department left he knew what to do—although he didn't really know why, or how his department related to the others in the plant. Now to learn why, he was plugging away at . . . one of the little mimeographed booklets which had been distributed throughout industry to improve people's knowledge of their jobs. . . .

When you walked through a Cuban factory, you didn't need to be told that it was under new management—you could see and feel it everywhere. In the Pheldrake plant for producing wire and cable, formerly owned by Dutch and American interests, the whole office of administration was filled by men in shirt-sleeves who were unmistakably workers; the engineers had gone and the workers had taken over. . . . In a large tobacco factory, the administrator was black; in the metal-working plant formerly owned by the American Car and Foundry Company, the head of a department turning out chicken incubators was black. Black people had not held such positions before the Revolution.

No contract was too small to notice for the U.S. Department of Commerce, whose responsibility it was to plug leaks in the Cuban blockade. When Cuba signed a contract with a British firm for a much-needed fertilizer complex, the United States required that no part of that complex, no screw or valve, could be used on which a United States citizen held the patent. The British and Cubans had to search through dozens of countries to find replacement parts with the same specifications. Ships bringing goods to Cuba were not allowed to trade at United States ports. United States trading partners were told that if they bought Cuban nickel they could sell no article that contained it to the United States.

These measures did not succeed in severing all of Cuba's trade with Western Europe. European businessmen were not about to let the Cuban market slip away just to do Washington a favor. Sweden, Norway, Finland, and Denmark refused to buckle under to the demands of the State Department and increased their trade with Cuba after the embargo was imposed.

The group of nations that responded most vigorously to Cuba's crisis, however, were the Soviet Union and the socialist countries of Eastern Europe.

FIDEL: You might ask, "If you were left without fuel, markets, sources of raw materials and everything, how did you manage to survive?"

Ah, this is because a small, isolated country such as ours, a small nation facing imperialism, isn't alone in today's world. We were lucky enough to make our Revolution at a moment when it was possible for us to receive extensive and generous aid from abroad. No need to say that this aid wasn't given to us by the bourgeois or the imperialists anywhere in the world. That aid was given to us by the only camp that could extend that aid—the socialist camp!

To meet Cuba's needs, the socialist countries had to adapt their industries. These countries used the metric system, while Cuba measured everything in pounds, yards, and feet; every industrial machine or implement had to be converted. The socialist countries use 50-cycle electricity, Cuba 60-cycle. Each electrical implement had to be rewired.

Trade with the Soviet Union and the European socialist nations expanded like a shock wave. In 1959, these countries had made up 2.2 percent of Cuba's foreign trade. This rose to 24.3 percent in 1960, 73.3 percent in 1961, 82 percent in 1962. Currently Cuba trades with more than eighty countries. Roughly 70 percent of Cuban trade is with socialist countries.

Thousands of technicians from the Soviet Union and other socialist countries began working with Cubans in many areas of the economy. With aid from the Soviet Union, development programs have been carried out in such areas of the economy as electricity, nickel, oil, automobile repair, textiles, mechanization of the sugar harvest, expansion of the sugar industry, ports, railroads, roads and dams, irrigation and drainage systems, geological prospecting, communications, educational equipment, computers, the steel and machine industries, fishing, airports, and more.

Many commentators have tried to prove that Cuba simply traded one dependency for another—that Cuba now stands in relation to the Soviet Union as it once did to the United States.

The Cubans are quick to point out, however, that the kind of aid and trade Cuba has had with the socialist countries is completely different from the economic relations it formerly had with the United States.

"It is true that the Soviet Union plays an important part in Cuba's economy," Fidel told several American journalists in 1974, "but we do not see this as a drawback. On the contrary, we are fortunate. We had someone to help us when the United States imposed the economic blockade."

How can one compare the relations we have with the Soviet Union with those that existed with the United States? The Soviet Union has given us easy payment terms, has helped us obtain credit elsewhere and has always had the greatest consideration for us in financial matters. The United States *owned* our electric plants, our telephone company, our major means of transportation, our major industries, our best lands, the bigger sugar mills. It *owned* our banks and controlled our foreign trade. In other words, it *owned* the Cuban economy. The Soviets don't own . . . a bank, a business, a public utility, or one acre of land. All the natural resources, all the industries and all the means of production are in our hands.

Before the Revolution, the United States' control of the Cuban economy had stifled all attempts to develop a national industry. Soviet aid, on the other hand, is aimed at building up Cuban industry. Aid from the Soviet Union has gone to build a massive factory in Holguín that produces 600 cane-cutting machines a year—ending after four centuries most of the agony of manual cane cutting. It has been used to lay a modern railroad the length of the island, to build ports and fertilizer factories, a satellite communications system, and many other basic industrial projects.

As a result, Cuban industry is more diversified than ever. Though sugar accounts for 86 percent of Cuba's total exports (1974 figures), the dollar value of her mineral exports has increased 5 times since 1958, seafood exports 10 times, and citrus exports 120 times (1976 figures).

The terms of Cuban–Soviet trade are especially beneficial to Cuba. In 1972, Fidel and Soviet President Leonid Brezhnev signed an agreement that deferred Cuba's payments on Soviet loans—interest-free—until 1986. The Soviet Union buys Cuban nickel and sugar at prices fixed well above the world market price. These advantageous, long-term trade agreements sheltered Cuba from the worst effects of the inflationary economic crisis that struck the capitalist world beginning in 1975. In 1979, Raúl Castro commented, "It is only because of the existence of a socialist regime here and our close economic relations with the socialist world, particularly with the Soviet Union, that the effects of the present world crisis have not let us into economic bankruptcy, with its sequel of starving people and hundreds of thousands of unemployed."

Today the blockade is no longer a major threat to Cuba's existence, but it continues to slow her rate of growth. There is no way to measure the price the Cubans have paid. The cost of transporting goods for thousands of miles is enormous. The energies that had to be put into reorganizing trade, retooling machines, reorienting technology, were vast. The lost markets and the shortage of dollars delayed Cuba's rise from poverty for many years.

"The enemy's propaganda is truly hypocritical," Fidel said in 1963, "putting all one's power into blockading a small, under-developed country, and then saying—'Look, it's having difficulties.' "

Nevertheless, simply by being free to concentrate resources and manpower on the essential problems and by the redistribution of the wealth it already had, Cuba was able within a few years to make dramatic advances in such basic areas as unemployment, health care, illiteracy, and education.

Within three years after the Revolution, unemployment had been reduced by two thirds. So great were the unused resources, the stilled factories, the piles of cement lying in warehouses, that little more than mobilization was needed to match idle workers with idle facilities and to begin work. Employment in construction increased 179 percent in three years. By 1965, unemployment in Cuba had practically vanished.

Fidel was even able to chide President Kennedy in 1961:

We might ask Mr. Kennedy: If your system is better than ours, why is it that the number of millions of unemployed in the U.S. is increasing?

If your system is better than ours, why are you heading toward a crisis while we are headed for progress?

Does Mr. Kennedy want to end unemployment in the U.S.? Then let him nationalize the big monopolies; let him nationalize the big utility companies; let him nationalize the banks, so the banks stop being private companies serving a few millionaires; let him stop the arms race; stop making rockets and battleships, pursue a policy of peace, and you will see how the problems and the crisis in the U.S. will be over.

Out in the rural areas, thousands of acres of cane were plowed under to make way for lettuce, beans, citrus fruits, potatoes, *malanga,* and other dietary staples. Agricultural employment increased 53% in the same three years.

More important, by 1960 the *tiempo muerto,* which like the hurricanes once seemed to be an unchangeable evil of Cuban life, had ended. Soon there would be a shortage of labor in the fields, foreshadowing the problem Cuba has today of too few workers— not too few jobs.

Eleven thousand women who had worked as maids in the homes of the rich were trained to work in more productive areas of the economy. Half a million workers were taking correspondence courses to improve their skills.

"At the end of two years, with no sugar quota, no spare parts, without replacements in machinery, without investments of private Yankee capital, without Yankee oil, without Yankee monopolies, without Yankee managers in our factories, without straw bosses, without foremen, without foreign administrators, without all these 'wise men,' " Fidel said a few months before the Bay of Pigs invasion, "our country has proceeded to solve problems to such an extent that its successes each day become a greater nightmare for our enemies."

Cuba's wealth in those days could not be measured in terms of consumer goods, but in the quality of life. Often when Fidel would drop into a factory or a school, he would ask those there, "What do you like most about the Revolution: the schools, the new hospitals, the conditions in the factories?" And many times the reply would be, "Yes, those are very important, but what I like most is that now I feel equal to everyone. I feel like a human being."

That enthusiasm was the Revolution's greatest natural resource.

CUBA IS NOT ALONE

The International Revolution

Every righteous man should feel on his cheek the blow given to the cheek of any man.

—JOSÉ MARTÍ

FIDEL: When we took up arms . . . we did so on our own.

When the first revolutionary laws were put into effect, we did this on our own.

When the dangers and the threats arose, we were ready to run every risk absolutely on our own.

What would have happened if the socialist countries hadn't existed, if the Soviet Union hadn't existed? Well, at least they would have had to kill us all.

But, this country that had made a revolution entirely on its own, encountered something extraordinary—something which is the greatest, most advanced and most generous revolutionary idea in human history. It encountered what is known as *internationalism,* what is known as international solidarity.

In the 1950's, as the July 26 Movement prepared and carried out the uprising against Batista, Fidel avoided any direct conflict with the United States government. Like most Cubans, he felt no love for the *Yanquis,* whose most familiar representatives in Cuba were tourists, gangsters, military advisers, drunken sailors, playboys, and the Sugar Trust. But for the time being, the leaders of the Revolution focused their efforts against their national enemy, Batista.

It was after 1959, when the United States began its escalating pressures against the Revolution, that Cuba encountered that "extraordinary idea, international solidarity." The Revolution's emissaries abroad felt like explorers of a new world: as their old alignment with the United States was severed, those on whom they had once looked as enemies turned out to be friends. They began to realize the international significance of what they had done on that small island.

Almost in wonderment, Che Guevara wrote from a conference in Indonesia in the summer of 1959:

> Could it be that . . . millions of Asians and Africans have the same hopes we have? Could it be that our brotherhood transcends distances, different languages, and the absence of close cultural links, and unites us in the struggle? . . .
>
> The man from another land . . . touches my beard and in a strange tongue asks, "Fidel Castro?" adding, "Are you a member of the guerrilla army that leads the struggle for freedom in Latin America? Are you our allies from the other side of the sea?" And I have to answer him, and millions of Afro-Asians like him who live in new and insecure atomic times, in the affirmative. Furthermore I tell him that I am his brother, one among many from this side of the world who await with infinite anxiety the moment when our continents will unite and destroy, once and for all, the anachronistic presence of colonialism.

The impact of Cuba's clash with the United States threw the island into the international arena, where Cubans learned of people fighting for liberation in the Portuguese colonies of Africa, in Vietnam, in the Congo, Algeria, Laos—and in all these cases found the United States and its allies arrayed against them.

FIDEL: Our country, looking at things clearly, could never have chosen to be at the side of France against the Algerians; at the side of Franco against the Spanish; at the side of Chiang Kai Shek against the great Chinese people; at the side of the imperialists against the Vietnamese of the South who are struggling for their independence; at the side of the Portuguese against the Angolans. . . .

In 1963, few Americans even knew of the existence of Vietnam, in whose mountains and jungles the United States government would later sacrifice the lives of 56,550 U.S. citizens, 1,000,000 Vietnamese, and 150,000,000,000 dollars. Had most Americans heard Che Guevara's speech at the Ministry of Industry in November of that year, they would probably have taken him for paranoid or hopelessly romantic.

After explaining the history of the Vietnamese revolution to his audience, Che predicted that the United States would begin the "mass use of Yankee expeditionary forces" in that conflict. He linked Vietnam to the future of Latin America:

There in Vietnam are being trained the [U.S.] troops that one day will be able to defeat our guerrillas—ours in all America. There are being tested the new weapons of extermination and the most modern techniques to fight against the people's freedom. . . .

We know . . . that . . . whatever the method used by North American imperialism, the final result will be the victory of South Vietnam and the reunification of the entire country.

Che did not live to see his prediction come true, but Cuba was the first country to recognize the Provisional Revolutionary Government of South Vietnam (PRG) and to establish an embassy in the jungle. When Fidel visited the PRG-controlled areas of South Vietnam in 1973, he was photographed carrying a medal-bedecked PRG flag. Two years later that flag rode on the first tank of the PRG armored column that seized Saigon.

Cuba could not offer Vietnam the same level of military, economic, and diplomatic aid as did the Soviet Union. However, Vietnamese students were (and are) enrolled in Cuban schools and universities. Brigades of Cuban workers built schools and hospitals in North Vietnam, and teams of doctors and nurses worked beside the Vietnamese under heavy bombing raids.

One Cuban team, the Tavito Medical Brigade, treated 8,500 victims of fragmentation bombs in Hanoi and Haiphong. "They took care of our children as if they belonged to their own family," the Vietnamese minister of public health said when he bade them farewell.

During the early 1960's, there occurred certain international events, both favorable and unfavorable to Cuba's interests, that gave rise to a new revolutionary vision in the minds of her leaders, particularly Che Guevara—of a global guerrilla war against imperialism.

What lay behind this militant strategy for which many Cubans laid down their lives, including Guevara himself?

First: In the year following the assassination of President Kennedy, United States foreign policy took a lurch to the right, displaying a new military aggressiveness.

On January 9, 1964, U.S. troops in the Panama Canal Zone fired on a demonstration of Panamanian students and workers who were trying to raise Panama's flag next to that of the United States. Twenty-two Panamanians were killed and hundreds wounded.

In February the United States air force secretly began bombing large areas of Laos near the Vietnamese border, a portent of the war to come. In March the left-leaning reformist government of Brazil was overthrown by right-wing generals trained and supported by the United States.

In July came the later-to-be-regretted Tonkin Resolution by the United States Congress, permitting the President to escalate the war in Vietnam. Che Guevara's prediction of a year before—that the United States would send masses of troops to Vietnam—was coming true.

That same month the Organization of American States (OAS) voted 15–4 to break all diplomatic ties with Cuba, suspend direct and indirect aid, and halt all sea transportation between their countries and Cuba. Bolivia, Chile, Mexico, and Uruguay voted no. Finally, only Mexico held out, never breaking relations with Cuba.

Then, in 1965, U.S. Marines were landed in the Dominican Republic, scarcely one hundred miles from Cuba, to crush the revolutionary movement there. It seemed as if the United States was returning to the old days of gunboat diplomacy.

Second: A political conflict among the socialist countries was boiling to the surface, adding urgency to Cuba's vision of the need for guerrilla wars.

The simmering dispute between the two largest socialist countries, the Soviet Union and China, burst into hostile argument. At the end of 1963, the Chinese called on Communists around the world to break away from their parties and form new ones favoring the Chinese side of the argument.

During 1964 this dispute cleaved through the Communist parties of Latin America. The Peruvian Communist Party split in January 1964, the Bolivian and Paraguyan parties the following year. The Brazilian party had broken apart two years earlier.

The Cubans saw this split as a greater killer of revolutions than any repression by the enemy. Cuba called for unity between the Soviet Union and China, which the Soviet Union welcomed and China rejected. Cuban-Chinese relations began to deteriorate. Though at times the Cubans strongly criticized some of their fellow Communist parties, the leaders of the Cuban Revolution could not agree with the Chinese policy of deliberately splitting revolutionary movements. They knew from their own experience

during the revolutionary war (for example, the disagreement between the guerrillas in the mountains and those in the cities) that
disunity could lead to defeat.

This threat of disunity lead the Cuban leaders to believe that aid
from the socialist countries to movements for national liberation,
particularly Vietnam, would be seriously weakened. This meant,
they reasoned, that other revolutionary movements and governments should move militantly to confront the United States. This
would compensate, they hoped, for the disunity caused by the
Chinese.

Third: Cuba's victorious example gave new impetus to guerrilla
wars in Latin America, though such wars were nothing new in this
hemisphere. The Mexican Revolution had been just such a peas-
ant-based insurrection that developed into a civil war. In 1931
Augusto Sandino had led a guerrilla war against United States
intervention in Nicaragua.

In the wake of Batista's overthrow, a guerrilla movement
caught fire in Venezuela early in 1962, as did an armed insurrection in Guatemala. By 1964 two guerrilla detachments were operating in the mountains of Colombia, and a peasant war was brew-
ing in Peru.

These movements sprang up in the heady atmosphere of Cuba's
example, but they were not begun, led, or organized by Cuba.
Occasional shipments of arms came from Cuba, and guerrilla
leaders were welcomed in Havana, but the level of aid never
approached the estimates of those in Washington who saw a
"Cuban conspiracy" behind every uprising.

Those who were fighting in the jungles and mountains of half
a dozen Latin American countries justifiably looked to Cuba for
advice and aid. Cuba with its infinitesimal resources, battered by
invasion, embargo, and isolation, watched these rebellions carefully and with sympathy. Isolated diplomatically from every Latin
American government except Mexico, Cuba no longer had any-

thing to lose by using its prestige and political influence to support these rebellions.

The events in Latin America, the guerrilla movements erupting in Vietnam, Laos, Cambodia, Indonesia, the Philippines, Angola, Guinea-Bissau, Mozambique, the Congo, and many other countries convinced the Cuban leaders that a revolutionary storm was rapidly approaching among the colonies and ex-colonies of Asia, Africa, and Latin America. "This is the hour of the furnaces and only light should be seen," José Martí said of his own turbulent period. The world seemed poised once again on such a time.

This was the basis of Cuba's new revolutionary strategy: The aggression by the United States had to be confronted, and the crisis created by the split between the two largest socialist countries compensated for, by the support of guerrilla wars against imperialism.

Pointing to Vietnam, then under murderous attack by the United States, the Cubans argued that the duty of Latin American revolutionaries was to defend Vietnam by creating "two, three, many Vietnams" throughout Latin America. This would force the United States to pull troops out of Vietnam and disperse them around Latin America and the globe.

That was the vision. It did not lack audacity or courage. No one ever accused the Cubans of being armchair revolutionaries.

Che Guevara returned to Cuba from a journey through Africa in mid-March 1965. He was usually not one to hide from public view. When in Cuba, it was his habit to do volunteer work in warehouses, on the docks, in factories, and in the cane fields. Now he did not appear.

Che would not be seen again in public view until his body, strapped to the outside landing rail of a Bolivian Army helicopter, was flown to the tiny Bolivian village of Villegrande, under the direction of an agent of the CIA.

Che did not prepare to launch a guerrilla movement in Bolivia with romanticism or illusion. He was "a master, a virtuoso in the art of revolutionary war," Fidel said later. Che knew that guerrillas in Bolivia would have a more difficult fight than had the twelve survivors of the *Granma* landing. For one thing, Che was not Fidel; a leader with such unifying ability could not easily be duplicated. Che was also aware that the United States had learned from its mistakes and would not be lulled into standing by while a powerful revolutionary movement grew up under its nose, particularly when it discovered that Guevara was involved.

He bade farewell to his parents in a letter, recalling the time ten years earlier when he had left them to join the Rebel Army in Cuba.

Dear Folks:

Once again I feel beneath my heels the ribs of Rosinante.* I return to the road with my lance under my arm. . . .

Nothing has changed in essence, except that I am more aware. My Marxism has taken deep root and become purified. I believe in armed struggle as the only solution for those peoples who fight to liberate themselves, and I am consistent with my beliefs.

Many will call me an adventurer, and I am, but of a different type, one of those who risks his skin to demonstrate his truths. It is possible that this will be the last time. I don't look forward to it, but it is within the logical realm of possibilities. If this be so, I send you a last embrace. . . .

A year and a half later, disguised as a balding Uruguayan businessman, Guevara made his way to a remote farm in the high plateau of southeast Bolivia—the headquarters of his guerrilla army. A month earlier, the U.S. Army had invaded Vietnam.

---

*Don Quixote's horse

Bolivia, like Cuba, was poor and underdeveloped, dependent on a single raw material, tin, and endowed with a highly political working class. Guevara saw the country, not as ripe for immediate revolution, but in a fluid, turbulent condition that a guerrilla struggle could catalyze into a revolutionary situation.

However, the revolutionary movement in Bolivia was not united. Unlike in Cuba, Che was not able to count on a strong organization in the cities that could supply the guerrillas and organize political support. He had difficulty recruiting reliable Bolivians for the guerrilla force.

A series of disasters and betrayals dogged the guerrillas from the start. A lengthy training march for new members in January 1967 proved disastrous, revealing their presence to the Bolivian army. The inhabitants of entire villages were seized by the army for questioning, and the area was sown with informers dressed as peasants.

Two guerrillas deserted to the army and led government forces to the farm while Che was away. On March 23, the rebels clashed with the army for the first time.

Though the guerrillas won that fight, the battle forced them prematurely into a combat for which neither they nor their sparse supporters in the cities were prepared. The word was out: there was a guerrilla movement in Bolivia, and it was led by Ernesto Che Guevara. Their single task now was to survive. They abandoned the farm.

As they left, Major Robert "Pappy" Shelton of the CIA arrived in Bolivia and set up an antiguerrilla training center in a deserted sugar mill. He was given six hundred Bolivian recruits, 20 United States Special Forces troops, and several Cuban exiles on the CIA payroll. The government placed all of southeast Bolivia under martial law.

The guerrillas survived—on the run. Che's hopes were still high. In May a political crisis broke out in the capital city, and Che wrote in his diary, "The Government is rapidly disintegrating. It's a pity we do not have a hundred more men at this moment."

Militarily, the guerrillas were in no worse shape than Fidel's Rebel Army had been in the months after the landing of the *Granma.* But their contact with the cities had been severed; they were alone.

Adversity combined against them. On April 15, Che had been forced to divide his forces, hoping to join them together later. He never did.

They kept on the move. There were clashes, in all of which the guerrillas came out ahead, but good men were killed. On April 25, Che lost one of his closest friends and best fighters, Eliseo Reyes, 27. Reyes, a member of the Central Committee of the Cuban Communist Party, had joined the Rebel Army at the age of sixteen, risen to captain, and become the head of State Security in Pinar del Río province after the victory.

Betrayed by a peasant, one of Che's guerrilla groups was ambushed by the army in late August while crossing a river. Only one survived. Meanwhile "Pappy" Shelton had graduated his six hundred Bolivian Ranger troops, who saturated the area in which the guerrillas were moving.

Later, after it was confirmed, Fidel told the story of Che's death:

Che wrote the last lines of his diary on October 7. The next day, at one in the afternoon, in a narrow canyon where they were awaiting nightfall in order to break out of their encirclement, a large body of troops made contact.

The small group of men who made up the detachment fought heroically from their positions at the base of the canyon and along its edges against a mass of soldiers who surrounded and attacked them. There were no survivors from among those who fought closest to Che. . . .

Those who defended the position at the far entrance to the can-

yon, several hundred yards from Che . . . resisted the attack until
dusk, when they were able to evade the enemy.

Che fought on, wounded, until the barrel of his M-2 was destroyed by a shot, rendering it useless. The pistol he carried had no
magazine. These incredible circumstances explain how they were
able to capture him alive. The wounds in his legs made it difficult
to walk without aid, but they were not fatal.

Carried to the little town of Higueras, he remained alive about
twenty-four hours. He refused to say anything to his captors, and
a drunken officer who tried to annoy him received a slap in the
face.*

According to Fidel's account, Bolivian Rangers ordered a sergeant to carry out the assassination. When the sergeant, drunk,
entered the schoolroom where Che was lying, the Cuban guerrilla
—who had heard the shots that killed his two captured comrades
in the next room moments before—told him calmly, "Shoot!
Don't be afraid."

The sergeant left, and was ordered back by his superiors. This
time he fired a burst of gunfire into Che's body, killing him.

The photographs of Che Guevara's body show him with his
eyes open peacefully, looking uncannily alive.

Of the tributes to Che by people who loved him, one of the most
beautiful was from Haydeé Santamaría:

Che: . . . How can I tell you that I have never cried like this since
the night they murdered Frank [País], and that this time I did not
believe it. . . .

. . . Fidel said it, so it must be true—what sorrow. He could not
say "Che"; he summoned all his strength and said "Ernesto
Guevara"—that is how he told the people, your people. . . . Later
in the evening meeting, the people did not know what rank Fidel
would confer on you. He gave you the rank of *artist.* I was thinking
that all the ranks were too low, too small, and Fidel, as always, said

---

*And in return shot Guevara in the arm with his pistol.

the true thing: all that you created was perfect, but you made a unique creation, you made yourself, you showed that the new man is possible, thus everyone could see that the new man is a reality, because he exists, he is you. . . .

After the death of Che, Cuba began to reevaluate its guerrilla strategy. The world situation was once again changing rapidly—in favor of socialism and national liberation. The United States was bogged down in Vietnam and losing the war. With 500,000 soldiers there, the United States had none to spare for military interventions elsewhere. The Sino-Soviet dispute had not weakened the ability of the socialist countries to aid revolutionary movements, nor had it seriously harmed the Communist parties around the world. Cuba was finding herself less isolated and more respected for her domestic achievements and anti-imperialist militancy.

Latin American countries that had lain under the domination of the United States were beginning to assert their independence. Military governments that challenged much of U.S. policy came into power in Panama and Peru. Both countries opened up contacts with Cuba.

The United States State Department looked on in dismay as country after country established diplomatic, trade, and cultural relations with Cuba. The wall the United States had so carefully built around Cuba was crumbling.

In Chile, an old friend of Fidel's, Salvador Allende, led a coalition of Communists, Socialists, and other left-wing parties into the government. Fidel made a triumphal three-week tour of Chile in November 1971, where he was welcomed by cheering crowds.

The ice was breaking all over Latin America, revealing fresh streams of discontent among all levels of society, not only the peasants. Cuba found herself admired and respected by the underdeveloped Third World countries of Asia, Africa, and Latin

America for her steadfastness and fierce opposition to the policies of the United States.

The war in Vietnam put the United States in the role of global "bad guy." Opposition such as Cuba's to U.S. policy was becoming a respected element in world opinion.

During this same period, the capitalist countries themselves began to be shaken by a series of crises—rising unemployment and inflation, oil shortages, fiscal and monetary disasters—that revealed on what insecure economic pillars even the most developed capitalist countries rested.

Hit the worst were the underdeveloped countries of Asia, Africa, and Latin America, who sold raw materials (oil, meat, grain, copper, etc.) to the advanced nations at a low price and were forced to buy manufactured goods from the advanced countries at a high price. Soon countries that produced raw materials were banding together in organizations such as OPEC, (Organization of Petroleum Exporting Countries) to demand a fair price for their products.

Underdeveloped nations increasingly looked toward Cuba as a possible model for economic development. Once a stagnant appendage of the United States economy, Cuba could now count on a stable, long-term market among the socialist countries. It was also impossible to ignore the fact that Cuba—a socialist country —had the best health care, housing, and educational systems in Latin America.

By the end of the 1960's, Cuba had defeated the attempts to isolate and crush the Revolution. Not only had Cuba survived, but it was solving the same social problems that oppressed many other nations in the world: hunger, malnutrition, disease, illiteracy, inequality, poverty, racial discrimination.

The nation was able to do all this, Cuban diplomats argued in such forums as the United Nations and the Movement of Non-aligned Nations, because the "balance of power" in the world had changed. The United States and the other developed capitalist countries were no longer all-powerful. They were wracked by social and economic crises; their economies were increasingly unstable, their people uneasy. The socialist countries, on the other-hand, were more prosperous and stable than ever. Every year more countries moved in a socialist direction.

A good example of this was Angola.

A nation of mixed African and Spanish descent, Cuba early identified with the revolutionary struggles of the African continent. In the sixties, she aided the Algerians fighting to free their country from French control. She supported the national liberation movement in Mozambique in 1963, that of Guinea-Bissau in 1965. Cuban troops later helped Guinea's president Sekou Touré repulse a mercenary invasion. Che Guevara spent almost the entire year of 1965 in the Congo, training, directing, and fighting alongside African revolutionaries.

In the year 1969 a young American journalist was visiting Cuba. "I was in the countryside thirty miles or so from Havana," he wrote, "visiting a small hospital on the grounds of a school complex. The patients were black men, some with limbs missing. They were, I was told, casualties of war. It took an awkward three way translation—from Portuguese to Spanish to English—to learn that these men were African guerrilla fighters convalescing with Cuban medical assistance.

"They were Angolans."

The men were soldiers of the MPLA (Popular Movement for the Liberation of Angola) which had led the war to drive the Portuguese out of their country. After the Portuguese withdrew in 1975, the MPLA was then forced to fight a civil war against two other Angolan groups openly supported by the CIA, the South Africans, and China.

Late in 1975, the MPLA had established an internationally recognized revolutionary government in the capital city of Luanda and was holding its own against its foes, until October 23 when the Union of South Africa launched a blitzkreig invasion from the south. By November 10, South African armored columns were twenty-five kilometers from the capital. Augustino Neto, president of Angola, asked Cuba for aid and she sent it.

To the Cubans lining up to volunteer to fight in Angola, it was the Bay of Pigs invasion all over again, this time in Africa. And they were aware that Africa was, in some sense, their homeland.

"Those who once enslaved men and sent them to America," Fidel said, "perhaps never imagined that one of those peoples that received the slaves would send its combatants to fight for liberty in Africa."

The Union of South Africa's social system of racial segregation, *apartheid,* was repugnant to the Cubans. The term apartheid, said Cuban foreign minister Raúl Roa, "carries with it the very negation of the human being, the reduction of the human being to the category of an instrument. The separation of people according to pigmentation under the supremacy of the white race is one of the most monstrous attacks on the essential unity of mankind that has ever been perpetuated."

Cuba's emergency airlift of troops, backed with arms from the Soviet Union and other socialist countries, helped turn the tide against the South African invasion. But Cuba was not alone. Battalions from Guinea and newly liberated Guinea-Bissau also joined the MPLA in driving the South Africans across the border.

Three years later, in 1978, Cuba sent troops to aid the revolutionary government of Ethiopia, whose country had been invaded by troops from neighboring Somalia. The Somali invasion was backed by the United States, Saudi Arabia, Iran, Egypt, China, Great Britain, and West Germany.

Most of the black nations of Africa supported Cuba's aid to Ethiopia. Writing in the U.S. magazine, *The Nation,* in 1978, Tanzanian president Julius K. Nyerere, one of Africa's most respected leaders, said:

Cuban and Soviet forces are also in Ethiopia, at the request of the Ethiopian Government. The reasons for their presence are well known. They have helped the Ethiopians defend their country against external aggression.

It is, then, on the basis of Soviet and Cuban forces in two African countries [Angola and Ethiopia] that there is a great furor in the West about a so-called Soviet penetration of Africa. And those forces are in those two countries at the request of the legitimate governments of the countries concerned.

Cuba has been called "a small country with a large country's foreign policy." It has not remained passive or on the sidelines in global politics, but has projected itself beyond the Caribbean, and by its audacity and willingness to take chances became respected as a leader among the countries of Asia, Africa, and Latin America. It has not forgotten the obscurity from which its own revolution came, nor the international aid that made it possible. It is determined that if other revolutions face a common enemy, they, like Cuba, will not have to fight alone.

The daughter of slain revolutionary José Luís Tasende hugs Raúl Castro at the ceremony turning the Moncada garrison into a school.
Prensa Latina

Cuban soldiers rescuing victims of the *Le Coubre* explosion
Prensa Latina

Demonstration in favor of the nationalization of U.S. corporations in Cuba
Prensa Latina

Cuban militia advance along the road to Playa Girón.   *Prensa Latina*

Captured Bay of Pigs invaders held prisoner by Cuban troops   *Prensa Latina*

Fidel visits an antiaircraft position during the Missile Crisis.

Prensa Latina

Meeting between UN Secretary General U Thant *(center left)* and Cuban
government leaders during the height of the Missile Crisis

Prensa Latina

Che Guevara (*right*)
doing voluntary work
in construction.
Prensa Latina

A Cuban textile mill
Before the blockade every spare part came from the United States.   *Prensa Latina*

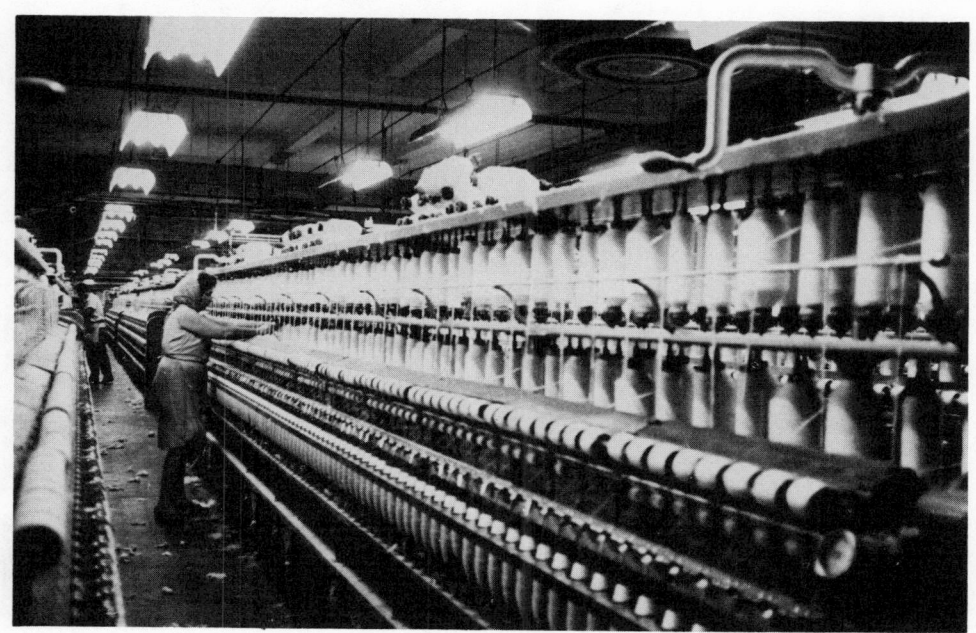

A Cuban medical team working in Vietnam

Prensa Latina

A crowd greets Fidel during his 1971
visit to Chile. *Prensa Latina*

Che Guevara in Bolivia in 1967
Prensa Latina

A literacy teacher reads from his teaching manual.

Prensa Latina

Students gathered in the courtyard of a School in the Countryside *Venceremos Brigade*

Students at a School
in the Countryside working in agriculture
Prensa Latina

A young volunteer works
in a sugarcane field
Prensa Latina

A modern rural hospital nestled in the mountains near Cienfuegos   *Prensa Latina*

Cuban labor leader Lázaro Peña
Prensa Latina

A 1969 demonstration by CDR members supports the nationalization of small businesses.
Prensa Latina

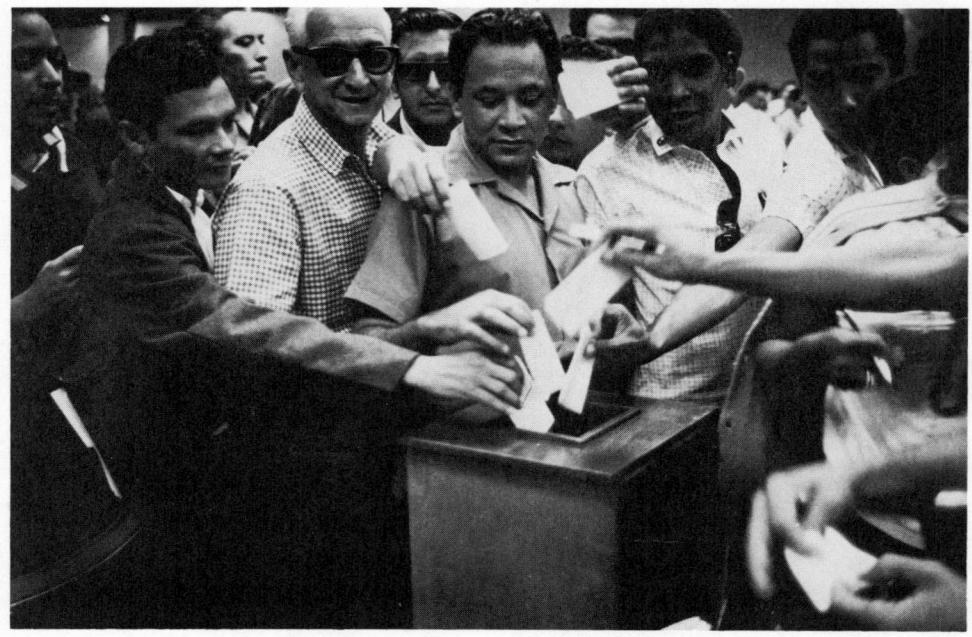

Delegates vote at the Thirteenth CTC Congress.   *Prensa Latina*

Voters gather outside
a polling station during
the People's Power elections
in Matanzas province in 1975.
Venceremos Brigade

May Day demonstration, 1975
Prensa Latina

Women marching in the International Workers' Day parade in Havana, 1975   *Prensa Latina*

(above)
By 1979 more than half the sugar
harvest was mechanized
Prensa Latina

Students at the 26th of July
School in Santiago,
formerly the Moncada garrison
Prensa Latina

(right)
Fidel cutting cane, 1965   *Prensa Latina*

PART III

EDUCATION

Revolution in the Revolution

To be educated is the only way to be free.

—JOSÉ MARTÍ, 1884

If you don't know, learn.
If you know, teach.

— CUBAN SLOGAN, 1961

Armando Hart, twenty-nine years old, fresh from the underground July 26 Movement and now suddenly Minister of Education, was holding his first press conference in the Ministry offices in Havana in January 1959. Gesturing at the halls around him, he said, "Such is the moral and civic corruption, so great the irregularities, the illegalities, the laxity, that the best thing we could do to start off is burn this building to the ground, so nothing remains of the evil that was done here."

Corruption and neglect had poisoned the educational system before the Revolution. The administration was chaotic; the teachers, bored and demoralized (ten thousand of them were unemployed); the students, those that there were, got the leftovers.

The rich sent their children to elite private schools in Cuba or abroad. The growing middle class took their children out of the public school system and sent them to mushrooming private schools, many of them church-run—like the one that Fidel attended—abandoning the public schools to the children of the working class, who were in turn abandoned by the Ministry of Education.

The last census before the Revolution, that of 1953, showed that there were 1,032,849 illiterate Cubans, 23.6 percent of the total population. Havana had only 9 percent illiteracy, Oriente 35 percent. The gap between the urban and rural populations was even more drastic: 11 percent illiteracy in the cities; 41.7 percent in the countryside.

Equally crippling, in the eyes of the revolutionaries, was the quality of the education that trickled down to those lucky enough to receive it: "nonscientific, learned by rote and memorization, intellectualistic and formalist," in the words of one Cuban educator, "uncoordinated and without any clear purpose."

Cuban children were taught that Custer was the hero of the Battle of Little Big Horn and that African tribes boiled heroic white explorers for dinner.

No educational system is better than the society that produces it. If the public schools were inadequate, the private and elite schools handed down the very values the Revolution was pledged to eliminate. "It is simply evil," Fidel said in 1961, "to imbue a human being with the idea that others have to work for him so he won't have to work for himself, that the clothes and shoes he wears and the bread he eats are not to be earned by his own toil, but will be provided by the sweat of other men's brows."

The revolutionaries did not burn down the Ministry of Education. Instead, they totally changed the face of Cuban education in a massive four-year effort probably unequaled by any other nation on earth.

The literacy campaign was one of the more remarkable mobilizations in the history of revolutions. One hundred thousand young people responded to Fidel's call, fanning out to the farthest reaches of the country, and in a single year taught 707,212 people to read and write. "It was perhaps the best thermometer of the people's faith in the Revolution," the editor of *Bohemia* has said, "given the threat of invasion—the Bay of Pigs invasion took place in the middle of the campaign—and the murder by counterrevolutionaries of several volunteer teachers in the mountains, and the Spanish family tradition that would never have imagined allowing young children—especially girls!—to leave home. It showed that a hundred thousand parents had confidence in the Revolution to protect their children. It also demonstrated the unity of city dwellers and peasants: most of the teachers were from the cities; most of the illiteracy was in the rural areas."

The effect was volcanic, requiring that the entire educational system be expanded. Public-school enrollment in 1962 was double that of 1958. The Revolution sent out a call for classrooms. Trade unions offered rooms in their union halls. Mansions of those who had abandoned the country were converted into schools, as were the old garrisons of the army of the dictatorship. Ten thousand new classrooms were created. The 1962 education budget was three times the budget of 1958. By 1973 it was eight times as large.

This inflow into an antiquated educational system was like trying to make an old car go at the rate of one hundred miles an hour. The inertia and privilege-ridden system was often slow to change. For a while, the three main universities continued to turn out lawyers and liberal arts majors, when the country desperately needed agricultural experts, chemists, agronomists and industrial engineers, mathematicians and statisticians—occupations once dominated by Americans.

The revolutionary government challenged the universities to open their doors to black, mulatto, and white Cubans equally.

In June 1961 the government nationalized the private-school system, breaking up those clots of privilege and discrimination.

Changing the university system from an elite producer of professionals and politicians to one that began to address the economic needs of the nation was part of an attempt to move the entire country in the same direction, to make all its institutions "vibrate" together, as the Cubans say, to make them respond to what was outside their walls. The radical changes came later, changes so profound that they made the massive turn-around of the educational system in the first years seem like nothing.

For the first time, the Ministry of Education began cooperating with the teachers; the teachers no longer fought the students. Discipline in the classroom disappeared as a practical problem. The students, finding themselves not only the object of popular enthusiasm and effort but being called upon to take the lead in educating others, responded with a new sense of their own importance and of the need to study to improve themselves and their country. The generation gap evaporated.

Young Cubans, free of the political quarrels of the past, were the first to unite. On October 21, 1960, shortly after Cuba nationalized the large American corporations, the revolutionary youth groups of the July 26 Movement, the PSP, and others merged into the *Asociación de Jóvenes Rebeldes,* or AJR (Rebel Youth Association). The young women and men of the AJR declared themselves an "anti-imperialist" organization, whose goal was socialism—six months before the Revolution was declared socialist.

So rapidly did the Revolution develop, that a year and a half later the AJR changed its name to the *Union de Jovenes Comunistas* (Union of Young Communists) or UJC, a full three years before the new Communist Party of Cuba was formed.

Speaking to the UJC two days before the Missile Crisis, Che Guevara offered his vision of what a young Communist should be, charged with his own faith in the perfectibility of humanity:

> There should be a great sensitivity to all problems, a great sensitivity to injustice; an independent spirit, whenever something arises that is not right, no matter what anyone says about it. . . .
>
> Together with all this, a great spirit of sacrifice, there ought to be a spirit of sacrifice not reserved for heroic days only, but for every moment. . . .
>
> This means that every Young Communist must be essentially human, so human that he responds to the best in human beings, brings out the best a man has to offer by means of work, study, and the exercise of continued solidarity with his people and with all the peoples of the world.

By 1975 there were 312,000 members in the UJC, 30 percent of them women. They participate in nearly every important activity—including voluntary work, running the school system, constructing the Havana-Santiago railroad, administrating special development campaigns in the sugar harvest, dairy projects, and reforestation.

Someone in Chile once asked Fidel whether Cuban universities were independent from the government—an important issue in Latin America where many governments meddle in university affairs. Fidel tugged his beard and said he couldn't really remember whether they were legally independent or not. The question no longer applied. "Maybe we should pass a law giving the government autonomy from the students," he quipped. "They're into everything, they run everything, you can't keep them away."

By 1965, Fidel could claim without contradiction even from his enemies that Cuba "has one of the most advanced teacher-training programs in the world."

Juan de Onís, Latin American correspondent for *The New York Times,* wrote:

> In many parts of Cuba today the books under the arm and the pencils in the pocket of the shirt are as much a symbol of the revolution as the rifle and the militia uniform. Adult education is one of the principle projects of the government and the mass organizations of Premier Fidel Castro's regime are mobilizing themselves to raise every man and woman worker to at least a sixth grade level. The organization of this enormous program is impressive. The teachers have been recruited from among the best-educated workers and receive special training.

Even this wasn't enough for Cuba. By opening the doors of education to everyone, the Revolution had burst the dam that kept the vast majority of Cubans in a stagnant pool of illiteracy and ignorance. When the dam broke, a tide of students began to sweep upward through the educational system.

This "baby boom" rolled on, placing an enormous strain on the Cuban economy. How could Cuba afford to educate this massive increase in students?

Cuba is a country of youth. Only one third of her people are in the work force, producing the wealth needed to support those in school and those too old to work. Furthermore, it contradicted the ideals of the Revolution to have some people only studying while others only work. As Fidel said:

> What should we do with certain people? Condemn them to be intellectuals for life? What should we do with the others? Condemn them to be animals for life?
>
> I believe that this goes against Nature. Our aspiration for human society is that every human being will some day do both manual and intellectual work.
>
> When the masses have access to culture, when they have the opportunity to study, when they have access to knowledge, instead of one genius, there are a thousand, there are ten thousand geniuses.

The answer lay in combining study with work: "Every worker a student and every student a worker."

The Cuban solution, when evolved, was brilliantly simple and unique: *Las Escuelas Secundarias Basicas en el Campo,* the Schools in the Countryside.

As the plane from Santiago lowers on the southern approach to the José Martí Airport in Havana, one can see the schools: bright orange or yellow H-shaped structures among fields of green banana groves or citrus orchards. Hundreds of these modern structures dot the Cuban countryside, hundreds more are being built each year. They house the educational revolution that began in 1970 when the first School in the Countryside was built. It was named *Martires de Kent* (the Martyrs of Kent), after the students shot to death at Kent State University in Ohio by the national guard that year.

Every School in the Countryside is built on a common architectural plan—an airy, open, colorful structure of prefabricated concrete. One wing contains the classrooms; the second, the kitchen and dining area and the living quarters for the thirty-six members of the teaching staff; the third, the dormitories for five hundred students, evenly divided between men and women.

In addition, each school plant includes laboratories, workshops, meeting rooms, a library, barbershop and beauty parlor, infirmary, movie theater, school store, and swimming pool.

The students come from the towns and villages in the surrounding area. In the Cuban educational system the Schools in the Countryside are roughly equivalent to our junior high schools: grades seven through ten. But these are schools for living and working, as well as study. The students live at the school during the week, returning home on weekends.

They awake at six in the morning, eat breakfast, and at seven group themselves in columns in the courtyard between the buildings for the morning assembly. Half the students—those in the seventh and ninth grades—are dressed in work clothes. The others —the eighth and tenth grades—are wearing blue and white school uniforms, ready for class. At lunchtime the tasks are reversed; those who have come in from work, study; the others are on their way to the fields.

> STUDENT: From the very moment you first enter a School in the Countryside, you feel what work is and what you really produce. Then you realize all the things that you didn't realize before.
>
> Let me pick out a recent example. Many times when you're young, you see things without understanding. . . . An orange, well, I drank the juice, but I never thought about where that orange came from. I bought it at the grocery store. But here you grow it, you fertilize it, you weed it, you take care of it, and you understand where the orange came from.

The tilling of the land by students is no make-work project. Depending on the nature of the crop, a single school can produce up to two million pesos' worth of citrus, tobacco, bananas, or vegetables a year. It is possible for schools not only to pay their own expenses, but contribute to the economy.

It was hoped that by 1980 almost all of Cuba's secondary school students would be housed in Schools in the Countryside and that the schools themselves would be economically self-sufficient.

On a spring morning in 1975, this author arrived at the General Bartolomé Masó School in the Countryside (named for a hero in the War of Independence) outside Holguín, in one of Cuba's fastest-growing areas, northern Oriente province. I met first with the leadership of the school: the director, a lively, down-to-earth man in his twenties (I don't think there was a member of the staff over thirty), the head of the UJC, and the production chief. The small front office was decorated with pictures and handicrafts made by the students and their parents.

"OK," the director said, with an open gesture, "You ask the questions—anything you want to know. . . ."

"What's the main problem you have with the kids?"

"Getting used to a new way of studying and working. Mostly at the beginning with the seventh graders. They're homesick. The children aren't used to working, or have bad study habits, or just aren't used to being away from home.

"We talk to them, explain how things are organized here. Mostly the transition is made with the help of the other students, the older ones with more experience. They make a special effort to talk, to entertain them, and take their minds off home. Then, once they get involved in the activities here, the homesickness disappears."

STUDENT: When I came to this school I had never held a hoe in my hands, never. I had never worked in my life, because I studied in a regular school. So I came here . . . and all the kids would tell me, "Look, Dania, let's work to produce."

At the beginning I didn't feel good when I had to work, because I used to say that the work made me tired. But with time, slowly, because this is a slow process, slowly I became more enthusiastic, I began to understand the importance of the work.

They explained to me how I would feel better if I worked harder and the truth is that I began to change. I began to feel a love for my work—a passion. Then it was I who would talk to the others, "Come on, girls, let's go to the fields!"

The school is governed by a council made up of representatives from the administration, the Young Communist Union, the student organization, the Communist Party, and the workers at the school. Another council brings together the parents and the community organizations from the surrounding area.

"Together they get all the parents and people from the community involved in the school," the director explained. "Every Wednesday a group of parents comes out. They decorate the school, fix furniture, clean, help in the fields. It's really good when the kids see their parents' interest in how things are going.

"During the time when we're evaluating the progress of the students we call a meeting of the parents, where we analyze whatever teaching or discipline problems we might have and ask for their cooperation to help deal with them. Sometimes a student might have problems that come not from the school but from the community. Then the parent who represents that community talks to the parents or whoever is involved and tries to straighten it out."

The members of the regular teaching staff are older than the students, but not much. The teachers live in a single dormitory, sleep on the same double-decker wooden bunks as the students (the only discernable difference between their quarters and those of the students is that the students' rooms are neater). The striking discipline of the school—the students file to and from class, march to work, are orderly, clean and respectful—is mingled with a camaraderie and informality in relations between students and teachers. Their discipline is self-discipline; infractions of the rules are dealt with by fellow students in group discussions. No one patrols the halls.

The teachers are evaluated by the students, and advanced students themselves teach courses from which they have graduated the year before.

Having brought work clothes, I went with a brigade of about forty students that afternoon to the banana groves where they were clearing away weeds from around the trees.

The visitor from the United States did little to increase production. Every time I asked a student near me a question or was interrogated in return, the entire group stopped weeding and pushed together to listen to the conversation.

Why is there so much juvenile delinquency in the United States? Is it true that people have to pay for hospital care and to get into college? Do workers go to school at their factories? Why isn't there a revolution?

Some of my answers shocked them. The oldest were sixteen, born the year of the Revolution and knowing no other way of life. They looked with wonder and a little suspicion (one of the Cubans with me had to reassure them that I knew what I was talking about) when they heard about the high cost of medical care and university education. "All the schools aren't free?" they asked. "But what if one doesn't have money?"

To American eyes, the most impressive quality of the students at the Schools in the Countryside is their personality, their demeanor. They give off a sense of calm dignity, an internal tranquility, a confidence that arises, I think, from two sources: (1) many causes of anxiety—fierce competition for grades, uncertainty about the future, racism, joblessness—have been generally eliminated; (2) their deep sense of connection—with their parents, their homes, their teachers, and the Revolution. They know they are the future of the country. They know that great things are expected of them, and they respond. They see around them a society mobilizing its resources for them. "If there is a privileged class in Cuba," I was told many times, "it is the children."

I was talking to a group of girls in the dormitory about why there was not yet a revolution in the United States.

"But we rose up against our government," one girl said, and then corrected herself. "Not *us,* our *parents.* They rebelled and gave their blood. They died so we could have this." She gestured at the school, the fields. The others nodded.

"That's why we study so hard, because we know what they sacrificed for us."

A lot of hands went up when I asked about Vietnam. Why did they want to help out a country on the other side of the world, where they speak a different language?, I asked.

"We feel Vietnam's victory as if it were our own. The Vietnamese have been like blood brothers for a long time, for everyone in Cuba. When they are fighting, we fight; when they have victories, we have victories. We feel proud and happy to see now that

Vietnam is liberated—they've been fighting for so long. We feel the pride just like them."

In the revolutionary literature I had read, the term "the new man" or "the socialist man" occurred often. It meant a person without destructive egotism, the opposite of what the Cubans saw as the product of capitalism—a person full of selfishness, "a wolf to other men." I asked the students what kind of person this *nuevo hombre* was.

"The most important quality of the new man is that, whatever the difficulty, he can resolve it."

Frankly, I think I saw some of the new men and women at the Bartolomé Masó School in the Countryside.

Even Fidel tends to get a little misty when asked about the Schools in the Countryside and the generation they are producing. "They're not like us," he told me. "They're different. Sometimes I don't know how to talk to them. They're calm. They speak out forthrightly. And they're not neurotic, like we were. . . ."

Were it not for the inescapable achievements of the Schools in the Countryside, these words might seem like wishful thinking, utopian rhetoric—and they are far from being achieved everywhere in the educational system. "The progress we have made is slight in relation to the work we have ahead of us," Fidel said in 1972. "The problems grow more complex and difficult day by day."

The dropout rate is still a severe problem. In 1972 there were 215,000 children between the ages of thirteen and sixteen who were not attending school. Promotion rates averaged only 70 percent, resulting in a serious problem of overage students. (The promotion rates in the Schools in the Countryside are dramatically higher: at the Bartolomé Masó School every student passed.)

On my return to Havana from Holguín, I met Melba Hernández and told her my impressions of the School in the Countryside. I got that same faraway look. I mentioned what Fidel had said about the children being different from the older generation.

"Yes, I feel the same," she answered. "I have to make a great effort not to seem ridiculous in front of them. It's an entirely different generation. Whenever I feel tired, I go and visit a School in the Countryside. I talk to the young ones, I listen to them. It's like having a party—it refreshes me. They're sure of themselves, very solid. When they speak they know what they're talking about. They are completely liberated. In my opinion they are the greatest achievement of the Revolution."

THE CUBAN WAY
OF HEALTH

Best in Latin America

Everyone has the right to the care and protection of their health. The State guarantees this right: By offering free hospital and medical services . . . . By offering free dental treatment; By developing plans for sanitary efforts, health education, periodic medical exams, general vaccination, and other preventive medical means. In these plans and activities the entire population participates through the social and mass organizations.

—ARTICLE 49 OF THE SOCIALIST CONSITIUTUON
OF THE REPUBLIC OF CUBA

Enrique Otero Fernández, a peasant born and raised in the Escambray Mountains of central Cuba, still becomes indignant when he talks about the past:

> He who was seriously ill was just stuck. To be treated one had to go to Cienfuegos, which in the spring, took 15 hours. One traveled by horse or on foot along a terrible path toward Gavilanes, then the boat to the Guanaroca lagoon, and from there to the Bay of Cienfuegos. We saw many people die on the road. Today one makes the trip by highway, direct, in less than an hour.

We *guajiros* of the Escambray didn't have the right to be born and not even the right to die decently. The women gave birth naturally, without any help, just like the cows in the pasture. Today the rural women have all their treatment guaranteed from the first moment to the birth, and even our cows now have veterinary doctors. If our women in those days had even the attention that our cattle do now, it would have saved the lives of many children and pregnant women.

It is one of the Revolution's most dramatic achievements that in fifteen years Cuban health care passed from medievality to what is recognized by international health organizations as the best in Latin America, and one of the best in the world.

Medical care was a lucrative business in capitalist Cuba. The wealthy had their psychiatrists and personal physicians, most of them in Havana. The Ministry of Health and Social Assistance was a land-office opportunity for enrichment through embezzlement, padded accounts, rake-offs, and the garnering of votes in exchange for hospital beds. (In return for a recommendation to a hospital, politicians received the sick person's voting card.)

Six thousand doctors were practicing medicine in Cuba when the Revolution triumphed, 64 percent of them in the city of Havana. When the Revolution challenged them to work for the health of the people as a whole, half chose to leave the country —a sad testimonial to the motives that made them doctors.

But others responded; a new generation of doctors was trained, dedicated to spreading medical care to the entire country. Beginning in 1960, the Ministry of Public Health (MINSAP) sent teams of doctors to towns and villages where no doctor had ever been seen.

Though they believed in preventive medicine, these early teams could do little more than attack the worst ills of a peasantry suffering from parasites, malnutrition, anemia, polio, gastroenteritis, respiratory diseases, malaria, typhoid, and whooping cough.

The doctor usually set up shop in a corner of the home of a *campesino,* traveling to the surrounding area by horse or mule or on foot. He treated a daily stream of people, sometimes able to do little more than sympathize, knowing that poor sanitary conditions, overwork, too little food, and poor nutrition were the real causes of their ills. He dispensed pills, delivered babies, gave advice on sanitary habits, and argued against those who believed that magic or potions or God were the means to health.

A doctor recalls those days:

> In the countryside it had been the custom, and in this area even more, for doctors to charge for a birth in proportion to the number of miles he had to travel, in addition to the medical care. One morning at six a *campesino* arrived on muleback asking me to go to his house to care for his wife. She was having contractions and he couldn't take her to a hospital.
>
> We made the journey on foot in three hours. The woman gave birth, happily, at three in the afternoon. When it was over, she asked for the *campesino* to take me back to the dispensary, since I didn't know the road. The man appeared at five in the afternoon, very worried.
>
> "Doctor," he said to me, "I'll bring you the money early tomorrow. I left to sell a cow, but they aren't going to pay me until tomorrow morning."
>
> I felt so embarrassed. I put my arm around him and told him, "My friend, you're mistaken. I'm a doctor that the Revolution sent to take care of you, not to rip you off."

The true enemy of public health, a 1969 MINSAP report noted, had been "economic underdevelopment, feudal exploitation, the *latifundia* and its consequences: illiteracy, the hundreds of thousands of unemployed, the terrible *tiempo muerto* with its inescapable companions: misery, hunger, and death. To deal with the problem at its root meant agrarian reform, public education, roads, communications, hygiene, full employment."

In that sense it was the Revolution itself that contributed most to health in the early years. Slowly things improved. Sanitary practices took root. The Revolution spread a network of roads, schools, medical posts. Agrarian reform gave land to the peasants; unemployment shrank.

The rural doctor began to be freed from his daily consultations, to plan with the villagers for the long-range needs of the community—to coordinate vaccination campaigns, to improve sanitary conditions, to hold classes on preventive medicine.

Mass campaigns were begun in 1962 against polio, malaria, and tetanus. The CDR (Committees for the Defense of the Revolution), the Federation of Cuban Women, and other organizations held vaccination drives in every section of the country: 2,216,022 children were immunized against polio that year, using the Sabine vaccine; 4,000,000 inoculations against diptheria, tetanus, and typhoid were carried out in a four-month period. As a result, there have been no cases of polio in Cuba since 1963. Malaria, which struck some 3,000 persons a year, was eliminated in 1968. Diphtheria was eradicated in 1971. Gastroenteritis, a major killer of children in underdeveloped countries, killing 4,157 Cuban children in 1962, 80 percent of them under the age of one, was curbed, causing only 761 deaths in 1975.

Behind these efforts lay a profound philosophical assumption: under socialism "the protection of people's health is the obligation of the socialist state," in the words of a 1969 MINSAP statement. The quality and availability of health care should in no way be affected by one's ability to pay or one's geographical location.

To carry out this obligation, the Cuban Revolution created a remarkable network of medical services that now reaches every Cuban man, woman, and child with comprehensive, preventive, and curative medical care, equal in quality and free of charge.

The rural hospital or polyclinic is the basic unit of the health system. Here is where most of the people of Cuba receive medical care. The polyclinic offers general medicine, pediatrics, gynecology, obstetrics, dental care, control of communicable diseases, hygiene, and health education.

In 1975 I visited such a rural hospital, the Mario Muñoz Hospital, named for the doctor killed in the attack on the Moncada garrison. The hospital lies near a sugar mill deep in the countryside north of Holguín, almost at the sea. The country is rolling, with sudden precipitous hills and stretches of pasture and cane. I had expected a small building, like a community clinic in a city, and was surprised to find a large modern hospital.

The social workers from the hospital, I was told, fan out over the rural area, visiting sick people in their homes, arranging for transportation to the hospital. When a mother needs to be treated, they arrange for the children to be housed by other families or at a day-care center while she's gone. When any prolonged treatment is called for, the social worker helps settle the home problems that may arise: providing a guaranteed salary from the Ministry of Work, school arrangements, child care, a job for another member of the family, special care for older dependent members of the family.

The explosion of medical services can be seen in a glance by comparing the statistics from the first year of the Revolution with those sixteen years later.

	1959	1975
National Health Budget	$22,000,000	$400,000,000
Hospital Beds	28,536	46,402
Blood Banks	1	22
Medical Schools	1	4
Physicians	6,000	10,000
	(3,000 left Cuba after the Revolution)	

Nursing Schools	1	34
Polio	300 cases a year	0
Malaria	3,000 cases a year	0
Diphtheria	600 cases a year	0
Gastroenteritis	4,000 deaths a year	761
Infant Mortality	60 per 1,000 live births	28.9
Life Expectancy	55 years	70

Cuba's network of health services extends beyond her boundaries. Cuba's first medical mission—sent to newly independent Algeria in 1962—has evolved into a permanent program of medical training and technical exchange. During the bombing of North Vietnam, twenty-one Cuban doctors and medical workers treated both victims of war and the general population. After the war, Cuba maintained a director and several physicians at the Vietnam-Cuba Friendship Hospital, training Vietnamese medical personnel.

Cuba has sent other medical teams to Peru, Guatemala, Nicaragua, and Chile to help during earthquakes and disasters.

At present, Cuba maintains medical missions in Vietnam, Ethiopia, Yemen, Somalia, Laos, Tanzania, Algeria, Guinea, Angola, Equatorial Guinea, Guinea-Bissau, and the Congo.

An American doctor who traveled to Cuba with a group from the American Public Health Association had high praise for the spirit of the doctors he met there:

Everyone I met seemed to be making their life decisions around what the community needs and wants. Doctors would frequently say, "I will work where the Revolution needs me." After completing their obligatory three years of rural medical service following medical school, they would, I think, be perfectly happy to stay on another five years if it was necessary. They receive satisfaction out of the group success and the group experience. That's a really exciting feeling, and to see it embraced by just about everybody I met made me think that socialism was a success in Cuba.

The practice of medicine, stripped of moneymaking, had been restored to its role of "healing art," as it seemed from a statement made by Cuban doctors in 1968:

Our medical service must be made more humane and scientific; each sick person should be cared for as if they were our own father, mother, spouse, or child. In this way, we will enrich ourselves, being more human to others.

WORK AND THE
WORKING PEOPLE

In the past, work was an instrument of exploitation of man. Today, it is an instrument for the redemption of man, for the elevation of man, for the progress of man.

—*FIDEL CASTRO, August 18, 1962*

Mayarí, on the northern coast of Oriente province: the Castro family came from these rich sugarcane plains that sweep from the green mountain chain of the northern Sierra—the Sierra de Nipe —to the coastal bays and beaches of the Caribbean. Before the Revolution, a single corporation—the United Fruit Company— owned these fields as far as the eye could see. Within these hold-ings stood the patches owned by poor peasants and the medium-sized lands of farmers like Fidel Castro's father. But the sea of cane belonged to United Fruit.

The people of the area called the company *Mama Yunaí,* (Mother United), dropping the English hard last syllable.

There are many who remember Mayarí before the arrival of the United Fruit Company, when there was no mill and no railroad.

In the spring of 1975 I passed through Mayarí, talking to old men about the time *cuando los americanos estaban aquí.* "Oh, yes, when the Americans were here. . . ."

I met Nino on a rainy day in his small wooden house in Mayarí. Within minutes the living room was crowded with his family— two sons who fought with the revolutionary army in the nearby mountains, women of three generations, children, neighbors, neighbors' children. The intermittent rain beat in gusts on the tin roof, making it almost impossible to hear; then it subsided, while everyone listened to Nino's stories.

Nino sat with one leg hooked over the arm of his rocking chair, a proud, vigorous patriarch, eighty-three years old, punctuating his remarks with powerful gestures and laughter, enjoying the rum we had brought. "Here I am," he said. "I was here before the Americans, before the Pseudo Republic, before Machado, before Batista—" He smiled and raised his glass. "And now they're all gone, and I'm sitting here drinking rum." He said it with the deep-rooted pride of one who had struggled and endured. "Oh, yes, when the Americans were here . . .

"When the Americans were here, they didn't associate with the Cubans; the Americans lived on one side, and the Cubans on the other. They had their system, and we had ours. What was it like? As if we were the dogs and they were the only real people. But I made them respect me, and they respected me.

"Only a few Cubans lived well, but really it was only the Americans who lived well because they had everything—the land, the sugar mill, the power with the government, and us living on whatever was around."

The listeners nodded. Now and then Nino would halt and announce that he had said enough and then be urged on: "Tell him about the time . . ." Or Nino would caution me, "We don't mean *all* the Americans, just the ones who exploited us.

"They had their private cops to guard their houses. You can be sure no poor or blacks or mestizos got in there." And laughing:

"They had so many guards not even the mosquitoes could get in the American district!"

Past times were not dwelled upon long. I suggested to Nino that there were those in the United States who thought socialism an evil system. This stirred him far more than memories of those who once had made life hell.

"Those who speak bad of socialism? You just have to tell them that this is the best there is!" he thundered over the tin rattle of the rain. "That the best there is is to live socially, each one looking out for the other without ambition as they are all humble, down to the littlest; that we have no millions—here there's none of that; here everyone is equal!

"What's of value here is the person"—his fingers drummed on his chest—"the honor, the dignity, the pride. Because before this, he who had money had everything, but Fidel came and said that here everyone is equal, and now we are all equal. There is no hunger. We have everything—doctors, medicine, and free for everyone. We endured more than thirty years trying to make a Revolution and justice, but we had no Fidel. Fidel came along, and now everyone has socialism. How could man live before, when there was no consideration for people . . . ?"

God help the person who would argue in favor of capitalism with old men in Cuba.

The road north from Mayarí parallels the tracks of the sugar railroad built by United Fruit through the rolling land that once was "Yunaí's." Nothing in the landscape has changed. The seedlings of next year's harvest glow green in the morning. It could be 1933 or 1895 until the car passes through a small village with its new school or polyclinic. It is as one draws closer to the Guatemala sugar mill, which slowly comes to dominate the landscape, magnetically drawing toward itself railroad and highway and houses, that the changes appear.

The barracks, the slums, and the shacks of years ago are gone. Nearby is the new Polytechnical Institute at which mill workers are trained and educated. The elegant mansion of the former mill boss, of dark Victorian tiled and paneled luxury, houses the community grade school. There was an exhibition of student projects in what had been the sunroom.

I had asked to meet with a retired or older worker who could tell me about the history of the mill, and I was introduced to three extraordinary old men: Joaquín Breff Guitierrez, aged seventy-seven; Manuel Fernandez Chaveco, sixty-nine; and Angel Leiba Cabrera, seventy.

We sat in the office of the administrator, a man in his thirties, my tape recorder trying to catch their words over the hum of a fan that stirred the hot air. Now and then a locomotive with a few cars would clank past under the trees outside.

As young boys they had lived in this zone before there was a sugar mill; each had worked here more than half a century, through labor struggles, dictatorships, coups, wars, revolutions, socialism. They were vigorous, engaged, and were pleased to tell their stories to an *Americano.*

JOAQUÍN: What was here before the company came? Only weeds and jungle. Then in 1905 they began to build the mill.

I started work in 1913 when I was fifteen years old. They let me work because they thought I was Spanish; they preferred the Jamaicans because they spoke English, or the Spanish; the Cubans, you see, weren't obedient. Cubans couldn't even work here at first. I began carrying firewood, because then the *central* used wood for fuel.

Later, when I started work as an operator of the evaporation tanks, there was racial discrimination; you had to be white to be in that department. What did I do during the *tiempo muerto?* I fished in the Bay. We went four, five, six months without work.

During that time I lived in the barracks for single men. The blacks lived in one area, called "Brooklyn" and the Americans in another, called "Washington." The head of the *central* lived in a two-story house, him and his wife and nine Jamaican servants, two cars with two chauffeurs. When the house needed repairs, the workmen had to take off their shoes before they entered and put on rubber slippers, and be quiet; you weren't supposed to talk.

ANGEL: We were living very oppressed here, very, very oppressed; you can't imagine it, my boy. When *Mama Yunaí* was here, the Rural Guards used to beat us with the flat of the machete.

When the Americans were here, they had these three recreational centers—one just for the Americans; I couldn't put my face in there. In "Brooklyn" there was a club for the blacks. The Pan-American Club—the one for the Americans—had a swimming pool, but of course it was only for them. There was a street on which only Americans could walk, Washington Avenue.

We had two cemeteries here. One was for the poor and the black, and the other for rich people. If you were a high-level Cuban employee, you could be buried in the rich American cemetery, but if you were poor, you went to the other one. They were four hundred yards apart. The funerals cost a lot of money.

Now, since the Revolution, of course the funerals are free, and we say, To die, all you have to provide is the corpse. Everything is taken care of by the Revolution. We don't want to die, of course, but when we do, everything is taken care of.

MANUEL: I started working in 1920, and I liked the idea of the union very much, and I've seen and been in many a strike. In 1921 we elected a union committee, and we planned to call a strike. Well, as soon as we had the meeting, the Rural Guard knew.

We were having a meeting in "Brooklyn" when Captain Sando brought the army out from Mayarí to break it up. We had to get out of there fast! We couldn't do a thing against their "Machete Plan."* A lot of comrades went to jail; they really smashed it.

But we took courage and went at it again. You know, we couldn't meet in public, so we had to meet during our baseball games. We'd hold a big game and during it hold planning meetings.

---

* *"Plan de machete,"* an ironic Cuban term describing repression, from the habit of the Rural Guards of beating people with the flat of their machetes.

The three men had saddened, recounting the bitter struggles of the past. I changed the subject to the Revolution—and it was as if someone beautiful had entered the room.

ANGEL: I was taken to Havana—something that had never happened in all the history of my people here! I have never seen any company taking the old people on such a beautiful trip as the one we had. They took us all over Havana, treated us so well, gave us everything we could have wanted.

I'd always think to myself, when I'm done working and retire, where am I going to live? This was always one of the things I worried about—*where am I going to live after I retire?* After the Revolution came, I saw fields of light open up! I saw that I had a house with five rooms, with water and electricity—without paying anything—all my life! What beauty is this—eh? And I'm here until I die. Truly a beautiful thing. Let me tell you, *chico,* I have been and will be a Communist, all my life!

The enthusiasm expressed toward the Revolution by the three retired old workers at the Guatemala sugar mill was shared by most workers in Cuba. It was so real, in fact, that for many years a system of "organized enthusiasm" kept the economy running against all odds. "I feel more free," another worker at the mill said. "Before, we worked for money, but now we struggle for the good of everyone."

This spirit caused Cuban men and women to make incredible sacrifices at the Bay of Pigs, during the Missile Crisis, Hurricane Flora, and in confronting the U.S. blockade. One could sense it every day in the factories, fields, and neighborhoods.

The leaders of the Revolution came to believe that tapping this enthusiasm was the major way to organize the massive work necessary to build a socialist society. People would be motivated to work by their love for the Revolution and by the good it did the people as a whole, rather than by the enticement of individual material reward.

This flowed from their vision of a Communist society in which all would live, "As if every one of his fellow citizens was really his brother."

As in a military campaign, they thought that the Communist Party could direct from the top a massive economic effort during the latter half of the 1960's, culminating in a record harvest in 1970, that would bring Cuba out of underdevelopment.

This is the story of why that massive effort failed.

It begins with the question of motivation: What makes a man or woman get up in the morning and work a full day?

Before the Revolution the answer boiled down to money— money to live on, money to improve one's lot in society, money to provide for one's family.

When there was high unemployment and poverty, there was another motivation: fear—fear of losing one's job, failing to support one's family, fear that one's children would not have the advantages sought for them.

Once unemployment was eliminated and free schooling and health care were provided by the Revolution, these old "material incentives" to work were lessened or abolished. Believing, as Raúl Castro said, that "we will never create socialist consciousness with a dollar sign in the minds and hearts of our men and women," the Cuban leaders tried to replace material incentives with "moral incentives."

They did not entirely abandon such material rewards as overtime pay, trips abroad, scarce commodities, such as refrigerators, or special vacations for those who made an extra effort or did high-quality work. But they placed their emphasis on moral incentives. Appealing to the "spirit of Playa Girón" and the "spirit of

October" (referring to the Missile Crisis), they would reward a factory that over fulfilled its quota with a banner. A community rally would be held to honor the workers. Newspaper articles would be written praising a worker who had given his free time to the factory or cut the most sugarcane. They did their best to restore honor and pride to work itself, to imbue it with heroism.

The people responded, as they had on so many other occasions, with enthusiasm, rallying as if under wartime conditions. Yet, ironically, the very way work was being organized began to make things go awry. The moral vision of the leadership and their desire for justice was not wrong, but as it turned out, they were ignoring certain laws and practices that had proved necessary in other countries building a socialist society. In Cuba, the first institutions that suffered from this neglect were the trade unions.

Before the Revolution, a trade union was the basic weapon a worker had with which to defend himself. Even when the union was corrupt, it was better than facing the employer alone, becoming an easy victim of layoffs, cutbacks, wage cuts, speed-ups, and bad working conditions.

The job of the union then was to defend the worker's rights, to increase wages to meet rising prices, to improve working conditions. But within a few years after the overthrow of the Batista dictatorship, all this was turned on its head.

Suddenly there were no more bosses. The owners of the factories, the rich plantation families, the landlords—all were gone, fled to Miami and points North. Workers were in charge of the factories and the sugar mills.

The best union before the Revolution was the one that fought the employer the hardest. Now this had changed. The new administrator was a man or woman who a month before had been cutting cane, or working on the assembly line.

What was the union supposed to do now? A strike would be a strike against the Revolution, against the people of Cuba themselves. Now that the profits were going to build schools, roads, houses, and hospitals instead being pocketed by the owners, the unions had a new responsibility.

The best interest of the workers now lay not in striking, not in lowering profits, but in higher production, working harder and with more efficiency, cooperating with the new administrator.

Since the task of encouraging higher production and harder work had been assumed by the Party, and since the union was no longer needed to defend the worker against the boss, the unions were allowed to wither and were replaced by organizations of "vanguard workers"—those who worked hardest and best.

Without strong trade unions, the workers lost the means to make their desires or their problems known. An important link between the workers and the government was severed.

The more committed workers gradually began to feel as if they were carrying the ball for those not so committed, since not everyone was equally motivated. The vanguard workers gave up their Saturdays to do volunteer work in the cane fields, or chipped in to do unpaid overtime work to make sure their factory filled its monthly quota. And they began to resent those who did not.

The less-committed workers, for their part, also became frustrated and resentful. No one was paying attention to them. They got no prizes for their work. They didn't get their pictures in the paper.

Meanwhile another problem appeared, which also affected people's motivation to work. Wages were gradually being increased, but the trade embargo against Cuba meant that fewer consumer goods were available. Workers had little on which to spend their money.

The surplus of money undermined the values the Revolution was trying to instill. Those less moved by moral incentives felt less compulsion to work. Why should a high school graduate go to work if the family had plenty of money? Why should a woman, trained as a teacher, work when her husband made enough for both of them and wanted her to stay at home and cook?

Some people found they could make more money by opening a little fried-fish stand outside the gates of a factory than by working inside. Others hired themselves out to stand in line for scarce commodities or to do people's laundry while they were at work. A thousand-and-one private businesses and services sprang up. To its horror, the Revolution discovered that it was spawning a growing class of small businessmen, who in turn were hiring others for profit, often paying more than the state paid. A new capitalism was thriving off the benefits that socialism had brought, promoting the values of private profit, selfishness, hoarding, and black-marketeering that the Revolution sought to eliminate.

By downgrading material incentives, the Revolution had unwittingly permitted the growth of incentives of the opposite kind, incentives to loaf and to profiteer. In Las Villas an investigation discovered an individual entrepreneur who farmed out work to three hundred women, supplying them with scraps of material he picked up here and there from which they were making rope and hammocks, all at a tidy profit!

Hoarding was common. The owner of a private shoe store would save the best shoes for his friends, or sell them on the black market for higher than the legal price. The result was an unequal and unfair distribution of scarce and needed items. Workers complained of the growing rudeness and lack of respect shown by small businessmen. Rather than wasting away as the Revolution advanced, half of these small businesses had popped up after the Revolution.

To solve this crisis, Fidel in 1968 called for a "Revolutionary Offensive," in which all these small businesses were nationalized. These nationalizations were completely unlike the seizures of big industry in 1960.

No troops were called in. There was little or no sabotage or resistance. The nationalization of the small businesses was carried out mostly by the CDR (Committees for the Defense of the Revolution).

Those who took command of the stores were in large part the consumers themselves. It was necessary only for a CDR representative to come to the store and be given the financial books and records. The bank accounts were frozen while the transfer of control took place. If it was felt the owner could be trusted, he stayed on as the manager—at a salary. Many shop owners, no longer able to make money off their fellow citizens, left the country.

The target the Cuban people had set for themselves, for which the massive work campaigns of the late 1960's were in preparation, was a ten-million-ton sugar harvest in 1970. That would be, by far, the largest harvest in Cuban history and would hopefully provide the income with which they could fully mechanize the sugar industry, pay off their foreign debts, reduce the unfavorable balance of trade with the other socialist countries, and lay the base for a leap forward in housing, social services, and consumer goods.

"The question of a sugar harvest of ten million tons has become something more than an economic goal," Fidel said in 1968.

> It is something that has become a point of honor for this Revolution. It has become a yardstick by which to judge the capability of this Revolution. Our enemies have bet that we won't reach it.
>
> A colossal effort is being made . . . thousands of men have been working intensively for months, day and night, throughout the island. . . . Havana workers can very often see the tractor lights as they work late into the night and even into the early morning hours.

It was not many weeks into the 1970 harvest, however, that they discovered they would not succeed in reaping the ten million tons. Though they did harvest over eight million tons of sugar—the largest amount in Cuban history—they were unable to meet the goal on which they had staked their honor.

At a mass rally after the harvest was completed, Fidel reported to the people that the leadership had analyzed what had gone wrong and why.

It was not the fault of the Cuban people, Fidel said, but of the leaders of the Revolution, particularly himself. The working people had not been consulted enough in making the plans for the harvest. Instead, the Communist Party had tried to run the whole effort from the top. This had to change. More power in decision-making must be given to the people.

He pointed out in detail how the effort to achieve the ten-million-ton harvest had disrupted the entire economy of Cuba. Production in every other area had decreased. Transportation had been disrupted. Inefficiency was rife.

Moral incentives alone were not enough. By relying on mobilizations, campaigns, and voluntary unpaid labor, the Cuban government had lost track of expenses and costs. This was no way to run a business, let alone a nation's economy.

"Our enemies say we have problems, and in this our enemies are right," Fidel said. "They say there is discontent, and in reality our enemies are right. They say there is irritation, and in reality our enemies are right.

"We couldn't care less about the enemy. The embarrassment will be welcome if we know how to turn our shame into strength, if we know how to turn the shame into a will to work, if we know how to turn the shame into dignity and into morale!"

A century earlier, Karl Marx, the originator of modern Communist and socialist thought, had put forth certain laws that a country should follow in order to build a socialist economy. In their desire to leap rapidly toward the goal of socialist equality and justice, the Cuban revolutionaries had ignored much of Marx's advice and the experience of other socialist countries.

Looking back at the failure to achieve the ten-million-ton harvest, Fidel later said, with painful honesty, that every revolution has its "utopian periods," when it seems as if "men's will, wishes and intentions . . . can accomplish anything."

"Without some dreams and utopia," he added, "there would be no revolutionaries."

But dreams are not enough.

"From the very beginning, the Cuban Revolution did not take advantage of the rich experience of other peoples who had undertaken the construction of socialism long before we had," Fidel said.

> Had we been humbler, had we not had excessive self-esteem, we would have been able to understand that revolutionary theory was not sufficiently developed in our country and that we actually lacked profound economics and scientists of Marxism to make really significant contributions to the theory and practice of building socialism. We would have searched with a modesty befitting revolutionaries for everything that can be learned from these sources and applied in the specific conditions of our country.

Beginning in 1970, the leaders of the Revolution began to rethink all that they had done. To correct their mistakes, they turned to the organizations of the Cuban people—the "mass organizations" of workers, women, students, and peasants. Five years later, they had created an entirely new government, changed the role of the trade unions, restructured the economy, written a new constitution, and even redrawn the map of the country.

WORKERS, PEASANTS, WOMEN, NEIGHBORS

The People of Cuba Organize Themselves

The secret is among the people. The great truth is there: in the people.

— *MELBA HERNÁNDEZ, 1975*

The mass organizations of Cuba—to which almost every Cuban belongs—are the bedrock of public activity. Without them there would be no Revolution. They are the people's organizations through which each major sector of the population—workers, peasants, women, and neighbors—defends and represents its interests and makes its feelings, problems, and opinions known.

In the agonizing reappraisal that followed the failure of the ten-million-ton harvest, the leaders of the Revolution moved to strengthen these organizations to give the people a greater voice in finding solutions to the crisis. The mass organizations grew sharply in numbers, strength, and importance.

Joining a mass organization is a matter of individual choice. Any woman who supports the Revolution can join the *Federación de Mujeres Cubanas,* (Federation of Cuban Women), or FMC.

Peasants owning their own land can join the *Asociación Nacionál de Agricultores Pequeñas* (National Association of Small Farmers), or ANAP. For workers there are the unions of the *Central de Trabajadores de Cuba* (Confederation of Cuban Workers) or CTC. The community organizations found on every block in Cuba's towns, are part of the CDR (Committees for the Defense of the Revolution).

A woman working in a factory might belong to the FMC, the CTC, and her neighborhood CDR chapter, and many do. The organizations overlap, but each embodies a basic role or condition in Cuban society: work—the CTC and ANAP; community life—CDR; or work, family, and the role of women—FMC.

They are indeed mass organizations. Four out of every five Cuban women over the age of fourteen belong to the FMC. Eighty percent of the population over fourteen are members of the CDR. Almost all the workers in the factories and the fields have joined the CTC and ANAP.

THE WORKERS

Sometimes we speak of developing the awareness of our workers, but the fact is that our workers' awareness has developed greatly. Often we must ask ourselves if it isn't we [the leaders] who must drink from that fount, from that revolutionary awareness that has developed among our workers.

—*FIDEL CASTRO, August 30, 1970*

From 1970 to 1973, the trade unions, the government, and the party worked furiously to revitalize the Cuban labor movement, which had gone into eclipse during the 1960's. In the process of creating a strong trade-union organization through which the workers could make their needs and opinions felt, they held a staggering number of meetings. In 1971 alone, meetings were held in 5,595 local work centers to discuss the workers' problems and complaints. New elections were held in 35,000 union locals to bring in new leadership. By May 1, 1973—the traditional workers' holiday—twenty-one new national unions had been formed.

A new vigor and dignity animated the trade-union movement as workers discussed wage policies, work efficiency, participation by workers in economic planning, the role of voluntary labor, and material and moral incentives. These discussions and reorganization culminated in the Thirteenth National Congress of the Central Organization of Cuban Trade Unions (CTC), held in November 1973.

For Lázaro Peña, the "grand old man" of Cuban labor (then in poor health and without long to live), the Thirteenth CTC Congress was the high point of a career begun as a teenager in the Havana cigar factories.

The most important decision made by the congress was to institute a simple but profound economic law that underlies the building of socialism. Formulated by Karl Marx, this law states, "From each according to his abilities, to each according to his work."*

In other words, since the fruits of labor are shared by everyone in the society, it is expected that each person will contribute to the best of his or her abilities, whether cutting cane, teaching school, or driving a bus. In return, society rewards the individual with wages that are proportional to the quantity and quality of his work.

This was the law that was ignored during the 1960's. Under the

---

*Marx, in his 1875 essay, "Critique of the Gotha Program," argued that in a *higher* phase of communist society, when there is abundant wealth, wages can be paid according to the rule: "From each according to his ability, to each according to his needs." Before that higher stage is reached, however, the society cannot meet all of a person's needs, and the wealth of a country is still distributed unequally, according to a person's work.

system of moral incentives, campaigns, and voluntary labor, one's wages had little relation to the work one did.

Marx's rule of work and wages is a sort of first cousin to the golden rule. To the individual worker it says, If you give more and better work to society, society will give you, in return, more and better. It also provides a way of measuring productivity that was lacking before.

How does this work out in practice in a Cuban factory that produces, for example, gears for a sugar mill? The workers and the management first meet and discuss all the problems involved: How many gears are needed, what the plant's capacity is, what shape the machinery is in, the health and safety of the workers, and their physical capability.

Together they work out a *norm:* each worker is expected to be able to produce fifteen gears in a normal eight-hour day. If the worker then mills fifteen gears in a day, he receives the normal salary. If he grinds eighteen, he is paid extra, in proportion to what he has done. If he makes only ten, his salary is proportionately lower.

Of those voting at the Thirteenth CTC Congress 99.1 percent approved this measure, which completely overhauled the old distorted wage policy. Under the old policy, two workers doing the same work often received different wages (because one had earned more before the Revolution). Another two might be paid the same, though one of them worked twice as hard.

By introducing self-interest, the plan encourages self-discipline. "To live well," it tells the workers, "you have to work well." The worker sees in his paycheck each week the immediate benefit of showing up on time and working with discipline and efficiency. With everyone working harder, the resentment between the more conscientious workers and the less decreased, and was replaced by a common sense of cooperation.

There are critics of Cuba who say that this is reintroducing selfish motives, making personal gain the reason for working, rather than love for society. The Cubans reply that they are being realistic. People come to love work by working, not by slacking off. Patriotic appeals and moral rewards only reach those who are already most responsive.

By the end of 1975, the new labor policy was bringing about sharp increases in productivity and morale. The rejuvenated labor movement was ready to take part in planning and carrying out the first economic Five Year Plan (1976–80).

A few months after the Thirteenth Congress, the ailing Lázaro Peña died. The body of the man who had founded the CTC in 1939 and faced company goons and police in the dock strike of 1948, was accompanied to the Colón Cemetery in Havana by thousands of mourners. "He wasn't born in a socialist regime," Fidel said at Peña's grave. "He was born and grew up under the cruel and ferocious capitalist society. And he was not born in a golden cradle; he was born poor, where being poor was synonymous with humiliation and anguish. He was born black in a society where human beings were discriminated against because of the color of their skin. . . .

"We're Communists. This means we're workers in the historic process that gets written with sweat, blood, life, and also with men's hopes. Some time ago we said there were many men like Camilo [Cienfuegos] among the people; now we say that there are many men like Lázaro among the workers."

THE PEASANTS

To the Rebel Army the peasant progressively gave his vigor, capacity to suffer, knowledge of the terrain, love of the land, and hunger for agrarian reform.

—CHE GUEVARA, 1960

When the ANAP (National Association of Small Farmers) was founded in May 1961, the leaders of the Revolution made a solemn pledge to the peasants:

> FIDEL: What is the policy of the Revolution? The most absolute respect for the will and the desires of the *campesino*. If he wants to spend his life alone, working and cultivating as he wishes, as he sees fit, the Revolution respects whatever the *campesino* thinks is best for himself, what he likes best.

The Revolution honored this commitment. In 1975, almost a third of the agricultural land of Cuba was still in the hands of 162,000 private peasant owners, who, with their families, raised 26 percent of the livestock, 18 percent of the sugarcane, 80 percent of the tobacco, 75 percent of the coffee, and slightly less than 50 percent of the fruits and vegetables (1975 figures). These members of ANAP were grouped in some six thousand "base committees" throughout the island.

In the spring of 1975, I traveled with an ANAP agricultural adviser to one of these base committees outside Holguín, in Oriente province. He picked me up in town in a new Toyota Land Rover. After about a twenty-minute drive we turned off the two-lane highway and entered a network of dirt roads, rutted by the spring rains. Another hour along roads that only a horse or a Land Rover could negotiate, fording swollen streams which at the height of the rainy season would be impassable, and we were deep in wooded foothills.

Over coffee and a noon offering of rum, I met with five representatives of the base—peasant men ranging from their mid-forties to seventy-five—in a clean-swept thatched-roof home just off the muddy road.

One of the first topics was the remoteness of the area, the seeming isolation.

"Listen," said the oldest and most animated of the men, chief of production plans in the area, "before the Revolution, we didn't even dream of visiting Holguín. There were people here who didn't know the city existed! All my life, for sixty years, we knew nothing of 'the plain.' We lived here, worked here, died here. Then, in 1959 I went to Santiago for the first time. There were thousands of us—peasants—staying in the homes of the city people there. I never thought I'd see such a sight!

"You can see how it's all changed. There's a young man from our area working, building a hospital, in Vietnam. Traveling by plane! Whoever imagined? We have children studying on the Isle of Pines; they go by plane. I got sick. I flew to Havana by plane, and the next day I was back. We have children studying in the Soviet Union, in the German Democratic Republic.

"What we have now seems like a dream. Before there was one school two miles away. Only a few children could go. There was no doctor, no hospital. You had to sell your vote to get into a hospital. After the harvest, if there was no one to buy your crops you had to throw them away. It was the worst, son, the very worst."

Though they own their own parcels of land, work is now communal for all but a very few. Most farmers have joined agricultural "plans" grouped by area or crops (tobacco, cane, fruits, vegetables). They buy their seeds, fertilizers, farm implements, and irrigation equipment from the state. Agricultural experts from the National Institute of Agrarian Reform (INRA) keep them up to date on advances in agricultural technology. The National Bank extends credit and loans for improvements in the land.

Crops not used for personal and family consumption are sold to government agencies at fixed prices. The peasants are no longer at the mercy of a market that seesaws with the weather, nor are they the victims of oversupply, which used to wipe out the result of a year's hard labor. They are also allowed to sell surplus crops privately, a recent reform that has increased the amount of vegetables available on the open market.

Cuba's population is now double the five million of 1953: The amount of agricultural land, however, cannot be increased. Cuba must feed her people by making her agriculture more efficient, by producing more crops per acre than ever before. Every inch of arable land must be used. This means that eventually the individual peasant farm will be a thing of the past, for such a system is too inefficient to produce enough food in a modern society. But because of the Revolution's pledge, this must be done slowly and voluntarily.

"Will you miss the old way of life, the old holdings?" I asked the men in the front room of the *bohio* in the hills near Holguín.

"No, no, no!" one answered, gesturing with hands grained like old wood. "We're going to have buildings, with electricity. The kids will go to school nearby, just like in the cities.

"That's what ANAP has decided. We're going to go step by step, carefully, planning it all. We'll unite all the land for progress. Everything is up to us. You see, we know how it will benefit us. We can touch the benefits. Everything is bigger now, better. The whole concept is grander. We can fertilize the whole area at once. Life will be easier, more productive."

(Later, back in Holguín, I ran into a middle-aged construction worker at the site where a new school was being built. Until a year before he had worked a small plot of land in the country. Then he had sold it to the state and moved to the city. "Don't you miss it?" I asked. "Are you kidding?" he replied. "What kind of life was that? All that hard work for a little patch of yucca. No, sir. I wanted to come here, *where the action is!*")

The agricultural plans and the Schools in the Countryside are radically changing an impoverished way of life whose passing no one regrets. By 1970, 165 new rural towns, built from scratch were making their appearance—models of a coming urbanization that will erase the hated cultural and economic boundary between the countryside and the more affluent cities.

If a peasant family want to leave their farm and move to these new towns, they may. If they want to remain where they are, that is their own choice.

There is a little ceremony for those who choose to move to the new rural towns. After their possessions have been removed from the old thatched hut, the family lights a torch and sets fire to their former home. In an instant, the past is burned away.

The typical new town to which they move contains a medical clinic, post office, barber shop, social center, laundry service, shopping center, school, and sports center. These services were unheard of to the average peasant family before the Revolution.

The small plot they leave is then combined with other state-owned land. Using large-scale equipment and modern fertilizers the yield per acre can sometimes be increased as much as twenty fold.

FIDEL: The country has to be completely transformed. Columbus is supposed to have said—we do not have a recording—that this was the most beautiful land human eyes had ever beheld. One day it will again be said that this is the most beautiful land human eyes have beheld, this time not for the beauty of the landscape, but for the work of man.

In the ANAP farmer's house outside Bayamo, a chubby little boy who had been peeking around the door edge into the front room decided to give the stranger with the note pad a gift—a pencil that he clutched as he made his way across the room and heaved himself up on the wooden bench beside me. With immense five-year-old seriousness he thrust the pencil forward, and I thanked him. The men chuckled.

"They are the hope of our hope," the eldest said.

The boy beside me would never scrape his living from a small plot of land as they had done.

"They have the whole future," the old man said, looking at the child who was now wondering if he could take the pencil back. "The future is all smiles to this new generation."

THE WOMEN

Hidden in the deepest woods, suffering hunger, nakedness, and sickness, exposed to the brutal rage of an inhuman soldiery who persecuted them without respite and mistreated them without pity, fleeing with their children through the rough brambled mountains, the Cuban women suffered, cried and prayed for the liberation of Cuba. With good reason it is said that this is the war of the women.

—A GENERAL IN THE 1868 WAR OF INDEPENDENCE

"Cuba's wars of independence were, one could say, *family* wars," a Cuban writer has said. "With the peasant, the woman left for the mountains, taking with her all those in her home." Vilma Espin, president of the FMC (Federation of Cuban Women), adds, "In the jungle she shared the dangers with her husband, caring for and curing the wounded, carrying out with admirable endurance the thousands of tasks that made more bearable the hard struggle of the rebel soldier."

Mariana Grajales, after whom the first women's platoon in Fidel's army was named, was one of the titanic figures in the 1868 war of independence. When the uprising broke out, she had her sons swear an oath that they would fight for their country "until they were free or were killed," and then followed them into the Cuban jungles, sharing the rigors of war for ten years. One by one she lost them, first her husband, then her grandsons, and finally her sons, including the best known—General Antonio Maceo.

Ana Betancourt worked underground in Camagüey province, sending arms, supplies, clothes, books, and information on the movement of Spanish troops to the liberating army. When the insurrection reached Camagüey, late in 1868, she abandoned her home and made her way to the mountains, where she stayed with the rebels for three years.

At an assembly of rebel leaders to frame a new Cuban constitution in 1869, Ana Betancourt addressed them, linking for the first time in Latin America the struggle of women to the movement for independence:

> Citizens: The Cuban woman, in the dark and tranquil corner of her home, has been patiently awaiting this sublime hour, in which a just revolution breaks her yoke and frees her wings. . . .
>
> The slavery of color no longer exists, you have emancipated the slave.
>
> When the moment arrives to liberate the woman, the Cuban who has done away with the slavery of birth and of race, will devote his generous soul to the conquest of the rights of she who today is his self-sacrificing sister of charity who tomorrow will be, as she was yesterday, his exemplary comrade.

Independence from Spain did not bring equality for women. Not until 1934, after the overthrow of the Machado dictatorship, did Cuban women receive the right to vote. Under pressure from the newly organized trade-union movement and the Communists, the constitution of 1940 wrote into law the principle of equal pay for equal work, declared discrimination by sex to be illegal, offered equal civil rights to married women, and protection for the working mother.

The laws stayed on the books, but were never enforced until after the Cuban Revolution.

In the fall of 1960 the several revolutionary women's groups were unified in the FMC. Vilma Espín, an organizer with Frank País of the 1956 uprising in Santiago and the underground movement in Oriente province, was elected president.

One of the first acts of the FMC was to establish the Ana Betancourt School for peasant women. The Ana Betancourt School brought thousands of young women from the countryside, teaching them reading, basic skills, and hygiene. By 1963, ten thousand women were entering each year. In return, the school asked one commitment: that each return to her village and teach ten other women what she had learned.

The FMC, to which 80 percent of Cuban women over the age of fourteen belong, has participated in every mobilization, campaign and day-to-day task of the Revolution: building the militia, mobilizing during Playa Girón and the October Missile Crisis, organizing the literacy campaign, educating peasant women and domestic workers for productive jobs, encouraging women to take jobs outside the home, supporting the educational and public-health campaigns, and raising the political consciousness of Cuban women.

The core of the FMC's work, around which all other tasks revolve, is the involvement of women in productive work—a prerequisite for the full equality of women.

The FMC early understood that equality of men and women on paper meant nothing as long as women were confined to the home, to domestic work, the kitchen, and the children. Women had to be drawn into a larger orbit. Like the peasant, they had to go "where the action is."

The Revolution could not simply decree that women find work outside the home. It had to provide day-care centers for the children, public laundry services, shopping and cooking services....

At the same time, the Revolution had to fight old cultural attitudes, habits, and prejudices of men and women alike. The FMC found that when men saw women ably carrying out jobs not traditionally theirs, the men's attitude began to change—and the women's also.

This struggle is still being carried on in every organization in Cuba: in the trade unions—to open up jobs for women and to convince male workers that it is in their interest to do so; in the CDR, the community organization—to work out problems in the home and help provide services that make it easier for women to leave the house; in the government—to provide services for working women and young children and to convince reluctant administrators to hire women; and in the Communist Party—to carry out educational campaigns against old prejudices.

By 1974, attitudes had changed sufficiently for them to be written into law in the form of a new "family code" that replaced the antique social code in force since the days of Spanish rule.

The family code eliminated legal discrimination against women and children. It gave men and women equal rights and responsibilities within the marriage, joint control over the property of the family, and equal responsibilities for child-rearing, education, and even housework. It established the rights of children to stability, care, love, health, and education.

What do Cuban men think of the provisions of the family code? It seems their greatest concern is the equal sharing of housework. In 1975, *Bohemia* magazine ran a frank series of "Man in the Street" interviews with men from all walks of life, which shows them to be grappling, more or less successfully, with a new image of themselves and women.

A Havana bus driver responded:

Well, my wife was working until 1964, but then the children came along, and there was no day care center to take care of them. So, little by little, she turned simply into a housewife, and me, well, I adapted to it, I got used to it.

But then something happened that at the time I didn't understand. My sister-in-law came to stay with us, and that produced sort of a spark in my wife. She got interested in a course she read about in a magazine. I was surprised a little, but when I started to think about it, I realized that I'd been egotistic, so I didn't try to oppose her desires.

Now she's working, the course is over. And you know what? She's a chauffeur for a car-rental service. That doesn't seem like a job for a woman, right? But it's not that way.

About your question on housework. Well, I help her. I even (please don't put this down) do some of the washing. She's a good cook, me,

I'm regular. But in my own defense, I wouldn't starve to death if she didn't cook. Nevertheless, you should taste my coffee. . . .

Can a woman work with the same ability as a man? Listen, I know a woman comrade . . . a little while ago she moved into a new building they just finished around here, in Vedado. And believe me, she earned it. She worked for two years on the microbrigade that built the building. That's the truth!

Even those who don't like the code feel the weight of public opinion on them. A thirty-two-year-old divorced man:

I don't agree that a woman should work outside and neglect her house, her husband and her children. I don't mind if she works as long as she takes care of my house. When I got divorced, my wife wasn't working. I learned how to take care of myself in the Army. Now I'm alone and I do everything around the house. Children? Three girls and a boy. Who should educate them? Their mama, the school. . . . I don't have anything to do with that. Sure I think the boy should do chores—little ones. Listen, wait! No, no! Don't take my photo!

There is no doubt that the campaign to bring women into the work force is making headway. By 1980 there were 800,600 working women in Cuba (30 percent of the work force), more than three times the number in 1953. Relations between men and women will be further improved by the new generation of young people graduating from the Schools in the Countryside—young men and women who have worked side by side in the fields, who have spent their school years in a more egalitarian environment, and on whom the prejudices of the past will have a far weaker influence.

NEIGHBORS

I want to tell you that the Americans always refer to you with great respect, and, I'd say, with fear. Each time they refer to the CDR

they say "the powerful Committees for the Defense of the Revolu-
tion." And really, you are.

—*RAÚL CASTRO TO THE LEADERS OF THE CDR, 1968*

A residential block of small stucco-and-frame houses across from
a neighborhood park on a tree-lined street in Holguín. A warm,
humid evening in May:

During the war against Batista, the body of a young revolutionary named Dagoberto San Fiél was dumped from a police car on
this block. Today the local chapter of the CDR (Committees for
the Defense of the Revolution) carries his name. It is meeting
specially tonight to explain their day-to-day activities to this
American writer, at the home of the chapter president.

There are at least twenty people crowded in the small living
room, some standing, others sitting on benches brought in from
outside. Within a few minutes, everyone is sweating and fanning
themselves. A few move just outside the front door and peer in.
When I ask my first question, "How did this committee come to
be formed?" everyone turns to a woman in her sixties, the founder
of the chapter and the mother of the current president.

"It began in September 1960," she says, "right after Fidel's
speech during which some bombs exploded. It was so easy to
organize; all the neighbors wanted to participate. During those
days it was a vigilance organization. Later we started working on
sharing supplies, distributing lard, and other activities as a result
of the blockade. Then came Playa Girón, and we joined the public
defense."

Playa Girón was the CDR's trial by fire, coming six months
after their founding. Their members' vigilance totally paralyzed
the domestic attempts of the counterrevolution to aid the invasion
force. That's when the CIA came to realize that the Revolution
had the overwhelming support of the Cuban population.

"During the Missile Crisis we did guard duty day and night; we kept the streets clean, working around the clock. Women went to the factories to replace the men who were called up for defense."

By that time, there were a hundred thousand CDR chapters, one in every neighborhood in the land. The first mass-vaccination campaign was carried out by the CDR at the height of the crisis, while ten thousand members donated blood for the armed forces.

"At the time of Hurricane Flora [1964], we set up a dormitory for refugees across the street in the school. Everyone cooperated, bringing supplies to the school, maintaining vigilance. The stores couldn't keep the food too long because of the damage, so the CDR chapters distributed the food to the neighborhoods." The next year the CDR mobilized half a million people to work in the sugar harvest on Saturdays and Sundays. Another three hundred thousand worked in the fruit harvest. That same year, in a period of seventy-two hours, they immunized two million children against polio. By 1965, the CDR had two million members and were concentrating on strengthening the educational system. Seven hundred thousand CDR members joined study circles; others helped in the construction and repair of schools, roads, and drainage ditches.

"We did an enormous amount of work for Vietnam, holding meetings, rallies, contributing blood donations. We all collected clothes, and donated part of our sugar ration for Vietnam. We told them we were ready to go there to fight if it was necessary. When the terrible earthquake happened in Peru, we also donated our blood."

In 1970, the year of the Peruvian earthquake, 1,005,747 people joined the CDR, bringing its membership to almost four million.

I asked about the day-to-day activities of the chapter. The president introduced those in the room who headed each of the group's activities.

The administrator was an older woman, very shy, who asked me to promise not to look at her while she gave her report. I promised, and stared fixedly at my note pad while she spoke.

She keeps what one could call the "Book of the Block," a remarkable inventory of all that takes place there. On this block, she explained, there are sixty-one people, belonging to sixteen families. When someone leaves the block, moves away or is traveling for a long period, that fact is recorded. Each person's responsibility for tasks on the block is marked down and checked off when completed. One gets the impression of a supra-family, large and perfectly organized. Everything is entered in the great Book of the Block; when people are born and die, when they move to the block and when they leave, how old they are, how many children, and if they are in school.

"The counterrevolutionaries used to be our primary task," the man in charge of vigilance told me, "but there are hardly any counterrevolutionaries anymore." He showed me a map of the zone, marked with the location of schools and commercial centers. Everyone did his or her turn on guard duty; women from eight to midnight, men from midnight to four in the morning. It was rotated so that each person on the average did guard duty about once a month. This was the oldest of the activities and a source of great pride. Knowing the city intimately, they felt completely safe.

The man in charge of political education was also shy, but the others, fanning themselves vigorously, encouraged him to speak. As each report was given, the atmosphere in the room became more close, friendly, and supportive. Some were eager to talk; others nervously reviewed their notes in anticipation, knowing they'd be next in line. People commented to one another about what was being said; children were shushed.

"We analyze and study all the national and international news and all the laws and measures taken by the government," he said.

"Right now we're studying the draft of the new Cuban constitution." He showed me the draft, which looked like a special issue of a newspaper. On the back was a study guide and a full-page form to fill out: Do you agree? Do you disagree? What measures should be taken out, changed, added?

"We try to help the children at school," the woman in charge of education said, "and we encourage the parents to take an interest in the children's education. If a child flunks a class (this doesn't happen on our block), we would try to find out what the problem is and see if there's some way to solve it."

Her committee also helps the children form ballet and dance classes, and musical and poetry groups, she explained.

She was very proud of the craft workshop, and I was taken outside to admire a kind of paper lamp the members made by the hundreds for festivals and celebrations, festooning the houses and streets.

"Then for the July 26 Carnival and the celebration of September 28 [the national CDR Day], a boy and a girl are chosen to be the stars. . . ." Everyone interrupted to make sure I understood that this wasn't a beauty contest.

"No, no! The stars are chosen for their qualities as students and neighbors and workers and people. It's a great honor and a real stimulus for the children."

It was after midnight. The sweat was beginning to blot out my notes, but no one had left. The conversation became more informal. I told them that they certainly didn't seem like the "dreaded vigilance committees" pictured in anti-Cuban propaganda. They laughed. From what I had heard that evening, I said, the Revolution seemed deeply rooted in the people.

"You see," said one softly to her neighbor, "he understands."

I found out later that there had been an undercurrent of hesitation at first: Should they tell the American stranger all the details of what they did? Would he report exactly what they said? They did, and I have tried. It was one o'clock in the morning when the meeting broke up. The children had long since gone to bed. Everyone went out into the air and down the block to their homes.

A neighborhood meeting in Holguín, Cuba.

BEGINNING AGAIN

How Cuba Organized a Socialist Government

We must be enemies of the old law and pillars of the new.

—FIDEL CASTRO

The men and women who overthrew the Batista dictatorship were not elected to the revolutionary government. They were in the government because they had led the Revolution. During its first fifteen years, the revolutionary government was a government *for* the people, providing services and laws in the people's interest. It was a government *of* the people, since the revolutionary leaders came from the ranks of the workers, peasants, and students. But it was not a government *by* the people, for the citizens of Cuba did not directly elect its members.

The revolutionary government led instead by a "moral mandate." Its leaders were respected for their sacrifices, their honesty and courage. The government was respected for its battles against illiteracy, racism, and unemployment, and for providing, together with free health care and education, a sense of pride.

During the first fifteen years, the Cuban people were preoccupied with defending their country, developing the economy, building schools and hospitals, and learning skills that had been denied them. Everyone knew that elections would come some day, but for those years learning, building, and defending their country came first.

During those years, they learned to have faith in themselves. They had raised themselves above poverty through their own efforts, without the help of the rich and powerful, the landlords, the industrialists, the *Americanos.* They had learned a great lesson, said Major Juan Almeida in 1967:

> The rich say it's impossible to organize a society without the owners of private property. Nevertheless . . . there are societies without the wealthy class, but none without the working class. We can live without the rich, but not without the workers!

Finally, however, the time came when it was necessary to organize a democratically elected socialist government. The failure of the ten-million-ton harvest in 1970 had shown, as Fidel admitted, that "sending a man down from the top to solve a problem involving fifteen or twenty thousand people is not the same thing as having those problems solved by the people themselves, who are close to the source of the problem."

An entirely new government had to be organized from the bottom up that would give the people the means to directly control the economic and social life of the nation. Such a government is only possible when the people as a whole own the factories, schools, sugar mills, and stores. It also demanded of the people a level of training and responsibility that had not existed fifteen years earlier.

How does the new Cuban government work? First, there are elections.

The election of representatives begins on the block at the local chapter of the CDR. All the voters on the block—whether CDR members or not—meet to nominate candidates. These candidates will stand for election to the municipal government, called the "Assembly of People's Power" *(La Asemblea del Poder Popular).*

There are no professional politicians at this nominating meeting, just neighbors. No one jumps up to announce that he or she is running for office. The voters nominate those they feel can best represent them. There is no limit on the number they can nominate. They freely discuss the merits and weaknesses of each nominee and then vote to nominate the best one.

Similar meetings are held at each of the CDR chapters within the election district, or *circumscripcion,* each of which consists of from five hundred to a thousand people. On election day, one candidate from among those nominated in a given *circumscripcion* is elected to represent that district in the Municipal Assembly of People's Power. In the 1974 Matanzas elections, 4,712 candidates ran; 1,079 were elected.

The election campaign itself is without the familiar trappings of campaign posters, buttons, and bumper stickers, multimillion-dollar campaign funds, rallies, and ads on TV. Each candidate provides a full biography and a photograph, copies of which are posted in public places. The work and achievements of each candidate are his or her only campaign propaganda. The people of the *circumscripcion* read the biographies, discuss among themselves their opinions of the candidates, and then make up their minds.

The candidates make no campaign promises nor do they take stands on issues. Their job when elected will be to represent faithfully the opinions and wishes of those in their *circumscripcion,* not to force their personal ideas on others. They do not pretend to be superior or to have professional knowledge. They are accountable to the voters and do not stand above them. It is not the candidate's personal opinion that counts here, but his experience and ability to resolve problems.

After the first People's Power election in Matanzas province in 1974, a journalist asked local voters how this election differed from those before the Revolution, and got this answer:

What? There isn't any way to compare the two. Before the Revolution, it was an outright circus: threats, payoffs all over the place. They'd promise anything—to build a bridge where there was no river. Whichever candidate had the most money or the biggest gangsters won. As soon as the election fraud was over, they forgot what you looked like.

In the first socialist elections in Matanzas, 93.6 percent of the eligible voters participated. The ballots were secret. No one was forced to vote.

Since those elected as delegates live in the communities they represent, they are naturally in close contact with their constituents. But the Cuban system requires more than that: each delegate must meet with the people in his *circumscripcion* once every three months to account for his activities. He is also required to hold smaller meetings at closer intervals and to set aside time to meet with individual voters to listen to their problems, complaints, and suggestions.

The principles of *accountability* and *recall* are central to Cuban democracy. Any delegate can be removed from office at any time by those who elected him, if in their opinion he or she is not doing the job well.

The delegates from the *circumscripciones* sit on the Municipal Assembly of their town or city. This assembly determines how all the municipal property and services in their area will be organized, directed, and controlled. The delegates are responsible for the running of:

the schools and educational activities; the radio stations, cultural events, bookstores, movie theaters; the restaurants, hotels, and tourist centers; internal trade; the gas stations and auto repair shops, garages and bus terminals; the post offices, telegraph offices, and press offices; the hospitals, polyclinics, and health centers; the centers for purchasing agricultural products, distributing produce; the grain mills; the power stations; the courts and the system of justice —and much more.

Every Municipal Assembly appoints trained personnel to administer each of these activities. The assembly delegates need not be experts in the technical ins and outs of running a transit system, for example, but they know from their constituents when the buses are late, the service inadequate, or the equipment faulty. The administrators of the bus line must carry out the decisions of the people's elected delegates.

One of the first things the Municipal Assembly does is elect from its members delegates to the two higher levels of the government: the Provincial Assembly, which governs their province, and the National Assembly—the national congress or parliament. One municipal delegate is elected to a Provincial Assembly for each 10,000 residents in the municipality; one is elected to the National Assembly for each 200,000 citizens.

At each level—municipal, provincial, and national—the delegates elected to that assembly are responsible for all the services and economic and social institutions that operate at that level. A taxi company in a town would be run by the local Municipal Assembly of that town; an intercity bus line would be run by the Provincial Assembly of that province; the Santiago-Havana railroad would be run by the National Assembly.

Though every Municipal and Provincial Assembly has the right to solve problems the way it sees best, standards are set, technical and scientific expertise is developed, and administrative methods are regulated at the national level in order to ensure uniformity and equality throughout the country.

For example, a city hospital is run jointly by the Municipal Assembly of that city and by the Ministry of Public Health (MINSAP). Before the creation of the Assemblies of People's Power, MINSAP tried to administer every hospital in the country from its offices in Havana. Bureaucratic quicksands of paperwork, delay, and overstaffing were the result. Now MINSAP provides the technical skills and the medical knowledge. People's Power makes sure that the hospital is properly staffed and run, that it meets standards of health care and efficiency, that it satisfies the people's needs.

At each level of the Assemblies of People's Power all questions are decided by a majority vote after full discussion. When the majority has decided, that is final. If a minority disagrees, it is bound to abide by the majority. There are no caucuses, factions, interest groups, or lobbyists. After debate, all delegates unite to carry out the will of the majority.

Does this system run the risk of breeding a "tyranny of the majority?" The answer lies in the nature of Cuban society.

Cuba is no longer composed of competing interest groups: business vs. labor, small homeowners vs. real-estate interests, tenants vs. landlords, plantation owners vs. small farmers, blacks or mulattoes vs. whites.

When the Revolution destroyed the power of the rich, it eliminated the most important source of antagonism among the Cuban people. Today, no one makes a living from the labor of others; everyone works and/or studies. The massive effort needed to transform the country and defend it against outside pressure and attack has produced a basic communality of interests. Factory workers, peasants, and students do not see their interests as opposed to those of one another.

Obviously, no people can be totally in agreement on everything. The exodus of 100,000 Cubans—one percent of the population—in the spring of 1980 revealed an unwillingness on their part to adapt to Cuba's socialist system.

On the other hand, the anger at those who left, demonstrated by the five million Cubans who took to the streets in May 1980 to show their support of the government, suggests that, no matter what the critics of the Revolution claim, the people do favor the new life the Cuban Revolution has created.

Overwhelming allegiance to the socialist revolution in Cuba is still the rule—discontent the exception—as it had been on February 15, 1976, when by referendum the voters of Cuba adopted the new socialist constitution.

A national constitution in its best sense is the voluntary agreement by the members of a nation as to what kind of society they wish to have.

The referendum on the constitution was conducted by voluntary secret ballot open to all over the age of sixteen. Ninety-eight percent of the eligible voters went to the polls that Sunday: 5,473,534 men and women (97.7 percent) voted yes—in favor of the constitution; 54,070 (1 percent) voted no. Interestingly, the 1 percent no vote coincides with the percentage who left Cuba in the 1980 exodus.

It is not easy to understand how a vote of 97.7 percent in favor of anything is possible in a general election. In Cuba, however, the referendum came at the end of a lengthy process of public debate, discussion, and revision that took months and involved everyone who wished to participate. The virtual unanimity with which the constitution was passed came not from blind discipline but from thorough participation in the discussion of every article.

Before the referendum, 160,000 meetings were held—in factories, union halls, farmers' associations, schools, military units, chapters of the CDR, and women's meetings. More than six million people—almost the entire population over the age of fourteen —discussed and made proposals on every article of the draft constitution. In the end, about sixteen thousand modifications were proposed and hundreds of these incorporated in the final version, which was then put to a national vote.

Article 1 of the constitution declares that "the Republic of Cuba is a socialist state of workers and peasants and all other manual and intellectual workers."

Article 4 establishes that "in the Republic of Cuba all the power belongs to the working people. . . ."

Among rights that the new constitution guarantees are:

• The right to a job, an 8-hour work day, a weekly rest period, and an annual paid vacation.

• The right to protection, safety, and sanitary working conditions on the job, with guarantees of adequate measures for the prevention of accidents at work and occupational diseases.

• The right to health protection and care—*free* medical, hospital, and dental care for all.

• The right to an education provided free to everyone at all levels —adults as well as children.

• The right to physical education, sports, recreation, and culture.

• The right to be cared for in old age.

• The right to be free from discrimination because of race, color, or sex.

These basic human rights alone guarantee the people of Cuba a dignified present and a secure future yet to be achieved by most of the people of Asia, Africa, and Latin America—or for that matter by millions in North America and Europe.

The Cuban constitution also guarantees to every citizen the right to personal ownership of one's earnings and savings and to one's home and personal property. It proclaims work as a right and duty of every citizen and declares the right of free speech, assembly, and religious belief.

The most important factor about the provisions of the new

constitution is that they are real and enforceable. "When our Constitution proclaims that every citizen has the right to health care, this is not a formal declaration," says Blas Roca, who led the drafting of the new document. "It is a reality, guaranteed in practice by a network of hospitals and doctors who offer their care free to the entire population."

The constitution does not, for example, now guarantee the right of each citizen to adequate housing, though this is a major goal of the Revolution, since Cuba is still underdeveloped and does not yet have the resources to provide good homes for everyone. When such a time arrives, I was told, the right to good housing will be written in the constitution.

Once enslaved in almost every aspect of their lives, the Cubans know that freedom is not an abstraction or an absolute. They ask instead, "Freedom for whom and to do what?" They paid with their lives to end the "freedom" of the military to repress them, of the politicians to manipulate them, and of their employers to exploit them.

That is why Cubans demand economic and social freedoms as well as the right to vote. The new socialist constitution and the People's Power government were created to ensure that never again will there emerge in Cuba a class of people that would live at ease on the hard work of others.

"I JUST CAN'T GET USED TO THAT WORD COMMUNISM"

Back in the early 1960's, when the words *socialism* and *communism* entered the vocabulary of the Revolution, there were many Cubans who had difficulty identifying with ideas that had been anathema for decades. One such Cuban was Pedro Martinez of Santiago. In August 1963 he decided to voice his concern in a letter to *Hoy,* the newspaper of the PSP (Popular Socialist Party).

I'm seventy years old. I'm a humble man of the people with very little education. I hold the Revolution in the deepest part of my heart. Every day I feel the Revolution doing things for the people. I won't permit even the littlest insinuation against the Revolution. The only thing I have on the door of my house is the Cuban flag, no pictures, nothing else. But despite how much I love the Revolution, I just can't get used to that word "communism." The question that I want answered is this: Can one be a good revolutionary without being a Communist?

"The old society of exploitation," *Hoy* editor Blas Roca replied, "turned communism into a spectre.

"All the intellectual servants of the regime, in books, plays, movies, magazines, newspapers, cathedrals, and pulpits dedicated themselves to presenting communism as the worst thing, as something repugnant, contrary to liberty, to human nature, to religion, the family, and the country.

"And their ideas, untiringly repeated for more than a hundred years, propagated in schools to the children, in the church, in the press, on radio, in films, on television, succeeded in penetrating people's minds so they acquired a horror, a fear and hatred for communism. . . .

"With regard to the concrete question by Pedro Martinez . . . : One cannot be a good revolutionary while hanging on to anticommunism, which is the ideology of imperialism and counterrevolution.

"One can easily aid the revolution without being a formal and conscious Communist.

"One can also be a faithful revolutionary without having arrived at or being a Communist.

"But one cannot advance resolutely along the revolutionary road if one maintains reservations or fears about socialism and communism."

ORGANIZER
AND GUIDE

The Communist Party of Cuba

The Party is a synthesis of everything. Within it, the dreams of all the revolutionaries in our history are synthesized. . . . The Party today is the soul of the Cuban Revolution.

—FIDEL CASTRO, December 1975

Most of Cuba's revolutionaries were not Marxists when they trudged ashore from the *Granma* to enter the Sierra Maestra, nor even when they entered Havana in triumphant columns. Instead, they found themselves acting like Marxists in the course of the war against Batista: uniting the poor in their own interests, distributing land to the landless, organizing trade unions, weakening the power and influence of the rich over Cuban life. This was carried out in the name of justice rather than Marxism, but the effect was the same.

"If we do that which is called Marxism," Che Guevara said in 1960, "it is because we discovered it here." This shock of recognition occurred to many leaders of the Cuban Revolution. Discovering Marxism, as Fidel said, was like finding a "map of the forest."

The revolutionaries also found that the spirit of Marxism did not clash with the humanism that had led them to the mountains.

"Who says that Marxism has no soul, no feelings?" Fidel said. "It was precisely love for man that conceived Marxism, it was love for humanity, the desire to combat misery, injustice and all the exploitation suffered by the working class that made Marxism arise from the mind of Karl Marx."

"The Marxist," wrote Che Guevara, "must be the best, the most complete of human beings, but always, above everything, a human being: a party militant who lives and vibrates when in contact with the people, a tireless worker who gives all to his people, a hard worker who gives his hours of rest, his personal tranquility, his family or his life to the Revolution, a man who is never alien to the warmth of human contact."

In the heat of the struggle against Batista, the revolutionaries also learned the necessity for unity.

FIDEL: The Revolution is the art of uniting forces. At the beginning we were only a small group. A small group which carried on the fight under very difficult conditions. And one of the factors which made for the triumph of the Cuban Revolution was the policy of uniting, uniting, uniting. And it wasn't easy. You should have heard the arguments we got tangled up in!

Many were the disputes, often painful and bitter, that were necessary to maintain the unity of the Revolution. People who are willing to die for a better life are often in harsh disagreement over how to achieve it.

During the war, all Cuban revolutionaries agreed that Batista must be overthrown, but those in the Rebel Army sometimes disagreed with their comrades in the cities over the method to use: general strikes or guerrilla war.

During the war, but more sharply after victory, there were disagreements with those who had opposed Batista but were afraid to confront the power of the United States and wanted a nonradical revolution. This conflict was won by those revolutionaries who wanted to "go to the root."

The most dangerous disunity, however, came after the overthrow of Batista when a conflict broke out inside the July 26 Movement over whether or not to unite and cooperate with the Communists of the Popular Socialist Party. A few, like revolutionary army leaders Huber Matos and Díaz Lanz were so anti-Communist that they betrayed the Revolution. Others were loyal to the Revolution, but feared the "Communist threat" and wanted to exclude Blas Roca, Lázaro Peña, and other Communists who had devoted their lives to the labor movement and the cause of socialism.

The majority, however, agreed with Fidel that the revolutionary forces should be united, not segregated. The older Communists, Fidel argued, had proven their commitment to the Revolution in battle and in the underground.

Like the American revolutionaries of 1776, the leaders knew they must all hang together, or they would all hang separately. They knew, moreover, that to create an entirely new social and economic system, they would have to act in unity, that to build a socialist system deliberately, consciously, and purposefully required that they serve together as guide and organizer.

The three revolutionary organizations—the July 26 Movement, the Popular Socialist Party, and the Revolutionary Directorate—therefore agreed that a new leadership body was necessary that would guide the country to socialism, using the ideas of Marxism as its "map." They would merge into a single party because there was a single goal—socialism—and a single constituency in power—the working men and women of Cuba.

BLAS ROCA: The party gathers the most convinced, the most revolutionary, the most decided—those who give the example, those who march in front, those who do not fear difficulties but who confront them and overcome them.

The party is the organization in which are gathered those who have no doubt about the virtue of our ideology and our position; those who have no doubt about the teachings of Marx, of Engels, of Lenin, our founders.

The new party would be completely different from the political parties of the United States, Great Britain, and similar countries. It would not be open to everyone, but would choose its members. It would be a *leadership* party.

The Communist Party of Cuba, as the new party was named when the three groups merged in 1965, is a tight-knit disciplined body, a long-distance runner, whose legs and head, having freely committed themselves, do not dispute the course.

Such a system of political leadership by a single party is only meaningful (or possible) in a society where the major causes of conflict of interests have been eliminated. In a country where workers clash with their bosses, whites with people of color, peasants with plantation owners, where private interests dominate the health system, education, and the military, to seek such unity is blind. Where economic interests clash, political parties will always arise to represent the opposing sides, or they will slug it out within a single party, each faction striving for advantage and control.

This free-for-all is often pointed to in capitalist countries as proof of democracy. The high level of unanimity in the Communist Party of Cuba, on the other hand, is sometimes taken as evidence of conformity and lack of freedom. There is, for example, no black caucus in the Cuban Communist Party as there is in the Democratic Party of the United States. Why? Because there is no racial discrimination in Cuba. Does this mean that there is less democracy in Cuba, or more?

The strength of the Communist Party lies in its internal democracy, in the right, as Blas Roca says, "to discuss every question within the Party, the right of each member to express his or her opinions in problems under debate, and to criticize any measure."

In the foreign press, Cuban socialism is often described as "Castroism" and Cuba itself as "Castro's Cuba," so identified is the Cuban Revolution with a single man. Since we will see in the next chapter that Fidel's role is changing, it is worthwhile pausing here to examine that role. Many Cuban revolutionaries have commented thoughtfully on the subject.

"Fidel's role was decisive in every moment in the early years," Angel Guerra, editor of *Bohemia* told me in 1975.

"What was his method?" said Guerra. "It was based on educating the people. He was always present in direct contact with the workers in the most dangerous situations, at Playa Girón in 1962 and during the Missile Crisis. He would talk to people, hear their problems, come up with solutions, and then speak on television. The solution would be broadcast. There was a direct connection between them.

"Fidel was on TV every week, talking for four, five, or six hours on solutions to the problems of the economy, on international policy. These were classes in politics—instead of commercials.

"The role of the mass media was important to us. Lenin didn't have it; Mao didn't have it. Television and radio made direct teaching possible—and after all, Marxism comes out best in explanations of concrete things, which is what Fidel did."

"The personal significance of Fidel Castro in the Revolution has been and is decisive," one of Cuba's best-known journalists, Jorge Timossi, wrote in the 1960's. "He moves constantly from one place on the island to another, unexpectedly, to be in daily contact with the problems. The average Cuban sees Fidel as an 'agitator.' "

"Fidel's relationship with the people can only be appreciated by seeing him in action," Che Guevara wrote in 1965. In big public meetings, you can see something like the dialogue of two tuning forks, whose vibrations summon forth new vibrations from each other. Fidel and the people begin to vibrate in a dialogue of growing intensity. . . ."

When I asked Melba Hernández why she had so much respect for Fidel, she answered: "What he sees at a given moment, sometimes we can't see. Then as time goes by, it turns out to be true. So he has our complete confidence.

"This isn't the cult of the personality. We couldn't behave toward him in a simple or subjective way, or because we let ourselves be carried away with our feelings. He taught us to be very sharp and critical, and every day he teaches us to be objective.

"He has a greatness for detecting his own mistakes, and he is very demanding of himself."

That Fidel has grown with the Revolution and has learned as much as he has taught can be seen from a study of his speeches and decisions and from talking with those who have known him.

Fidel is unusual in that he has taken responsibility when things go wrong as well as right. Despite the continuing economic difficulties, the mistakes of the leadership in certain areas, and the discontent of a few, most Cubans feel free to come up to him in the street and talk about what concerns them. They may be in awe of him, but he is one of them, the "agitator," whose honesty is taken for granted and whose trust in them is returned in kind.

Though Fidel may have been "decisive," it is the two hundred thousand men and women who belong to the Cuban Communist Party who actually lead and guide the nation. They are workers in factories and farms; they are teachers and fishermen and cane cutters and poets who have emerged from the ranks as leaders. They have no special privileges or powers. They work a full day at their regular workplace and live in the same communities as those who are not party members.

Since the party members are drawn from all sections of the population, and are the most active and exemplary citizens, the party's example and influence are felt at all levels—in the factories, the government, the army, the mass organizations, and the schools. They are the initiators of new ideas.

How does one become a member of the Cuban Communist Party? First, a person must be nominated by fellow workers—Communist and non-Communist alike—at the workplace. The workers meet to discuss the merits of each candidate, and everyone has a chance to express his or her opinion. A vote is then taken, and the workers' recommendation is submitted to the party organization in the area, which makes the final selection. Reasons for the party's decisions are reported back to the workers.

Each member of the Communist Party belongs to a "nucleus" of party members in his or her place of work. The party does not lead from afar. Its members are there at the next lathe, or in the office down the hall. They are in a position of leadership because the people they work with say they are the best.

But haven't the people already elected those they want to lead them as their delegates to the Assemblies of People's Power at the municipal, state, and national levels?

Here we encounter the difference between the government (People's Power) and the Communist Party. The Assemblies of People's Power are the administrative and state authority. They run the Cuban state, and they have the power to enforce the laws through legislative and legal means.

The party, unlike the state, has no coercive power. It has no army, no police force, no judges. It does not hire and fire. It's authority is political and ideological. It leads by education, example, and persuasion.

As Raúl Castro explained to a group of People's Power delegates, "The party can and must make suggestions, proposals, recommendations . . . but it must never 'hand down' decisions, never impose decisions, never take any manner of reprisals as regards an Assembly of People's Power or members of such organs who do not agree with or carry out something the party has suggested."

If the party has a proposal it thinks should be carried out, it submits it to the Assemblies of People's Power through its members who have been elected as deputies of People's Power.

The Communist deputies argue for their proposal. All the deputies discuss it with their constituencies and in their assemblies; then a vote is taken.

If the proposal is not accepted, the Communist Party can reintroduce it at the next higher level of People's Power. But if it consistently runs into disagreement with a particular proposal, that is a clear signal to the party members to sit down and reevaluate the proposal itself.

Once a proposal put forward by the party is accepted, the decisions about how to implement it are up to People's Power, not the party. The party does not interfere with the administration.

Given the transcendent role the party plays at every level of Cuban society, it's easy to see why the First Congress of the Communist Party of Cuba, held in December 1975, was called "the most important meeting in the history of Cuba." Three thousand delegates elected by every party nucleus in the country met to analyze every aspect of life in Cuba, and to develop guidelines for the coming years.

Though a party congress is formally an internal party event, almost everyone in the country participated in the preparations for it. The discussion papers of the congress were submitted to every party member for study and discussion months in advance, and many were circulated for discussion among the members of the mass organizations and the Union of Young Communists.

What the congress decided had to be done in Cuba over the next five years (1976–80) was nothing less than the total reorganization of the country.

THE REVOLUTION
MATURES

The people always produced its leaders in every stage of our revolutionary struggles. Leaders do not shape peoples; it is the peoples that shape their leaders. . . . At times the difficulties are incredibly great, and you may be dealt bitter reverses. The forms of struggle may even change frequently, but there is only one path: to struggle, struggle and struggle.

—*FIDEL CASTRO, January 1, 1979*

The First Congress of the Communist Party of Cuba began by redrawing the map of Cuba. The division of the country into municipalities, regions, and provinces was a holdover from the days of Spanish rule. By 1970 it was clear that these geographical lines no longer matched the new society. Oriente province, for example, equal in population to Matanzas in 1877, now had six times as many people.

By the time of the congress in 1975, the Revolution had built 153 new rural communities and a whole new city—Alamar—outside Havana, tripled the network of highways and roads, erected industrial complexes where none had existed, and altered the entire face of Cuba. The old boundaries were obsolete. New ones were drawn that matched the reality of modern Cuba.

The congress created fourteen provinces from the six original ones. This required eight new provincial capitals and governments, elections; a complete reorganization.

Redrawing the lines on the face of Cuba was the most visible of changes proposed by the congress. Less visible, but far more profound, was the reorganization of the entire economic system.

The new *Sistema de Dirección Económica,* or SDE ("System of Economic Management") replaced the system of "organized enthusiasm" described earlier with a rigorous system of bookkeeping and management based on methods developed in the Soviet Union and other socialist countries over many decades.

The old way of organizing the economy—relying on voluntary labor, mass campaigns, and moral incentives—had resulted in the failure of the 1970 ten-million-ton harvest and the disorganization of the economy. How is the new system, the SDE, different? Basically it has to do with the use and role of money.

The leaders of the Revolution, who came from and overthrew a profoundly corrupt society, felt a deep distrust of money. Hoping eventually to eliminate money from the economy, they abolished money transactions between agencies and factories. They urged workers to give up overtime pay; they eliminated taxes on farmers and payment of interest on loans. If a factory making truck bodies needed tires, the manager simply requested the tires from a tire factory; there was no payment. Without payment, bookkeeping was impossible. Without bookkeeping, there was no need for a national budget or a ministry of finance: both were eliminated in the mid-sixties. The schools of public accounting were closed down at the universities. Who needed accountants when there were no books to keep?

This seemed radical, but as Fidel later admitted, "When it seemed as though we were drawing nearer to Communist forms of production and distribution, we were actually pulling away from the correct methods for the construction of socialism."

Under the old system, a factory producing shoes, for example, had no way of figuring its costs, its efficiency, or the amount of waste. The Revolution called on the factory management and workers to produce ten thousand shoes a year. They did—but at what cost? The management had no way of calculating whether shoes that sold for five dollars actually cost seven dollars to make. If that was true, then the shoe factory was draining away the resources of the people, leaving them poorer than before.

Without cost accounting, the management had no idea how much leather it was wasting, no way to measure the cost of oil or tools. If some workers left for a month to cut sugarcane, how much did that cost the shoe factory? Suppose the workers put in six Saturdays of free voluntary labor at the factory. Could their labor have been better spent somewhere else—building a school, for example? There was no way of telling.

Under the new system, Cuba has returned to the use of certain old "capitalist" methods of bookkeeping, using the categories of profit, interest, prices, and wages. Now, each factory is supposed to show a "profit." If it uses the product of another factory, it has to pay a "price." If it borrows money from the national bank, it must pay "interest."

Though the names are the same and the bookkeeping methods are similar to capitalist economics, the content is completely different. Take "profit" for example. Before the Revolution, profit meant the amount the owner of the factory took for himself. Now that the "owner" is the people as a whole, profit measures the difference between the value of the shoes and the expenses that go into their making; in other words, the contribution of the factory to the society. If the factory uses a million dollars in labor and resources to produce one and a half million dollars worth of shoes, it has contributed half a million dollars to Cuba.

Where does the profit go? Part of it goes to the government which uses it to build schools, hospitals, highways, and apartment buildings, to provide special aid for students, to maintain the national defense, to buy needed goods abroad, or to build more factories.

The other part goes into a "collective incentive fund" for the workers at the factory and their families. The workers themselves decide how it will be used. It may go for special classes to upgrade their skills, or for a housing project or cultural activities. Some may go into individual rewards for those among the workers and management who have especially helped to increase production. It may go back into the factory to improve working or safety conditions there, or to buy more efficient and modern equipment.

When the economy was nationalized in 1960, profit in Cuba ceased to be the hated contribution made by workers to a rich man's comfort. The SDE has made profit a tangible reality that every member of the work force and management can see and feel. It becomes the immediate interest of everyone in the factory to cut costs, minimize waste, and boost production. A poor country cannot afford to waste a single drop of oil, scrap of metal, piece of leather.

Profit, money, taxes, interest, and wages, kicked out the front door with the capitalists in the early sixties, have returned, humbled, by the back door to serve as a way of measuring, of keeping track, or making more efficient an economy whose purpose has wholly changed.

It wasn't easy to admit the mistakes the leaders of the Revolution had made in their enthusiasm. "I know, comrades, that some of you were hurt as we analyzed our mistakes," Fidel told the First Communist Party Congress. "As a revolutionary principle, self-criticism is always a thousand times preferable to complacency. And being humble is always preferable to praising oneself!"

Socialism is a planned economy, and planning the economy is one of socialism's major headaches. Cuban leader Osvaldo Dorticós once told a gathering of Cuban economic planners that if one were theoretically to choose a Latin American country in which to plan a socialist society, the choice would certainly not fall on Cuba. The lack of technicians, experienced personnel, adequate statistics, efficient institutions, and the destabilizing pressure of the United States trade embargo made it impossible until 1976 for Cuba's economists to plan more than a year ahead.

The congress introduced Cuba's first Five Year Plan (1976–1980), made possible by the massive construction efforts of the previous fifteen years, the achievements in education, the defeat of the embargo, and Cuba's integration into the world socialist economic system.

Planning requires a delicate, flexible balance, rather like a juggler and a tightrope walker combined. Social and political needs must be harmonized with the need for heavy industry (another steel plant, or more aid to Angola?); investment with consumption (build more ships or import more television sets?); regions with one another (locate a textile mill in Oriente or in Pinar del Río?). These decisions are no longer up to individual businessmen or corporations. They are the central responsibility of the party and the government.

Once the party has drawn the outline, the central planning agency (JUCEPLAN) fills in the details and the timetable. It then consults with the government agencies to see if the plan is practical and seeks the advice of the workers in the production centers who must carry out the actual labor. The final plan has the force of law.

During the first four years (1976–79) of the Five Year Plan, Cuba both achieved startling successes and suffered bitter reverses. The economic crisis that struck the capitalist world during those years severely affected Cuba. Though Cuba sells most of its sugar to the socialist countries, at prices well above the Western market price, a significant proportion is sold on the open market. During the years 1976–1980, the price of sugar on that market plunged to lower than the average world cost of production. Sugar, which on the average costs fourteen cents a pound to produce, was selling for seven to eight cents a pound.

At the same time, inflation rose dramatically, increasing the prices of manufactured goods Cuba must buy on the open market, as well as the freight charges it must pay. These economic blows, Raúl Castro reported in November 1979, have "harmed our economy to a greater degree than was the case over the last few years."

At the same time, Cuban agriculture was attacked by a menacing series of natural disasters. Blue mold devastated Cuba's tobacco plantations in the 1978–79 season, totally destroying 27 percent of the tobacco crop, a loss to Cuba of $100,000,000. A plague of sugarcane smut—a fungus disease—attacked the sugar crop in 1979, just as an outbreak of swine fever curtailed pork production. At the moment the political and economic reforms seemed about to put the Cuban economy "over the top" into a more prosperous period, these manmade and natural disasters suddenly reduced Cuba's financial resources and lessened its purchasing power. Once again the Cuban people, through no fault of their own, had to tighten their belts.

The twenty-year battle against the blockade and poverty, coupled with the economic turndown, natural disasters, and disappointments, took a certain psychological toll among the people. In November 1979, Raúl Castro talked frankly about this at a rally in Santiago:

> To the objective factors we've described we must add the presence of indiscipline, lack of control, irresponsibility, complacency, negligence, and buddyism which . . . generate justified irritation on the part of broad sectors of the population, being the principle cause for the notorious lack of efficiency in important areas of our economy.

This was not the fault of the workers, he emphasized, but was "the responsibility of managers and all of us who have not set up the most adequate work and salary mechanisms and have not known how to organize things and create a certain sense of political and work responsibility on the part of the workers."

Though the goals of the Five Year Plan could not be reached, the Cuban economy still grew during the 1976–1980 period. In December 1979, Humberto Pérez, president of JUCEPLAN, the central planning agency, reported that important areas of the economy had shown "significant advances, important growth." To prove this, Pérez compared the five year period of 1971–75 with the *four* years between 1976 and 1979.

In the latter four years, Cuba had produced more sugar than during the previous five, he said. It had invested 50 percent more in industry, produced 400,000 tons more fertilizer and 2.3 million more tons of cement. It had built 7,340 buses in four years, compared to 5,485 in the previous five. Electricity production was up. In addition, Cuba had provided eight times as many child-care centers and fifteen times as many hospital beds as in the previous five years.

While raging inflation and rising oil prices were devastating the other underdeveloped countries of the world, Cuba's economic situation "with all the difficulties is incomparably better than that of other [underdeveloped] countries," Fidel reported late in 1979.

Cuba is virtually "the only non-oil-producing underdeveloped country in the world today,' Fidel reported to the National Assembly in December 1979, "that can say with tranquility that it can provide its fuel needs for the next five years."

The economic crisis was but another challenge that the Cuban Revolution has faced since 1959. The first socialist country in the Western Hemisphere has weathered an economic blockade unprecedented in peacetime, it has fought armed attack, counterrevolution, assassination attempts against its leaders, and threats of nuclear holocaust. It has overcome serious errors and miscalculations. It has survived, maintained its base of support, and continues to make progress. The Revolution, moreover, raised Cuba from an island colony of the United States to a major force in world affairs.

There were many who gave their lives along the way. Seventy-six in the attack on the Moncada. Twenty thousand during the Batista regime. Over one hundred at Playa Girón. Those who died and those who lived produced a nation that demonstrably has the most advanced and egalitarian society in Latin America.

If there has been one quality that has marked Cuba's leaders and people during the entire revolutionary process it has been the ability to admit errors and overcome them. They have been neither rigid and orthodox nor lacking in courage and audacity. Against those who opposed the Revolution they have been firm, with those who support it, flexible. The rapport the Cuban leaders have established with the overwhelming majority of Cuban people they have earned by defending the people's interests and by listening—carefully—to them.

Speaking on the twentieth anniversary of the Revolution, Fidel concluded:

> We would feel more satisfied on celebrating this twentieth anniversary if we had made better use of every year, month, day and minute; if all our actions, without exception, had been the wisest and most intelligent ones possible. The measures and initiatives of each of us weren't always the most correct, but we never lacked the ardent desire to do the most and to do the best we could for our people and our beloved Revolution. . . .
>
> The joy and optimism we feel today will not lead us into the error of underestimating the struggle that lies ahead. Our difficulties will still be enormous, but we will overcome.

A B O U T   T H E   A U T H O R

Terence Cannon, journalist and free-lance editor, has lived, worked, and traveled extensively in Cuba. The author of many articles on Cuban affairs and political events in Latin America, he has written for Latin American news services and magazines, and served as a correspondent at the United Nations. Mr. Cannon was graduated from Cornell University with a degree in mathematics, and during the 1960's founded and edited *The Movement* newspaper. He is presently a Charles H. Revson Fellow at the Greenburg Center for Legal Education and Urban Studies at the City College of New York.

Selected Bibliography

Abel, Elie. *The Missile Crisis.* Philadelphia and New York: J.B. Lippin-
cott Co., 1966.

Aguilar, Luis E. *Cuba 1933: Prologue to Revolution.* New York: W.W.
Norton & Co., 1972.

Bonachea, Rolando E., and Valdés, Nelson P., eds. *Che: Selected Works
of Ernesto Guevara.* Cambridge, Mass. The MIT Press, 1969.

———, eds. *The Selected Works of Fidel Castro.* Vol. I, *Revolutionary
Struggle.* Cambridge, Mass.: The MIT Press, 1972.

Boorstein, Edward. *The Economic Transformation of Cuba.* New York:
Monthly Review Press, 1968.

Cabrera, Guillermo. *Hablar de Camilo.* Havana: Pluma en Ristre, 1970.

Cannon, Terence. "U.S. Cuban Policy: A Future Stalled in the Past."
Cuba Review, March 1976.

Cannon, Terence, and Cole, Johnnetta. *Free and Equal: The End of
Racial Discrimination in Cuba.* New York: Venceremos Brigade,
1978.

Cannon, Terence, et al. *Democracy in Cuba.* New York: Venceremos
Brigade, 1977.

Castro, Fidel. *Aniversarios del triunfo de la revolución cubana.* Havana:
Editora Política, 1967.

———. *The Cuban Revolution, National Liberation and the Soviet
Union.* New York: New Outlook, 1974.

Castro, Raúl. *En el octavo aniversario 26 de julio.* Havana: Editorial de
Ciencias Sociales, 1973.

Comisión de Orientación Revolucionaria. *Cuba–Chile.* Havana: Ediciones Políticas, 1972.

Comités de Defensa de la Revolución. *10 años de trabajo.* Havana: CDR, 1971.

De Onís, Juan. *The America of José Martí.* New York: Noonday Press, 1954.

Departamento de Divulgación de la CTC Nacional. *Congreso de la CTC: Memorias.* Havana: CTC, 1973.

Discursos de Fidel en los aniversarios de los CDR 1960–1967. Havana: Instituto del Libro, 1968.

Divine, Robert A., ed. *The Cuban Missile Crisis.* New York: Quadrangle Books, 1971.

Dubois, Jules. *Fidel Castro.* Indianapolis: Bobbs-Merrill Co., 1959.

Eisenhower, Dwight D. *The White House Years: Waging Peace 1956–1961.* Garden City, N.Y.: Doubleday & Co., 1965.

Escuelas de Instrucción Revolucionaria del PCC. *Cronología de la Revolución.* Havana, 1966.

First Congress of the Communist Party of Cuba. Moscow: Progress Publishers, 1976.

Foner, Philip S. *A History of Cuba and Its Relations with the United States.* Vol. I, *1492–1845.* New York: International Publishers Co., 1962. Vol. II, *1845–1895.* New York: International Publishers Co., 1963.

Franqui, Carlos. *El libro de los doce.* Havana: Ediciones Huracán, 1969.

Gerassi, John. *Venceremos! The Speeches and Writings of Ernesto Che Guevara.* New York: Macmillan Co., 1968.

Gonzalez, Luis J., and Sanchez Salazár, Gustavo A. *The Great Rebel, Che Guevara in Bolivia.* New York: Grove Press, 1969.

Guevara, Ernesto Che. *Guerrilla Warfare.* Translated by J. P. Morray. New York: Vintage Books, 1969.

———. *Episodes of the Revolutionary War.* Havana: Ediciones Union, 1963.

———. *Obras 1957–1967.* Havana: Casa de las Américas, 1970.

Hart Davalos, Armando. *Education Since the Revolution.* Havana, 1963.

History of an Aggression. Havana: Ediciones Venceremos, 1964.

Hunt, Howard. *Give Us This Day.* New Rochelle, N.Y.: Arlington House, 1973.

Johnson, Haynes. *The Bay of Pigs.* New York: Dell Publishing Co., 1964.

Johnson, Leland. "U.S. Business Interests in Cuba and the Rise of Castro." Santa Monica, Calif.: RAND Corp., 1964.

Kennedy, Robert F. *Thirteen Days.* New York: W. W. Norton & Co., 1969.

Langley, Lester D. *The Cuban Policy of the United States.* New York: John Wiley & Sons, 1968.

Le Riverend, Julio. *Economic History of Cuba.* Havana: Book Institute, 1967.

————. *La República.* Havana: Editorial de Ciencias Sociales, 1971.

Lorenzetto, Anna, and Neys, Karel. *Methods and Means Utilized in Cuba to Eliminate Illiteracy.* UNESCO report. Havana: Cuban National Commission for UNESCO, 1965.

Mankiewicz, Frank. "Conversation with Fidel Castro." *Oui* Magazine, January 1975.

Ministerio de Educación. *Cuba: Organización de la educación, 1973–1975.* Havana, 1975.

————. *La educación en Cuba.* Havana, 1973.

————. *Revolución y educación.* Havana, 1970.

Ministry of Education. *A Decade of Adult Education in Cuba (1962–1972).* Havana (no date).

North, Joseph. *Cuba: Hope of a Hemisphere.* New York: International Publishers Co., 1961.

Pensamiento revolucionario cubano. Havana: Editorial de Ciencias Sociales, 1971.

Perkins, Dexter. *The United States and the Caribbean.* Cambridge, Mass.: Harvard University Press, 1947.

Pino-Santos, Oscar. *El asalto a Cuba por la oligarquía financiera yanqui.* Havana: Casa de las Américas, 1973.

Public Papers of the Presidents of the United States: John F. Kennedy 1962. Washington, D.C.: United States Government Printing Office, 1963.

Reinoso Hernandez, Edith. *Testimonio de una emigrada.* Havana: Editorial de Ciencias Sociales, 1974.

Roca, Blas. *Aclaraciones.* Havana: Editora Política, 1964.

————. *The Cuban Revolution.* New York: New Century Publishers, 1961.

Rodríguez, Carlos Rafael. *José Martí and Cuban Liberation.* New York: International Publishers Co., 1953.

————. *La clase obrera y la revolución.* Havana, 1960.

———. *4 años de reforma agraria.* Havana: INRA (no date).

Roig de Leuchsenring, Emilio. *Martí anti-imperialist.* Havana: Ediciones Políticas, 1967.

Rosell, Mirta. *Luchas obreras contra Machado.* Havana: Editorial de Ciencias Sociales, 1973.

Schechter, Danny. "The Havana-Luanda Connection." *Cuba Review,* March 1976.

Scheer, Robert, ed. *The Diary of Che Guevara.* New York: Bantam Books, 1968.

Seis leyes de la Revolución. Havana: Editorial de Ciencias Sociales, 1973.

Smith, Robert F. *The United States and Cuba.* New York: Bookman Associates, 1960.

Sobre el Partido. Havana: Ediciones de la Comisión de Orientación Revolucionaria, 1963.

Sundelson, J. Wilner. "A Business Perspective." *Cuba and the United States,* Brookings Institute, 1967.

Tellería, Evelio. *Los Congresos obreros en Cuba.* Havana: Editorial de Arte y Literatura, 1973.

26. Havana: Editorial de Ciencias Sociales, 1970.

Vignier, Enrique, and Alonso, Guillermo. *La corrupción política y administrativa en Cuba, 1944–1952.* Havana: Editorial de Ciencias Sociales, 1973.

Cuban periodicals: *Granma, Hoy, Pensamiento Crítico, Juventud Rebelde, Mella, Revolución, Bohemia, Economia y Desarrollo, Casa de las Américas, Cuba Socialista, Educación.*

Index

Cuba (*cont'd*)

underdeveloped countries
and, 180

Vietnam and, 170–71, 174,
197–98, 205, 235

"war of economic
independence" of,
125–32, 160–67

women's organization in,
220, 221, 229–31

work and working people in,
207–33

Cuban Communist Party
(before 1965), 42, 43, 45,
48, 51–52, 53, 57, 62, 66–
67, 83, 96–97, 102, 114,
127

see also Communist Party of
Cuba

Cuban People's Party
(Orthodox Party), 56–58,
59–61, 65–66

Cuban revolution (1952–1959),
59–110

agrarian reforms in, 97

cities' strategy in, 71, 78, 82,
83, 85, 87, 89–90

conspiracy in Batista's
military and, 86–87

emigrés and, 68–71

final campaign in, 91–102

general strikes used in,
89–90, 102

guerrilla warfare plans in,
77–78, 87, 89–90

invasion of cities in, 95–
102

as July 26 Movement
(M-26-7), 67–110,
113–14, 136, 250–51

Cuban (*cont'd*)

November 1958 election and,
98

political aspects of, 81–82

popular support for, 76, 86,
88–89, 102, 127

public tribunals of, 108–9

underground activities in,
83–86

women's platoon in, 95, 98

see also Cuba, Republic of

Cuban Revolutionary Council,
142*n*

Cuban Revolutionary Party
(1892), 33

Cuban–Spanish war (1892),
33–36

Czechoslovakia, 128

"dance of millions" period, 39,
41

Declaration of Independence,
U.S., 15

de Onís, Juan, 191–92

Depression, Great, 40

Desnoes, Edmundo, 59

Diaz Balart, Mirtha, 57

Dominican Republic, 54, 94,
172

Dorticós, Osvaldo, 119, 151,
260–61

Douglass, Frederick, 27

Du Bois, Jules, 109

Du Bois, W. E. B., 14

Dulles, Allen, 66

Dulles, John Foster, 98

Echeverría, José Antonio, 71,
79–80

economic conditions, 40, 43,

Ex Libris...
Lake County ...

ULISYS

11541950

Ex-Library: Friends of
Lake County Public Library

APR 5 '82

972.9106 CANN   81
CANNON   T.   16.95
REVOLUTIONARY CUBA

NP00 ∑

MAY 17 1982

A33636

JUN 6 1982

X

LAKE COUNTY PUBLIC LIBRARY
INDIANA
972.9106 CANN   81
CANNON   T.   16.95
REVOLUTIONARY CUBA

AD	FF	MU
AV	GR	NC
BO	HI	SC
CL	HO	SJ
DY	LS	CN L
	ME	

APR 5 '82

THIS BOOK IS RENEWABLE BY PHONE OR IN PERSON IF THERE IS NO RESERVE
WAITING OR FINE DUE.   LCP #0390